Turkey

CRUISING COMPANION

A yachtsman's pilot and cruising guide to the
ports and harbours from the Çeşme peninsula to Antalya

Emma Watson

WILEY NAUTICAL

Photographs © 2010 Emma Watson

Additional photography:
Page 41 (bottom) ©Turkish Tourist Board London, www.gototurkey.co.uk; Page 52 ©Ali Mutlu, Alaçatı Marina; Page 58 ©Setur
Kuşadası Marina By:Kadir KIR; Page 96 ©Milta Bodrum Marina; Page 162 (top) ©Netsel Marmaris Marina; Page 162 (bottom)
©Offshore-Sailing Albatros Marina; Page 180 ©Port Göcek Marina; Page 181 ©MarinTurk; Page 184 ©Ece Saray Marina;
Page 186 ©Yes Marina; Page 207 ©Setur Finike Marina; Pages 209 & 211 ©Rob and Amanda Smith/*Wavedancer*;
Page 213 ©Kemer Turkiz Marina; Page 216 ©Çelebi Marina; Page 221 ©YY

For Wiley Nautical
Executive Editor: Miles Kendall
Project Editor: Juliet Booker
Associate Editor: Drew Kennerley
Content Editor: Claire Spinks

For Nautical Data
Cartography: Jamie Russell
Art Direction: Lucinda Roch and Jamie Russell
Cruising Companion series editor: Lucinda Roch

ISBN-13: 978-0-470-721667

IMPORTANT NOTICE

This Companion is intended as an aid to navigation only. The information contained within should not solely
be relied on for navigational use, rather it should be used in conjunction with official hydrographic data.
Whilst every care has been taken in compiling the information contained in this Companion, the publishers,
author, editors and their agents accept no responsibility for any errors or omissions, or for any accidents
or mishaps which may arise from its use.

Neither the publisher nor the author can accept responsibility for errors, omissions or alterations in this book.
They will be grateful for any information from readers to assist in the update and accuracy of the publication.

Readers are advised at all times to refer to official charts, publications and notices.
The charts contained in this book are sketch plans and are not to be used for navigation.
Some details are omitted for the sake of clarity and the scales have been chosen
to allow best coverage in relation to page size.

Correctional supplements are available at www.wileynautical.com and on request from the publishers.

ACKNOWLEDGEMENTS FROM THE AUTHOR
As I don't have a boat of my own I am particularly grateful to those who have let me use theirs in order to visit the harbours and
anchorages included in this book. Special thanks in this respect go to Sunsail, MTM Yachting, and to the yachts *Wave Dancer* and
Serafina Pekkala. I would also like to extend particular thanks to: My colleagues, past and present, who have made working in this
industry such fun and who have taught me so much over the years. Special thanks go to the charter base managers, flotilla lead crews
and skippers in Turkey who have shared their knowledge of the area with me; Penny Blackmore, who has sailed with me in and out of
more harbours than I can count – and to Lucy the dog for being a good sport even when it got windy; Jes Holman, who has travelled
hundreds of miles with me up and down the coast on research trips and has never once lost his patience or good humour; my parents
John and Maureen, who introduced me to sailing at a young age and over the years encouraged me to stick with the sport and keep
working in the industry; everyone at Nautical Data and Wiley Nautical for their professional help, expertise and support with this project
and for giving me such a good excuse to visit and re-visit all these places in Turkey that I have been wanting to get to for so long!
Printed in Singapore by Ho Printing Singapore Pte Ltd

Contents

Sarsala, one of the beautiful bays in Skopea Limanı

Yachts moored on a restaurant jetty beneath the citadel at Bozuk Bükü (Loryma)

Introduction

The Aegean and Mediterranean coastline of Turkey is without doubt one of the finest cruising areas within this region. With almost 600M to explore, there is something for everyone here: consistent summer winds offer excellent cruising conditions for all kinds of sailing vessels; popular resort areas have top class marina facilities and plenty of nightlife; traditional fishing villages have a timeless quality and may still be inaccessible by road in even the 21st century; and you will be able to find plenty of uninhabited and remote anchorages where you can escape the world for days of solitude until your provisions run out.

History buffs will be pleased to note that Turkey is famous for having more and better preserved ancient Greek and Roman ruins than Greece and Italy do, and over the years has also been a destination for Persian, Celtic and Byzantine Greek invaders who have all left their marks on the landscape and culture of this wonderfully diverse place. Natural beauty abounds too, from the green wooded Mediterranean coastline backed by impressive mountain peaks, and its protected beaches, to the distinctive landscapes

Travertine terraces at Pamukkale

of Pamukkale's travertine terraces and Capadoccia's rock chimneys that feature on many postcards and are frequently included on 'Top 10' lists of the world's natural wonders.

Finally, there is no point discussing Turkey unless you can talk about its inhabitants. Almost without exception they are a friendly, generous and affectionate group of people who will take you into their hearts and treat you like family from day one. It may be the sailing conditions or the historical and cultural attractions that entice visitors to Turkey in the first place, but it is the warmth and generosity of the Turks themselves which encourage people to return time and again, and leads so many of us to start calling the place home.

CRUISING AREA OVERVIEW

The harbours and anchorages covered in this book lie between the Çeşme peninsula, near the major commercial port and NATO military base of İzmir,

Turkish fishermen

and the large resort and port town of Antalya. For the sake of convenience we have divided this coastline into four sections named after different civilisations that colonised them in antiquity. Although there is inevitably a degree of overlap between these, as you are travelling along the coastline you can sense that each of these sections does indeed have its own atmosphere and identity which can be noticed today. Historical information about these major civilisations is given below, and cruising information is provided at the start of each chapter.

The Ionian coastline:
Çeşme peninsula to Güllük Körfezi

The Ionians were the first Greek-speaking people to settle on the Anatolian mainland. Coming predominantly from the Aegean islands and the city of Athens (which was the only Ionian settlement on mainland Greece), they were driven out by the rise of the Dorian civilisation from around 1050 BCE. Their civilisation comprised a group of around 12 city states that administered to their surrounding areas and included Smyrna (modern day İzmir), Ephesus, Priene, Miletus, Didyma, Aphrodisias and Teos. Remains can be seen in many of these locations today.

The Ionian civilisation flourished for around five centuries, before being destroyed by the invading Persians in the 4th century BCE. It is known for giving rise to the discipline of natural philosophy; that is the study of the world through reason and observation untainted by religious bias and preconception. This revolutionary way of thinking allowed mankind to make the first steps along the road of scientific knowledge and understanding, as can be shown by the natural philosopher Thales' use of the new techniques of mathematics and geometry to make the first ever prediction of a solar eclipse. Art and literature were also important to this civilisation, as demonstrated by the existence of the great Celsus library at Ephesus. Ionian architectural styles continue to be influential in modern day design and can be seen in many of the remains from this period.

The Carian coastline:
Bodrum peninsula and Gökova Körfezi

For the purposes of this book the Carian coastline includes these areas, but in actual fact Carian settlements and influence can be seen far to the north and south of here. The Carian civilisation was established in Anatolia before the arrival of the Greek Dorians and Ionians, and continued to prosper under the later rule of the Persians who drove these other settlers away. Part of their success may have stemmed from their ability and willingness to adopt and adapt the customs of whatever other group seemed to hold influence and power. Perhaps it is for this reason that our knowledge of them remains slim compared with other civilisations of the same era that we know much more about.

Even the origin of the Carian people is unclear: the Greek historian Herodotus claimed that they were descendents of Minoan subjects that had been exiled to Anatolia by the ruler of Crete, but the Carians themselves always maintained that they were of Anatolian descent. We also have yet to decipher the Carian language, which Homer once described as 'barbarous'. Modern thinking tends to side with the Carians' view of themselves as an indigenous race that spread its influence through seafaring prowess and adaptability.

Whatever mysteries may remain, we do know that a number of cities in this region were populated by Carians at the same time as by other civilisations. One of the most well-known Carian cities is Halicarnassus (present-day Bodrum), which was ruled during the Persian occupation of Anatolia by the Carian King Mausolus from 377-353 BCE, and was also one of the six members of the Dorian hexapolis of ruling city states. King Mausolus was famously buried by his wife (also his sister!) in a grand tomb (interestingly this was of Ionian architectural style) that was known as one of the seven wonders of the ancient world and has conferred the name 'mausoleum' on all similar tomb constructions in the world today.

The Dorian coastline: Hisarönü Körfezi to Marmaris

The Dorian people were one of the three main ethnic groups of ancient Greece (along with the Ionians and the Aeolians). From around 10,000 BCE the Dorian civilisation expanded throughout the Aegean and towards the coast of Anatolia, driving the Ionian Greeks before them as described above.

Rather than occupying one section of coastline, the Dorians spread themselves around various states that became known as the hexapolis, or group of six influential city states. These included the cities of Lyndus, Lalysos and Camiros on the Greek island of Rhodes (opposite the modern-day Turkish town of Marmaris), the city of Kos on the Greek island of Kos, the city of Halicarnassus (which was also considered a Carian city and came under Persian rule as described above) and the city of Knidos on the tip of what is now known as the Datça peninsula.

Of all these settlements it was the city state of Knidos that was considered the most important, and in fact there were Dorian settlements throughout the peninsula, which had a population of over 70,000 inhabitants 3,000 years ago (today it is less than 15,000).

The Celsus Library at Ephesus

The Lycian coast – Ekincik to Antalya

The Lycian coastline is a steeply mountainous and rugged one that must have been a challenging place in which to eke out an existence, let alone create one of the great ancient civilisations. It is not surprising then that the people who managed to do just that were regarded by their contemporaries as a fierce, independent and warlike nation. On more than one occasion Lycian armies were reported to have slain their women and children, razed their cities to the ground and fought to the death rather than surrender to the much larger armies of invading Persians and Romans.

Piracy was also a long-standing feature of this coastline, which had many secret bays and coves where local vessels could wait to prey on passing trading ships. The Egyptians, Greeks and Romans all tried to tackle this problem with varying degrees of success, but it was not until the British Navy established a presence here in the 18th and 19th centuries that piracy was finally eradicated from this area for good.

One thing that the Lycians did bequeath to the world was the first known democratic union of the Lycian federation. The principles combining free-government with the needs of the population were admired and copied by the neighbouring Greeks and have developed into the democratic systems that we know today.

Lycia was the last region in the Mediterranean basin to be incorporated into the Roman Empire, and continued to function more or less independently within the empire for several centuries, even retaining its own language for many years. A dominant feature along this coastline today is the distinctive rock tombs carved into cliff sides that are so typical of Lycian remains. The Lycians regarded ancestor worship as important, considering the female line of descent to be more important than the male.

There are many interesting Lycian sites that are within easy reach of the coast. Xanthos was considered the capital of the region for much of its history and is today a UNESCO World Heritage site along with neighbouring Letoon. Remains of ancient Simena and Teimiussa can be observed underwater and along the shore in the region known as the Kekova Roads (see page 199). Myra was situated near the present day location of the town of Demre and is known for having the largest amphitheatre in Lycia as well as being part of the diocese of St Nicholas, commonly identified today with Father Christmas.

In all there are about 20 sites of historical interest in this region, most of which are sufficiently well preserved to be of interest to the casual visitor as well as the scholar.

ANCIENT HISTORY

During the 6th century BCE the Persian Empire swept across Anatolia from the east, led by the Persian King Cyrus. Some of the civilisations mentioned above, such as the Ionians, disintegrated under this onslaught, whilst others such as the Carians and Lycians managed to endure either through a degree of assimilation or by fierce and unending resistance.

Despite this the Persian Empire continued to rule both directly and through the appointment of *satraps* or regional governors for several hundred years, until the Macedonian general Alexander the Great crossed the Hellespont (Dardanelles) to conquer the Middle East as far as India. According to legend, Alexander reached the province of Phrygia and encountered the famous 'Gordian knot' of which it was said that the one who could untie this would gain dominion of the land. Alexander's solution was purportedly to cut through the knot with his sword, giving us the metaphor that we use today ('cutting the Gordion knot').

After the death of Alexander in 323 BCE the region descended into civil war for more than a century, with a succession of small kingdoms growing up only to be replaced by others. In the second half of the second century BCE the Roman Empire absorbed many of the Anatolian kingdoms into the province of Asia. The capital of this province was the city of Ephesus (see page 28), which is where disciple St John is reported to have written the fourth Gospel of Jesus Christ, and where he brought Mary, Jesus' mother, to live after Jesus' crucifixion in Golgotha.

The Roman Empire held sway here for several centuries, and in 324 CE, after decades of decline, became reunited under the Emperor Constantine. Constantine had famously converted to Christianity under the influence of his mother and founded the city of New Rome (later to be called Constantinople, and subsequently İstanbul) on the site of Greek Byzantium on the shores of the Bosphorus, declaring it to be the new capital of the region. By the seventh century CE the Eastern Roman Empire had become progressively more Greek in character compared with the declining Western Roman Empire, even adopting Greek as its official language in place of Latin.

For another 400 years the Byzantine Empire continued as a bastion of Christianity, a repository for Greek and Roman art and knowledge, and as a bulwark against the encroaching Muslim threat from the east. Towards the end of the 11th century CE, however, the Byzantines were defeated by the Seljuk Turks from Persia. Although their empire was short-lived, it is notable for being the first real Turkish state in modern-day Turkey, and for giving the world the poet-astronomer Omar Khayyam and the philosopher, cosmologist, physician and mystic al-Ghazali (these descriptions were not as mutually exclusive then as they may be today!).

Throughout this period the city of Constantinople was repeatedly attacked and violently 'liberated' during the Christian Crusades against the Holy Land and Muslim civilisations in general. By the end of the 13th century CE the Seljuk Empire was greatly weakened and was eventually defeated by the leader of one of the Ghazi Emirates (Muslim principalities) that had grown up in the decline of the Empire. This Osman I made his capital initially in the city of Bursa, and gave his name to what would be known as the Ottoman Empire, which would last for 500 years.

The Ottoman Empire rose and fell through several cycles, and extended at its height to cover much of South-Eastern Europe, the Middle East and North Africa. The city of Constantinople became the capital of the Empire after it was captured by Sultan Mehmed I in 1453 (at the age of only 21!), and for centuries the civilisation spanned east and west in much the same way as modern Turkey does today.

The Empire reached its height under Sultan Suleiman I (Suleiman the Magnificent), who ruled from 1520 until he died in 1566. He led victorious armies to conquer kingdoms in Hungary, Rhodes and North Africa (almost doubling the land mass governed by the Empire), and his navies ruled the Mediterranean Seas and Persian Gulf. He was also a man of culture and political awareness. As a poet himself he did much to sponsor the arts, including literature and architectural design. He also introduced many new laws concerning education, taxation and social and criminal law.

After his death the Ottoman Empire never again produced a ruler to match his achievements, and although the sheer size and might of the Empire ensured its continuation, it became greatly weakened over the following centuries by poor governance and military decline. Gradually parts of the empire broke away to form nations of their own, supported by the newly powerful Western nations that looked to profit from the division of the Empire they had once feared. Various attempts at modernising the structure and governance of the Empire came to nothing as the hereditary Sultans refused to share their power with any democratically-elected government of the people and internal struggles started to tear the system apart.

RECENT HISTORY

The piteous state of the Ottoman Empire at the start of the 20th century led to much dissent and subterfuge amongst the younger members of the Turkish elite, culminating in the founding of the Young Turks' Committee of Union and Progress in 1906. This was aimed at modernising and westernising the governance of the Empire, and at shifting the balance of power away from the Sultanate and towards the ambitious young military generals who felt they were better able to steer the Empire towards future greatness.

A Turkish flag flies over the citadel at Bozuk Bükü

All this came to a head when the leaders of the Young Turks (Mehmed Pasha, Ismail Enver and Ahmed Djemal) pronounced a military coup in 1913 and promptly steered the nation into an alliance with Germany and the Central Powers. Turkey's involvement in World War I is notable for the disastrous Gallipoli campaign in which the Allies attempted to capture Constantinople and the Bosphorus. Initially intended to be a brief naval attack masterminded by a young (and subsequently disgraced) Winston Churchill, the campaign turned to disaster when tens of thousands of troops from Australia, New Zealand, France, Britain and Newfoundland became entrenched along the new front that was vigorously defended by the Ottoman armies until the eventual evacuation in December 1915. Conditions on both sides were beyond appalling, with each nation involved losing at least 25% in casualties, and the overall death toll estimated at around 130,000 in a period of around eight months.

The Gallipoli campaign resonates to this day with all the nations that were involved. The peninsula is a place of pilgrimage for Australian and New Zealand citizens who return to hold remembrance services each year on ANZAC day (25 April). For modern Turks the campaign is associated (amongst other things) with the emergence of a young military captain named Mustafa Kemal. He was regarded as a military hero for his successful exploits in the Gallipoli area (known as Çanakkale in Turkish), and was heavily involved with the progressive Young Turk movement as well, although not always in favour with the leaders because of his strong temperament and outspoken opinions.

As World War I came to an end the victorious Allies occupied the city of Constantinople and carved up the diminished Ottoman Empire between themselves in the 1920 Treaty of Sèvres. Amongst other things, this Treaty greatly restricted the military capabilities of the remaining Ottoman army, granted the Allies control over the Empire's finances and established zones of foreign influence around south-eastern Anatolia (to France), much of the Mediterranean coast and the major ports of Anatolia (to the Italians), and the important trading city of Smyrna (now İzmir) to the Greeks.

In the end the Greeks refused to accept the limits placed on their presence in Anatolia, and guided by an ideal of reuniting the lands of ancient Byzantium, they pushed inland and began an occupation that if not condoned by the other allies, was certainly not condemned either. This proved to be too much for the tattered remains of the Ottoman army, who could not abide this challenge by what had recently been a subordinate state, and so began the Turkish War of Independence.

Once again the military and strategic prowess of the now Inspector General Mustafa Kemal came to the fore. He became the figurehead and organising force of the resistance movement, which quickly turned into a national independence movement, and for this he became a wanted man by the Ottoman government and was forced to resign his post in the Ottoman army. Promoted to Commander-in-chief of the newly formed Turkish army, he fought against the Allied and Greek advance towards his seat of power in centrally-located Ankara. Final victory against the Greeks was won in 1922, and the following year the Treaty of Lausanne was signed, which provided for the formation of an independent Republic of Turkey and ensured her recognition by the Allied nations that so recently had hoped to possess parts of her.

This was followed in 1923 by the infamous exchange of populations between Greece and Turkey. Ethnic Turks who had been living happily for generations in parts of Greece, such as Salonika (now Thessalonika, and the birthplace of Mustafa Kemal), were forced to leave their homes and decamp to parts of Turkey that had been emptied by ethnic Greeks being forced to go to Greece. Many modern coastal towns such as Kaş and Kalkan were originally founded by Greek fishermen, and some settlements remain abandoned to this day.

With the founding of the Republic of Turkey, Mustafa Kemal became its first President and instigated a number of forward-thinking and sweeping reforms to the culture and government systems of the new country. Amongst many other reforms, he adopted a variation of the Latin alphabet in place of the Arabic script that was widely used under Ottoman rule, and westernised the names of many towns and cities, including İstanbul (from Constantinople), İzmir (from Smyrna) and Ankara (from Angora); he encouraged gender equality in all areas, including education and the right to vote; he forbade the wearing of the fez for men, headscarves for women and all other expressions of religious faith in public life; and he insisted that all citizens adopt a surname or family name in the western style. His own surname was given to him by the Turkish parliament: Atatürk, meaning the Father of Turks.

Atatürk died in 1938 at the age of 57, and since then the country has had a difficult ride. Turkey managed to maintain an uneasy neutrality during World War II and from 1946 the rules forbidding the formation of opposition political parties were relaxed, leading to the election of the new Democratic Party in 1950. However, the military in Turkey has long regarded itself as the guardian of Atatürk's ideals and principles, and has never been afraid to take action to protect these. In 1960 it staged a military coup and executed the elected party leader Adnan Menderes (who now has an airport named after him in İzmir). In 1970 there was another brief coup, and in 1974 the troubles in Cyprus came to a head when a Greek nationalist proclaimed himself president of the country and the Turkish army went in to declare otherwise; a deadlock that continues to this day.

During the 1980s, political and economic turmoil formed the backdrop for a rise in Kurdish separatism from this ethnic group indigenous to the eastern part of Turkey as well as to neighbouring countries such as Iraq, Iran and Syria. Today the terrorist group known as the Kurdistan Workers' Party (PKK) is responsible for the occasional violent act such as bombs planted in locations selected for their importance to Turkey's image abroad. Thankfully these events are rare, and increased military action has been taken against PKK strongholds in eastern Turkey and Iraq in the last two years.

In 2002 the country elected a new party to power in a landslide victory that said much about the population's views on the political and economic roller coaster it had been forced to endure during the previous decades. The AKP party is headed by two charismatic leaders, Abdullah Gül, the current president, and Recep Tayyip Erdoğan, who is the party leader and current prime minister. Since their election there has been a reduction in inflation and the introduction of a new currency (see page 26) domestic and political reform aimed at progressing Turkey's entry into the European Union, and the long slow restructuring of Turkey's economy.

There has also been controversy. In 2007, after another landslide election victory, foreign minister Abdullah Gül was nominated for president and the country was outraged that his wife openly wore a headscarf. Ironically enough this would be quite acceptable in most western Christian countries, but is banned as a public expression of religious faith in Muslim but strictly secular Turkey.

In June and July 2008 the ruling AKP party was indicted in the Constitutional Court for activities opposing the secular nature of the Turkish constitution, and a five year political ban was sought for the party and all members. The world waited with baited breath as the court returned its verdict of guilty as charged, but failed to return the number of votes to ensure the banning of the party or any of its members.

This leaves things in an interesting political position for the future. Turkey is unique in that it is the only major Muslim nation to be governed according to principles of secular democracy, which are enshrined in the constitution established by Atatürk. The superpowers of the east and west watch closely to see how this drama between the views of the educated urban minority and the rural central and eastern majority will be played out.

Nautical matters

WEATHER AND CLIMATE

The Aegean and Mediterranean coasts featured in this book enjoy a typical coastal Mediterranean climate, which is to say short, mild, wet winters combined with long, hot, dry summers. The mountainous coastal backdrop is often covered with snow during the winter, although the coast itself rarely sees any more than the occasional slushy rainfall.

The hottest months are July and August, when temperatures can soar to almost 50°C and the humidity can near 100%, particularly in the more southern regions. Many people find that this is simply too hot and head for cooler climes for a couple of months, returning in September when the extreme heat and waves of tourists have started to subside.

WEATHER FORECASTING

VHF Broadcasts

The Turkish State Meteorological Service broadcasts several weather observations and forecasts for shipping each day from radio stations in İstanbul, Samsun (on the Black Sea) and Antalya. They are broadcast on VHF Ch 67 in Turkish and English at 50w power.

Antalya station broadcasts observations from Bodrum, İzmir, Kuşadası, Marmaris and Finike (amongst others) at 0730, 0930, 1130, 1330, 1530, 1730 and 1930.

It also broadcasts a general marine forecast for the Black Sea, Sea of Marmara, Aegean Sea and

Mediterranean Sea at 0700 and 1900, and a 72 hour forecast for the same areas, but in Turkish only, at 0900 and 1930.

The Turkish Coastguard broadcasts a forecast in Turkish and English at 0900 and 1800 on VHF Ch 08.

Navtex

Official weather reports for Aegean and Jason sea areas are broadcast from İzmir station at 518 KHz at 0120, 0520, 0920, 1320, 1720 and 2120.

The forecast for Taurus sea area is broadcast from Antalya station on the same frequency at 0050, 0450, 0850, 1250, 1650 and 2050.

Internet

Many cruising yachts these days have excellent communications equipment on board and may be able to access internet weather sites either from on board, or at least from a WiFi connection in a nearby café or restaurant. Internet weather sites have improved greatly and some have the advantage of being updated more regularly than you can receive forecasts in more traditional ways. The following sites are generally reliable and up-to-date:

www.weatheronline.co.uk/Turkey provides wind and weather forecasting for up to eight days for the following areas: İzmir, Bodrum, Marmaris, Dalaman, Fethiye, Finike and Antalya.

http://www.poseidon.hcmr.gr is maintained by the Hellenic Centre for Marine Research and displays a useful chart showing the sea areas between Greece and Turkey which can be projected up to four days ahead and can be filtered to show wind speed and direction as well as sea state.

www.windfinder.com has been developed to give wind and watersports enthusiasts the latest information about conditions in their sailing area. It is updated frequently and gives wind speed and direction information for the coming week for the following areas included in this book: İzmir, Çeşme, Alaçatı, Bodrum,

Gökova, Datça, Marmaris, Finike and Antalya. **www.windguru.com** is a similar site to windfinder and gives comparable information for the following areas: Çeşme, Alaçatı, Gündoğan, Yalıkavak, Akyarlar, Ortakent, Bitez, Bodrum and Datça. It is rather more aimed at windsurfing and kitesurfing enthusiasts than anyone else, so the locations are more restrictive.

Greek forecasts

Whilst sailing along the Turkish coast, for much of the time you will also be able to pick up Greek forecasts, which cover the sea areas surrounding the Greek islands lying very close to the Turkish coast, such as Chios, Samos, Kos and Rhodos. VHF forecasts are transmitted in Greek and English by Olympia Radio four times a day at 0600, 1000, 1600 and 2200. Listen on VHF Ch 16 for the sea area in which you are interested and then tune in to the appropriate channel as instructed.

PREVAILING WINDS

The prevailing winds in this area blow from the north to north-west and are a fairly reliable force 3-5 during the summer months. The general pattern follows a roughly six hour cycle, with calm weather in the morning replaced by building winds during the afternoon. There may be another lull in the evening with a stronger breeze developing again during the night. When the wind direction switches to a south or south-easterly it is usually the sign of an incoming front, so be prepared to expect a period of unsettled weather which

Stormy seas at the entrance to Antalya's harbour

can include rain storms and strong winds sometimes lasting for several days.

The *meltemi* is the name for this north-westerly wind, which blows frequently across the seas between Greece and Turkey. In technical terms it is the result of high pressure systems sitting over the Balkans combining with low pressure ridges extending over central Turkey, funnelling strong winds down from the north following the pressure gradient between the two. In practical terms it means clear skies, low humidity and reliable (if strong) winds for sailing.

The deeply indented and mountainous nature of the Turkish coastline results in these winds being continually bent, twisted, shielded, funnelled and accelerated by the land around which they blow. Winds are funnelled up the deep gulfs such as Hisarönü and Gökova Körfezi so that they blow in a more westerly direction through the central channels, although they may be different close in to the shore. In addition the winds are speeded up as they blow around headlands, making the western areas of Bodrum, Knidos and Bozukbükü notoriously windy. Local katabatic winds can develop, flowing off steep hillsides in the afternoons, and even light breezes can be squeezed and accelerated as they get funnelled down valleys and through gaps.

All of this means that it is generally much more pleasant to be travelling 'downhill' from north-west to south-east rather than in the other direction, particularly during the late afternoons when the sea has had the opportunity to build up as the winds strengthen. The simple answer to this is to ensure that you get an early start if you have a long passage to make in the 'wrong' direction to enable you to get as many miles as possible under your belt before the conditions start to get exciting. In fact this is a must for some areas such as the stretch along the Yedi Burunlar coastline to the south-east of Fethiye Körfezi.

TIDES AND CURRENTS

At this end of the Mediterranean you can almost discount the effects of tide on the water heights, which are liable to be as much affected by atmospheric pressure as anything else. Prolonged blows into a confined bay will tend to raise water levels as well.

In general you will not encounter strong currents along this section of coastline. What you do experience will tend to be driven by the prevailing anti-clockwise movement at this end of the Med, which can be modified or even reversed if the *meltemi* is blowing strongly against the prevailing currents from the north-west. Areas where you are likely to experience stronger currents than usual include the Dilek Boğazı channel between the Dilek peninsula and Greek island of Samos (see page 61), and also the sea areas around the tips of the Bodrum, Datça and Hisarönü peninsulas.

A south cardinal marker buoy

NAVIGATION CHARTS

The Turks have a long history of involvement with hydrography and the charting of coastlines. In the 16th century the Turkish Admiral Piri Reis published his *Kitab-ı Bariye* (Book of Navigation), which contains detailed and accurate charts of the Mediterranean Sea. His first world map was produced in 1513 and is known for its accurate positioning of the continents as well as for being the first Turkish map to include the Americas, and possibly the first map at all to include Antarctica, which was not officially 'discovered' until almost three centuries after Piri Reis' world map was produced.

The modern day Office of Navigation, Hydrography and Oceanography (TN-OHNO) publishes a series of nautical charts that cover the entire Turkish coastline, as well as several collections of Leisure Charts published in A2 Folio size.

The British Admiralty also publishes a series of charts covering this coastline as well as the Leisure Folios NE Aegean, SC 5776, and SE Aegean, SC 5773. Alternatively, the English publisher Imray offers a range of charts for Turkey which are printed on water-resistant paper and stand up well to the rigours of cruising usage.

NAUTICAL CONVENTIONS

Lights and buoyage

Turkey uses the International Association of Lighthouse Authorities (IALA) System A buoyage convention, in accordance with other Mediterranean countries. This means that as you approach a port or harbour the port-hand lateral marks will be red and the starboard-hand marks will be green (and vice versa as you depart).

WAYPOINTS AND CHART DATUMS

All waypoints included in this book are referenced to the World Geodetic Survey 1984 (WGS84) datum, which is the default setting for most electronic navigation aids.

Waypoints should always be plotted onto a chart to check that they are correct before entering into a GPS or navigation system and hitting GOTO. Always make sure to check that the datum of the chart you are using matches with the datum of the waypoint. Some charts of this area use an alternative datum such as the European Datum (1950), in particular charts from the Imray-Tetra series. In this case you need to adjust the waypoint before plotting onto the chart.

You should never depend on waypoints alone for navigation purposes, and should always rely on your own eyes and common sense to confirm that you are where you expect to be and that the way ahead is still clear of dangers as anticipated.

Bearings and Variation

All bearings given in this book are True, which is to say that they can be plotted directly onto a navigational chart. You must apply a correction for Magnetic Variation before using any such bearings as courses to steer. Magnetic Variation is currently around 3½°E in this area.

TURKISH VESSEL FORMALITIES

Transit logs

All vessels in Turkish waters, whether they are private or commercial vessels, and foreign- or Turkish-flagged, must have a valid transit log at all times. A transit log is a collection of A4-sized carbonated paper forms, written in both Turkish and English. It should be completed as follows:

• The top section contains the name of the harbour authority, the date and whether the log is to be used for entry, exit or a domestic trip.

• Section I concerns the vessel and insurance details, and should be completed according to the vessel registration and insurance certificates.

• Section II concerns the owner of the vessel and/or the captain of the vessel (see note below), plus a list of destination ports. Only main ports of call need be noted, and it is understood that the vessel may visit and remain overnight in smaller harbours and anchorages en route.

• Section III concerns the details of the skipper and crew. Full names, nationalities and passport or ID numbers should be noted. Any changes to this list should be authorised by a local harbour master (see below).

• Section IV concerns items of the vessel inventory.

• Section V concerns the declaration of any health issues and must be authorised by the owner or captain to confirm that all other information is correct.

Below this is space for the various official officers to place their stamps of approval, and for the harbour master to sign to indicate that the necessary payment has been received.

At the time of writing (2009) a Foreign Flag Private Vessel Transit Log costs 78 YTL (45 Euros) and can be purchased from any Chamber of Shipping office, as well as through the reception offices of some marinas located at Ports of Entry and through official customs agents.

Transit logs are valid for 12 months from the date of issue, and must be renewed before the expiration date in order to avoid penalty fees. Once completed and authorised, the transit log should be kept with the rest of the boat papers and shown to harbour and customs authorities on demand.

As of 2009 most harbour masters have started to insist that boat owners employ the services of a customs agent for all transit log formalities, and will no longer deal directly with private owners. This is connected to the on-going computerisation of the transit log system. Registered customs agents are able to enter a vessel's details directly into an on-line system, and to make payment this way as well. Eventually the paper transit logs will be phased out completely and the whole procedure will be recorded electronically. As of October 2009 paper transit logs are still in use, but keep an eye on the official websites for changes in this system.

Entry formalities to Turkey for vessels arriving from overseas

Vessels arriving in Turkey should fly the yellow 'Q' quarantine flag until all vessel entry and immigration procedures are completed. These procedures should be completed immediately upon arrival at an official Port of Entry to Turkey (see the list on page 17).

First of all you should purchase an appropriate transit log and complete it as described above. You should then prepare a file containing the following documents:
• Completed transit log.
• Vessel registration certificate.
• Vessel insurance details.
• Passports and visa payments for each crew member (the passports must be valid for at least three months from date of entry. For visa requirements see page 21).
• Signed authorisation to deliver the boat if the registered owner is not part of the crew.

Along the bottom of the transit log is space for different authorities to add their stamp. You should visit these authorities in the following order:
• Coastal health authority to declare that you have had no infectious diseases or deaths on board.
• Passport and immigration control to purchase the necessary entry visas and have them stamped into the crew passports.
• Customs patrol to declare the vessel and its contents on arrival into the country. Technically the customs patrol has the right to insist on an inspection, although in practice they rarely do this.
• Harbour master to have your proposed route accepted and authorised.

Once you have received all four stamps your transit log is complete and you are ready to start sailing. Do not lose your 'Entry to Turkey' transit log, even if you renew it after 12 months (see below). When you finally clear back out of the country you will need to produce it to show that the vessel has not overstayed the permitted five years. It is a good idea to make a copy of this log, just in case.

Transit log formalities within Turkish waters
Transit log change

Foreign-flagged vessels are permitted to remain in Turkish waters for up to five years, but individual transit logs are valid for only 12 months. If your boat will be in the country for longer than that then you must complete a transit log change formality. You do not need to be at a port of entry, but you do need to visit a customs patrol and harbour master.

You should purchase a new transit log and complete it in the usual way. If there has been a crew change since the original transit log, be sure to note the new crew detail on the latest transit log. Then put together a file containing the following documents:
• Completed new transit log.
• Old transit log about to expire.
• Entry to Turkey transit log if different from above.
• Vessel registration certificate.
• Vessel insurance details.
• Owner's passport OR signed authorisation for skipper to deliver the boat if the owner is not on board.

Firstly you need to have the new transit log authorised by the customs patrol, who will note the log change in their ledgers. Then you can visit the harbour master to have your new sailing route authorised.

Crew change

If you are planning to spend some time cruising the Turkish coast then it is likely that you may have visitors who will fly out to join you for a week or two's sailing. As long as you are already in possession of a valid transit log it is easy to alter the existing crew list.

Several of the pages of the transit log are marked in the lower right-hand corner as 'Change Pages 1-3', and allow up to three changes in crew. Simply copy the details from the first page of the transit log and include the new crew details in the appropriate section. You should then have the change pages authorised by the nearest harbour master.

Sale of the vessel

Owners of foreign-flagged boats are permitted to sell their vessels within Turkish waters, but it is important that the correct procedures be followed to save the new owner from running into difficulties with the authorities at a later time. Once the sale is completed and the new owner has obtained a registration for the boat, a new transit log must be acquired to show the change in ownership of the vessel.

You should put a file together containing the following documents:
• Most recent transit log (supplied by the previous owner).
• Entry to Turkey transit log, if different from above (supplied by the seller).
• New transit log completed with new vessel and owner details.
• Bill of sale to show change of ownership.
• New insurance details.
• Passport of new owner OR signed authorisation for skipper to deliver the boat if the owner is not on board.

The new transit log should be authorised first by the customs patrol, who will note the change in their ledgers, and then by the harbour master. The new owner should be aware that the change in ownership does not affect the length of time the boat can remain in Turkish waters before clearing out.

Placing a vessel into Customs bond

It used to be the case that the details of a temporarily imported vessel would be written into the owner's passport, in the same way that they still do today for imported cars or motorbikes. The reason for this was to prevent the owner departing the country without his vessel, which would leave it open to be used or chartered in his absence. The only way for an owner to leave the country without his boat in this case would be for him to enter the boat into customs bonds at an officially licensed boatyard or marina.

Today the customs agents no longer note any vessel details in the owner's passport, so they are free to come and go from the country as they please. However, the customs bonding system is still in place and is still required for owners who plan to leave their vessels unattended in Turkish waters. Although many marinas have become rather lax about enforcing this in recent years, it remains the law and may be insisted on more strongly at some locations.

The customs bonding formality is done by the marina or boatyard agency, and requires the old transit log, the vessel registration and the owner's passport or signed authorisation for another to complete the formality on his behalf. The transit log will be surrendered to the customs patrol and must

be replaced with a new one when the boat is released from customs bond.

It is worth noting that a vessel can remain within customs bond for up to two years, and that the 12 month transit log validity and five year permitted stay in Turkish waters are suspended whilst the boat remains in bond, so there will be no fines to pay when the vessel is unbounded (although it may be necessary to clear out of the country immediately).

Clearing a vessel out of Turkish waters

Foreign vessels must clear out of Turkey at least once every five years, although there is currently no set time they must remain out of the country before returning. The procedure for clearing out of Turkish waters can be completed at any official Port of Entry, and is basically the opposite as that for clearing in. First of all you should ensure that you have a valid transit log with the correct crew details – see page 14. Then prepare a file with the following documents:
• Valid transit log with the final section (Departure from Turkish waters) completed.
• Entry to Turkey transit log (if different from above) to show that the boat has remained in Turkey less than five years.
• Vessel registration document.
• Passports with valid visas for all crew members, including the registered owner.
• Signed authorisation for the skipper to deliver the boat if the owner is not on board.

You should visit the harbour master to inform him that the vessel will be departing Turkish waters. Then visit the customs patrol to declare the same and surrender your transit log. They will note the vessel's departure in their ledger and cross reference this with the original arrival date. Finally visit the passport and immigration control so that the crew passports can be stamped.

Regulations on waste disposal

The 1 March 2010 will see the introduction of the Blue Card environmental protection scheme to the area of coastline between Bodrum and Fethiye. This is planned as a pilot scheme that the Turkish government hopes to extend to the country's entire coastline by 2015. The point of this scheme is to control the waste produced by vessels and to prevent contamination of the bays and coastline of the area. All vessels within the pilot scheme area will be required to purchase a Blue Card for 70TL (a one-off payment), and to have this card swiped by an official waste collection facility each time that waste from the vessel is discharged. All dumping of black and grey water into the sea will be forbidden anywhere along this coastline, with hefty fines promised for those who disobey. In effect this scheme will require that all vessels within the area are fitted with holding tanks that will collect black water from the toilets and grey water from sinks and showers, and it will not be permitted to wash decks or hulls with any kind of detergent, including those described as 'marine-friendly' or biodegradable.

This scheme is obviously going to affect cruisers planning to visit Turkey in their boats and those already there. The authorities will be able to monitor the amount of waste collected from each vessel, and will levy fines or refuse to issue transit logs to vessels suspected of illegal dumping at sea. Although most modern cruising vessels already have black water holding tanks fitted, very few have grey water tanks fitted as well. Their owners will therefore need to consider the implications of this scheme as all vessels (including foreign flagged and non-commercial vessels) will be subject to these new laws and penalties.

The Turkish Marine Environment Protection Agency (TURMEPA) website (see page 28) has published a list of around 30 licensed waste collection facilities along the coast, including contact phone numbers. Further details of the scheme have not been published yet (for example, the cost of pumping out waste and the amount of the fines to be levied have not yet been confirmed), but the reality is that any vessel owner planning to visit Turkey in the future should check the latest information and should ensure that his or her boat is adequately prepared to prevent unpleasant discoveries upon arrival in the country. I would suggest monitoring the TURMEPA website for up-to-date information as the agency is closely involved with implementing the scheme. You will also find on-line discussion of the issue on cruising forums such as Noonsite, and if your boat is already in Turkey then contact the marina or boatyard where it is located for the latest information on the facilities that it will be supplying in connection with this scheme. At the moment there is no information about the scheme available on Turkish government websites, although hopefully this will be amended as the deadline approaches in 2010.

Dealing with Turkish authorities

As a rule you will find the Turkish authorities pleasant and helpful, and it goes without saying that you should always be courteous and respectful in your dealings with them. Remember that Turkey is a country of Muslim sensibilities, and that bikinis and skimpy attire are never appropriate clothing for dealing with the authorities. Both men and women should be fully clothed, as common sense dictates.

Although many of the rank and file officials you deal with will speak only Turkish, an increasing number of them have made the effort to learn some English, so you should be able to get by in this language at least. If you can memorise a few Turkish pleasantries to use

here you will find that this goes a long way towards establishing a rapport with these officers, and will make things go much more smoothly and speedily.

Fines and penalties

If you have violated any of the rules regarding the transit log system (such as failing to renew the transit log after 12 months, failing to clear a vessel out of the country within the permitted five years, or keeping a boat under customs bond for longer than the permitted two years) then you will need to pay a penalty fee before you can complete any further paperwork, such as clearing the vessel out from the country.

Penalty fines are generally a standard 166 TL, although they can be compounded if more than one infraction has occurred. The customs patrol will inform you if they notice anything out of line as they process your request and will then issue you with an invoice showing (in Turkish) the nature of the infraction and the amount to be paid. The penalty fee is not paid at the customs patrol office, but rather at the local tax office (*vergi dairesi*), which can often be some way away from the port and harbour area within a town and may require a taxi or bus ride to get to. Once you have paid the fine you will receive a receipt that you present to the customs patrol to allow them to complete your formalities.

It is worth mentioning that even though the customs and harbour master offices are generally open during the weekends and on public holidays, the tax office will certainly be closed. If you are planning to complete any formalities at these times then you should check in advance to be sure that there are no outstanding problems that could potentially delay your departure because of inability to pay any penalty fees.

Please also note that any fines relating to the overstaying of visitor visas are dealt with by the immigration authorities, as covered on page 21.

Sailing a vessel if the owner is not on board

The Turkish authorities are very keen to prevent the illegal chartering of vessels in Turkish waters. They enforce this by insisting that the owner of a boat should be on board whenever it is sailed, and by demanding to see the owner's passport whenever any vessel formalities are completed with the customs or harbour master's offices.

The logic behind this is understandable, but at times it is necessary for an owner to employ a delivery skipper to collect his boat and move it if he is unable to do this himself for some reason. Sometimes it may be the case that a boat has more than one owner, as is the case with many 'fractional boat syndicates' that are becoming a popular compromise between owning a boat outright and chartering a different boat each year.

Turkish law allows for any foreign-flagged vessel

to have up to four owners, who may make use of the boat independently. You should ensure that each of the owners is clearly named on the registration certificate, and that if the vessel is owned by a company or syndicate, each of the directors or members is clearly named on an official document, which should be shown each time a formality is completed for the vessel.

If the owner of a vessel is arranging for someone else to collect and move the boat in his or her absence, then he or she should be sure to provide the skipper with a signed authorisation to do so, preferably accompanied by a copy of the owner's passport as well as originals of all the other necessary documents as described above.

Presenting documents to the authorities

Whilst sailing in Turkish waters, you should carry original documents at all times and be prepared to show these to the authorities upon request. It is a good idea to make a number of copies of your passports, vessel registration and crew list, so that you can leave one with the authorities if requested.

Most of the time the authorities will be prepared to accept documents written in English or other foreign languages, as long as they are presented in a standard format (such as a passport, registration document or bill of sale), with the pertinent information easy to identify and read.

For more complicated documents such as certificates of incorporation, syndicate membership lists and skippered delivery authorisations, it may be necessary to have these documents translated into Turkish and certified as true copies by a Turkish notary. Translation services and notary offices can be found near most good-sized harbours, and the procedures can be completed fairly quickly as long as the language to be translated from is not too exotic (in which case try to have an English translation prepared in advance as this will be easiest to translate again into Turkish). You can have any number of official copies notarised for a small fee, and this will save time and aggravation when dealing with the authorities on otherwise mundane matters.

VAT and KDV

VAT is a European tax applied to goods and services sold within the European Union. KDV is the Turkish equivalent of this tax and is generally levied at 18%.

Much has been written regarding the complexities of VAT law and its application to pleasure and commercial craft, and this is not the place for such a discussion. The most important thing to note is that as Turkey is not yet a member of the EU, VAT is not applicable to any vessels bought or sold within its waters. KDV is applicable only to Turkish registered vessels that have been officially imported into the country, so is unlikely to affect most readers of this book.

Duty free fuel and parts

Turkey is well known for having vigorous importation regulations and hefty taxes and fees, but the owners of foreign yachts are entitled to import spare parts from abroad without paying duty, on the understanding that these parts will be fitted to the vessel and will later be cleared out of the country on that vessel.

This is fine in theory, but is often more complicated in fact, and it is best to do some groundwork to avoid delays and unanticipated costs. If you are having work organised through an agent then they should be able to make arrangements for you, or you can consult an official customs agent for the same.

The usual procedure is to ensure that the package in question is clearly addressed to the name of the yacht and the marina or boatyard where it is lying (must be an official customs authorised facility). The marina management will then hold the parts until they are collected by the owner of the boat. If someone other than the owner is to collect the parts then they will require an official power of attorney, arranged through a local notary office. Arrange this in advance before you leave Turkey, as it is more difficult and more expensive to do this once you have left.

Duty free fuel is available to all foreign yachts upon their departure from Turkey, however, it is best to check the facts in advance to avoid disappointment. The fuel must be ordered by tanker through the local customs authority and is subject to a minimum amount that is far in excess of what most pleasure craft can carry. It is not permitted to split the fuel order between several boats, even if they are all departing Turkey, so this is a perk engineered for the benefit of larger commercial vessels and superyachts only.

Ports of Entry to Turkey
(along the coastline covered in this book)
İzmir
Çeşme
Kuşadası
Didim
Güllük
Turgutreis
Bodrum
Datça
Marmaris
Fethiye
Kaş
Finike
Antalya

MARINAS, HARBOURS AND ANCHORING
The Aegean and Mediterranean coasts of Turkey have a wealth of berthing and anchoring possibilities, but practices here may be slightly different to what you are used to if you have done most of your sailing in

Northern Europe or the Americas. In general you can take your cue from those around you, but here are a few guidelines to get you started:

Anchoring

The waters in Turkey are generally deep until you are very close to shore, which means that depths suitable for anchoring may be limited even in comparatively large sheltered bays. For this reason most vessels tend to anchor quite close together and quite close to the shore, rather than spread out evenly across the bay.

To prevent damage to themselves and others, the majority of vessels secure themselves by taking a line ashore and tying to a suitable tree, rock or post provided for this purpose. In this case you can tighten up on your anchor after securing the shore lines in a similar way as you will do when anchoring stern-to in a harbour (see below). This has the advantage of digging your anchor well into the ground and providing extra security in the case of wind shifts or a build up of swell overnight.

If there is plenty of space and you are planning to stop only for a couple of hours during the daytime, then you may be able to get away with simply free-swinging at anchor for a short while, but it is considered polite to leave space for other vessels to anchor if they enter a bay after you have settled and retired for the night, so usually taking a line ashore is the best option.

Berthing stern-to with an anchor

The relative scarcity of large shallow areas means that many harbours have only a single protected quay to which vessels are expected to tie up to stern-to, thus maximising the space available for other vessels. The lack of significant tidal range and currents mean this is feasible simply by laying an anchor out and using this to hold the boat off the quay.

Of course it is never that simple in practice and the technique of laying the anchor in the right place and approaching at the correct speed and angle must be learnt before you are really proficient at it. Here are a few tips:

1. Get everything prepared well in advance before you start the manoeuvre:
• Have your fenders deployed along both sides to protect yourself and the boat you will moor next to.
• Have two stern lines attached, fed correctly through the fairleads, loosely coiled and ready to throw.
• Move the tender forward to prevent running it over, but not so far that the anchor falls into it when released!
• Ensure that the anchor is untied and ready to deploy on the helmsman's signal. Using a free drop mechanism is better than lowering the anchor using the windlass control, as if the boat is moving quickly and the anchor dropping slowly it may not reach the sea floor until the vessel is almost at the dock and will have to be re-laid.

• Ensure that all crew members are briefed on the manoeuvre and know their role. It's best to keep young children out of the way so that they do not cause a distraction at the vital moment.

2. Approach from some distance in reverse. This allows you to get a feel for helming the boat in reverse and time to overcome any prop walk. You will also be able to judge how the wind conditions affect the steering of the boat and gauge your speed to prevent the bow being blown off as you approach.

3. The anchor should be laid approximately three boat lengths from the quayside and directly opposite the berth. It takes practice to get used to judging the correct moment to drop the anchor but you can bear the following in mind to help you:
• Unless you have a well-trained team there will usually be some delay between the helmsman making the call and the anchor operator getting the anchor to fall, and there will always be another short delay before the anchor actually reaches the sea bed. Bear this in mind and try to err on the side of calling the drop slightly early rather than late.
• As you approach the dock the distance between the helm and the anchor is one boat length, and the distance between the dock and the bow of the boat you are berthing next to (unless wildly different in size) is likely to be another, so the helmsman can concentrate on judging the distance of one boat length between himself and the bow of the boat next door. This is much easier than trying to judge three boat lengths from the dock.
• If you have to enter the harbour parallel to the quay then try to stay approximately three boat lengths from the dock. As soon as the helmsman can see directly into the berthing space over his or her shoulder, he or she should turn the wheel hard to steer directly into the berth, straightening up a few moments before the vessel is lined up perfectly. At this moment the anchor should be in the perfect position to drop.

4. When you reach the quay you should always hand the windward line ashore first, and make it fast immediately. If you are having to deal with crosswinds then the helmsman will be able to put the engine into forward gear and control the boat by motoring into the wind direction at this point, as long as the windward line is made off securely so the boat will not actually go anywhere. If all has gone well there will be plenty of time to get the other line secure and take up on the anchor until it bites before re-adjusting the windward line. If the anchor is not laid correctly or has not dug in correctly then it is simple enough to motor back out, pick up the anchor and begin the process again.

5. The person at the helm should be the one who controls all aspects of the manoeuvre, including when to drop the anchor and which lines to take ashore. They are best placed to judge what is happening. If

things are going wrong then it is never too late to pop the engine into forwards, pick up the anchor and go out to try again.

Remember that practice makes perfect and if you are new to this technique, or a bit rusty since the last holiday, then it is best to find a quiet quayside somewhere and have a few practice approaches in order to get used to the handling of the boat so that all of the crew can learn their roles in the manoeuvre.

Berthing stern-to with lazylines

Many of the restaurants and all of the marinas in this area have installed lazylines onto their jetties and docks, which allows them to fit more boats into the same space and makes it easier for vessels to tie up securely as well.

A lazyline is simply a length of rope that is run from the quay to a pre-laid secure anchor point. Visiting yachts do not have to lay their own anchor; they simply reverse up to the dock, pick up the lazyline from there, pull up tight on the end that it attached to the anchor point in the water and secure the line at the vessel's bow.

You should prepare for berthing in the same way as if you were dropping anchor, and have somebody ready to collect the lazyline and take it immediately to the bow as soon as you reach the dock. Without an anchor to hold the bow off the dock, it is important to take up on the lazyline as quickly as possible, particularly if there is any crosswind. In this case it is useful to get the windward line made off straightaway and motor forwards on this to control the boat as described in the section above. Be careful not to foul the propeller on the lazyline of course.

Berthing bows-to

Many boat owners prefer berthing bows-to rather than stern-to, and there can be several reasons for this: in busy harbours you may not want to give passers-by a clear view down your companionway or into your cockpit; some boats are very difficult to manoeuvre in reverse; and in some places it is necessary to avoid damaging the rudder on rubble that has accumulated at the base of the quay.

In this case you should prepare for berthing as described above, but you will need to rig your kedge anchor to drop cleanly over the stern (be sure to tie off the bitter end of the anchor rode securely before you drop!) Judging distance from the helm can be more difficult when mooring up this way, so good communication between the bow and helm is vital to avoid crunching into the quay. It's a good idea to agree on a countdown system and to use hand signals rather than shouting loudly across the harbour.

How to recover a crossed anchor

Crossed anchors are an unfortunate fact of life in many of the harbours along this coast. Mooring space is limited and the harbours were generally designed for small fishing boats rather than cruising yachts. If the weather is calm and the other boat's crew are awake then you can ask them to slacken their anchor chain, which should allow your windlass to do the work for you and bring the tangle to the surface.

Once you can see the offending chain hooked over your anchor, it is tempting to try to hold it with your boat hook, or even your hands. Don't do this as it is a sure way of losing your boat hook or worse. Take a length of warp to the bow and make one end off on a bow cleat. Pass the other end underneath the offending chain (not through it), take up the slack and make this off on another bow cleat. You should then be able to lower your anchor on the windlass and free it whilst the rope holds the chain. Once your anchor is free you can release one end of the rope and allow the chain to fall back to the bottom of the harbour. It will probably do this very quickly, so make sure that the rope ends are free to run and will not trap any limbs or boat equipment as they do so.

FACILITIES FOR VESSELS

Yachting tourism is a growing source of income for Turkey, and the government has encouraged the establishment of facilities and provision of services. More and more people are starting to discover Turkey as a cruising destination, so to some extent the demand is starting to outstrip the supply. But new marinas are already under construction and further plans to increase the berthing capacity of the area are under discussion. Generally you will find yachting services in Turkey equal to or superior than elsewhere at this end of the Med.

Water

Fresh water is available in most of the places mentioned in this book. Marinas will have a supply to every berth,

Vessels berthed using lazylines rather than anchors

but public harbours may have fewer points available. In both cases you will usually have to provide your own hose, although if there is one attached you will be welcome to use this. Sometimes the water will be metered, sometimes included in the price of the berth, and sometimes it will be available free to any yachts using the restaurant's facilities. Be aware that several of the more remote restaurants are not connected to mains water supply, so will have none to spare for yachts. This is mentioned in the appropriate section.

Fuel

Most marinas will have their own fuel dock where you can buy diesel and usually petrol and sometimes gas as well. In town and village harbours where there are a number of gulets and day tripper boats a tanker will often visit to fuel up these boats. If you are able to squeeze amongst them on the same dock there is no reason why you cannot take advantage of this, but be aware that the tanker may not be able to access other parts of the harbour used by visiting boats. If in doubt you can check with the harbour master on arrival. Most of the harbour masters usually speak some English and may be willing to call the tanker on your behalf. Local restaurant owners may also be able to help, particularly if they advertise provision of fuel when no other source is apparent. All boat fuel is sold at the normal road price, and although duty free fuel is available in theory, the practice of obtaining it means that it is usually impractical for anything other than commercial vessels or large motor boats – see page 17.

Fuel stations are located at most commercial marinas in the area

Gas

Bottled gas is widely available in Turkey, where there is no mains gas supply because of the risk from earthquakes. There are a number of different supply companies such as BP, İpragaz, Aygaz and others. Be aware that the gas regulators required in Turkey are different from those you may have used elsewhere such as in Greece or Croatia. The bottles are a different shape as well. Occasionally you may be able to get an

Electricity and water are available at most harbours in Turkey

old bottle refilled, but if you are planning on spending any length of time in the country it makes sense just to buy a new regulator and a couple of Turkish bottles. You may even be able to find someone who is heading off towards Greece who will be willing to swap bottles with you. Gas bottles can be purchased directly from the main suppliers but are also often available from small mini-markets close to the harbour where you can swap your empty bottles for their full ones.

Shore power

Mains electricity supply in Turkey is 50Hz alternating current at 230v, and household sockets take round two pin plugs as in the rest of mainland Europe. Shore power supply is available in most marinas and harbours where there is a mains supply, but rarely in more isolated areas without mains connection. Sometimes the electrical installation can look rather 'home-made', which is one of the joys of being away from EU restrictions I suppose!

Technical services and yacht chandlery

Turkey has a long tradition of wooden boat construction, which continues to this day, and many of the skills and techniques are applicable to modern cruising yachts as well. Turkish tradesmen have also woken up to the fact that providing services to yachts means good money for them and the main yachting centres along the coast have an excellent provision of services available. Be aware though that the industry is barely regulated and that it can be difficult to obtain any kind of guarantee of the quality of the work to be done. Word of mouth is always the best recommendation, and most of the marinas and yachting centres have a visible and active cruising community from all nationalities who will be happy to share their experiences and advice with newcomers. There are also a number of accredited marine surveyors in the area who will oversee jobs on your behalf and ensure that professional standards are adhered to.

Yacht chandlery facilities are generally pretty good, and where original parts are not readily available there is usually a Turkish-made equivalent that will do the job, or you can have something made specifically for you. Some imported parts can be more costly to buy in Turkey than within the EU for example, but it is possible to import spares for yachts duty free (see page 17), so check this with your marina or local agent if necessary.

Most Turkish towns have an industrial area known as a *sanayi* on their outskirts. This is where you can get almost anything repaired or fabricated, usually for a very reasonable cost. Most *sanayi* areas have a selection of carpentry, metalworking, mechanical and even upholstery workshops. Don't expect the *ustas* (trade specialists) to speak much English, but if you can take along a similar part or a drawing to use as a pattern you can usually manage to convey your requirements easily enough.

Rubbish disposal

Turkey has a very efficient rubbish collection system, organised by the *belediye* (local council). There will usually be general waste disposal bins located near the harbour, with others throughout the town or village. The concept of recycling has been accepted by Turkish councils, and there are several recycling plants located along the coast that can accept rubbish from the surrounding areas. Recycling bins are generally situated close to the general waste disposal bins and are normally colour coded and labelled in Turkish (with pictures).

Even in remote bays, some restaurants do advertise a rubbish collection service. However, their own facilities are limited and it is far better for everyone if you can keep your waste with you until you reach

Rubbish disposal in Skopea Limanı

a large port with regular collection services. It goes without saying that you should never dispose of inorganic waste overboard.

Waste disposal

As noted on pages 15-16, the Turkish government is introducing a scheme to control the disposal of waste water from vessels cruising its coastline. At the moment there are around 30 licensed waste collection facilities in the Muğla area listed on the TURMEPA website and in government leaflets about the scheme, where you will be able to discharge your waste and have your blue card swiped. It is planned that more facilities will be built and licensed by the time the scheme is introduced, and that further facilities will be developed along other parts of the coast in anticipation of the expansion of the scheme over the next five years. For the time being it is still permitted to discharge black and grey water overboard from vessels outside the Bodrum-Fethiye area as long as you are more than 3M offshore, but you can expect the pilot scheme to be expanded in the future.

General information
VISA REQUIREMENTS

Most visitors to Turkey will require a visa before entry to the country. Generally these can be purchased on arrival at the Customs and Immigration entry point (ie, at the airport or ferry terminal). You should make sure that you have the correct payment available in cash to avoid delays. You can check visa requirements directly at the Ministry of Foreign Affairs website. http://www.mfa.gov.tr/MFA/ConsularInformation/ForForeigners/VisaInformation/visafees.htm

Do be aware that a three month visa is interpreted as 90 days rather than three calendar months, and that overstays will be penalised on a per day basis. Also be aware that if you overstay your visa by more than a couple of days the Immigration authorities may insist that you do not return to Turkey for up to three months, so make sure that you keep a note of the expiration date and aim to clear out of the country with days to spare to avoid problems.

Your visa is usually valid for multiple entries, but does not entitle you to work during your stay. Residence permits for longer stays can be obtained after your arrival in Turkey. Visit the Ministry of Labour and Social Security website for details on how to obtain a working permit. www.csgb.gov.tr

TRAVEL – LOCAL AND INTERNATIONAL
Airports

International airports are located close to the towns of İzmir, Bodrum, Dalaman and Antalya. Each of these airports is served by daily international charter flights from all over Europe during the summer season.

Regular domestic flights to İstanbul continue throughout the year, and there is a limited schedule of flights to the UK during the winter.

İstanbul has two airports, the larger of which is Atatürk International located on the western European side of the city. Atatürk airport has both domestic and international terminals and is the main hub for the national carrier, Turkish Airlines. Direct flights are available from most European countries as well as the USA, Australia, the Middle East and the Far East. Sahiba Gökcen airport is

Distinctive yellow taxis at a taxi rank

located on the eastern side of the Bosphorus and also has both domestic and international flights. If you are transferring between the two airports you should allow at least an hour to cross the city by taxi (approximately 80 TL fare).

Airline websites

Easyjet	www.easyjet.com
British Airways	www.ba.com
Turkish Airlines	www.thy.com
Cyprus Turkish Airlines	www.kty.com
Onur Air	www.aegeanflights.com
Atlas Air (domestic)	www.atlasair.com
Pegasus Airlines (domestic)	www.flypgs.com
German Wings	www.germanwings.com
Condor	www.10.condor.com
First Choice	www.firstchoice.co.uk
Thomas Cook	www.flythomascook.com
Monarch	www.monarch.co.uk
Thomson	www.thomsonfly.com

Taxis

Licensed taxis operating in Turkey are yellow in colour and are plentiful in towns, cities and resorts. They are usually metered, although in some areas a specific price is set for various journeys (especially between airports and surrounding resorts). The Turkish for 'taxi' is *taksi.*

Driving in Turkey

There is so much to see in Turkey that it is well worth taking a couple of days to explore some of the ancient sites and natural attractions that lie inland. Hiring a car and driving there yourself is the most flexible and convenient way of doing this, and you can usually find some overnight accommodation to allow you to spread the journey over two days.

However, you should take utmost care and precaution when driving in Turkey, as it has one of the worst road safety records in Europe. Towns are congested and other drivers can be erratic. The standard of roads along the coastal areas is improving, but road marking and lighting is often poor, and unlit tractors or motorcycles are not uncommon after dark.

The national speed limit in Turkey is 90km/hr if you are driving a standard car (it is less for goods vehicles). Although you will regularly see others driving far in excess of this, speed traps are not uncommon and result in on-the-spot fines of up to 200 TL. Speed limits in built-up areas vary and are rarely enforced, but do take care of pedestrians, cyclists, motorbikes and scooters who can all appear without warning from side roads. Be aware that on roundabouts in Turkey the traffic on the roundabout must give way to other traffic joining the roundabout. Signage is usually unclear so keep your eyes open and give way where necessary.

Do not let this deter you completely, however. The Turkish countryside is just as beautiful and dramatic inland as it is along the coast, and there are some spectacular places that are well worth making the effort to see whilst you are visiting the country.

Car hire

Most of the big international car hire companies such as Avis, Hertz etc have agents in Turkey and there are plenty of local outfits as well, especially in the main tourist resorts along the coast.

Hire fees are generally reasonable and include insurance. Extra drivers can usually be added for a fee, and don't forget to check if there is a mileage limitation. You will need to show a valid licence for each named driver. Almost all cars have air-conditioning, which is essential in the summer time. The rental offices can usually provide maps, or at least directions for how to reach the main tourist attractions, which are usually well signposted.

For shorter distances or running about town then hiring a scooter or moped is also popular. Insist that the rental company provides a helmet for the driver and passenger and do wear these whenever you are driving. Although this law has been widely disregarded in the past, the police are finally starting to enforce it and even wear helmets themselves these days. If you have travel insurance, not wearing a helmet could invalidate a claim for injury.

Railways

Turkey does not have a national rail network, but does have several regional networks operating mainly in the inland areas around İstanbul, Ankara and the east of the country. Work is underway to expand and integrate these, as well as to construct a high-speed link between İstanbul and Ankara. A suburban network serves the city of İzmir from outlying districts, but does not extend further along the coast and is unlikely to be of use to visitors.

National coach services

The easiest way to travel around Turkey is by coach and there are a number of companies operating routes between most towns and cities. Longer journeys such as between İstanbul and the Aegean coastline are usually scheduled to run overnight, and the coaches themselves are modern, comfortable and air-conditioned. Most towns have an *otogar* or coach station, which acts as the departure point for all of the different companies and routes. Services are regular and frequent, so advance booking is not usually required apart from during public holidays. Tickets can be paid for in advance or on the coach itself, and there will usually be several pick-up and drop off points along the way. Meal breaks are scheduled on longer journeys.

Local bus services – Dolmuş

Smaller towns and villages are connected by an excellent minibus system, also known as *dolmuş* (pronounced *dol-mush*). These are often colour coded according to the route they operate on, and will have the destination printed on a board next to the driver. There are no set departure times or stops along the route. The buses leave from the main depot when the driver feels he has enough people on board, and will pick up or drop off passengers on demand. Fares are cheap and paid directly to the driver. The name *dolmuş* comes from the Turkish word for 'stuffed', which gives an indication of how busy the buses can get on popular routes at peak times of the year.

COMMUNICATIONS

Telephone

The International Direct Dialing code for Turkey is 90. All Turkish phone numbers have 11 digits, which are usually grouped 4-3-2-2. If you are calling a Turkish number from abroad you should leave out the first 0 from the number (eg 00 90 (0) 252 555 55 55). To dial overseas from a Turkish phone first dial 00, then the area code (eg 00 44 for the UK) and then the rest of the number.

For land lines the first four numbers are the area code (eg, 0252 for Mugla area). If you are calling from a landline within the same area you can omit the code and just dial the seven digit number that follows. If you are calling from a mobile phone you will always need to dial all 11 digits. All Turkish mobile phone numbers begin 05**.

The national telephone company in Turkey is called Türk Telkom. Public phones are widespread and are usually operated either by a phone card that you can buy in most kiosks and mini-markets, or sometimes by credit card.

In larger towns such as Bodrum, Marmaris and Fethiye you will see Türk Telkom offices where you can make and receive international calls at a special rate. You can usually send and receive faxes from these

Public telephones are widely available in Turkey

The PTT is the national post office in Turkey

to join. Registration is free but you will need to show your passport and it can take several weeks for the registration to be completed so you may still spend some time without connection.

Internet

Turkish businesses and individuals have taken to the internet in a big way, and even the smallest restaurant is likely to boast its own website these days. Most towns and even some villages will have at least one internet café where you can send and receive emails from one of their PCs. If you are travelling with a wireless enabled laptop then you will find that many restaurants, bars and cafés offer free wireless connection to their customers, although signal strength can vary. Most commercial marinas also offer this service to their customers.

Post office (*postane*)

The national post office in Turkey is known as the PTT and has a conspicuous yellow sign that you will find in the majority of towns and villages. Post offices are generally open seven days a week from 0800-2200. During this time you can buy stamps, make phone calls and send packages from the main counter. You will usually find post boxes outside, with different slots for local, national and international mail. You may also see some post boxes at kiosks where you can also buy stamps and postcards, but using official ones at the PTT might help to ensure that your cards do not reach home long after you do.

Mail sent from Turkey generally reaches its destination quite reliably, but the service for incoming mail is rather more erratic. If you are waiting for important documents it is always worth paying extra to have them couriered so you can be sure of when and where they will be delivered. Major companies like Federal Express, DHL and UPS all have agents throughout Turkey. It is possible to rent a post box in the local PTT office if you will be there for some time, and most marinas will also hold onto mail delivered for their customers – make sure that your mail is clearly marked with your name and your boat's name as well as the marina's full address.

offices too. It is possible also to make and receive calls from most larger PTT post offices.

These days many people travel with a mobile phone, particularly on cruising yachts that may be out of harbour for days or weeks at a time. Network coverage in Turkey is generally good along the coastline and even in many smaller villages.

The main network providers in Turkey are Turkcell, Vodafone and Avea. You should expect to pay the usual roaming charges for making and receiving calls and text messages. Longer term visitors often like to purchase a local pay-as-you-go SIM card to use in their own phone in order to avoid these roaming fees, but beware of doing this in Turkey. Turkish networks will automatically detect and shut down any Turkish mobile line that is being used in a foreign handset. This is intended to prevent the illegal import of large numbers of cheap handsets from abroad (like many luxury items in Turkey, mobile phones are quite heavily taxed), but it is inconvenient for foreign visitors wanting to use their existing phones with a Turkish number.

One solution is just to purchase a cheap handset from a Turkish supplier, as this will automatically be registered on the network and so will not be cut off. Beware of purchasing cheap second-hand models as they may very well have been traded in by another disgruntled foreigner after being blocked by the network. It is also possible to register your own phone on one of the Turkish networks. You can do this in a main outlet store for whichever network you decide

PROVISIONING

Provisioning in Turkey is simple enough; even small villages will have some sort of mini-market where you can buy general provisions, and mid-sized towns and above are likely to have at least one supermarket. The big supermarket chains include Migros, Tansaş, Kipa and Carrefour, and sell everything you would find in a British supermarket, including electrical and household goods, refrigerated, dried and frozen produce, toiletries and even garden furniture. Larger stores will usually have separate bakery, butcher and

General provisions are available from mini-markets all around Turkey

seafood sections as well as a beer, wine and spirits aisle.

Few foodstuffs are imported into Turkey from abroad, but you will usually be able to find a locally produced equivalent of things you are accustomed to at home. If there are any particular brand names or products that you cannot live without for a week though, then it is best to take them with you. Do remember that as Turkey is a Muslim country, pork products are generally unavailable.

Fresh produce is available seasonally in Turkey, and tastes all the better for it. The best place to purchase fruit and vegetables is at one of the local markets that are held regularly in most towns and villages (details are provided in the appropriate sections). Not only will there be a wider range of produce in fresher condition than you will find in any supermarket or mini-market, but it will be much cheaper as well. Dried foods, dairy products, clothing and household goods will also often be on sale at these markets and the atmosphere is usually inviting and entertaining.

HEALTH CARE AND INSURANCE
Turkey is not part of the EU and has no reciprocal health care arrangements with EU countries, so it is important to make sure that you have good travel insurance if you are visiting the country for even a short period. You should make sure that your insurance covers you for activities such as sailing and watersports, which are sometimes excluded.

Health care in Turkey is generally good in all the main tourist areas along the coast. Larger towns and cities such as İzmir, Bodrum, Marmaris, Fethiye and Antalya have private hospitals as well as a state run one, and some of those in İzmir and Antalya are used as teaching centres for the universities located in these cities. Private hospitals normally have interpreters and many of the staff there will speak some English. The outpatients' department can usually deal with most issues without the need for an appointment or a long wait.

Smaller *polikliniks* can also be found that deal with general health queries and these will often offer other services such as dentistry. Most towns will have a number of specialised dentistry clinics as well (*diş hekimi*). These are much cheaper than in the UK and on the whole provide a good quality of care. Pharmacies (*eczane*) are widespread in Turkey, and you can buy a greater range of medicines (including antibiotics) without prescription than you can in the UK. Try to provide the generic drug name if possible as brand names can vary between countries.

EMERGENCY SERVICES
National emergency numbers are shown below. There is no national ambulance service, but ambulance services are provided by private and state hospitals in each region.

Coastguard	154
Fire Service	110
Traffic Police	154
Police	155
Jandarma	156

Turkey has several police forces which deal with different jurisdictions as shown below:

The *Jandarma* is a military police force which has jurisdiction mainly in rural areas between towns and villages.

The general police force (*emniyet/polis*) is responsible within towns, cities and other urban areas.

The *Zabıta* is a municipal police force concerned with enforcing local regulations relating to trading standards, sanitation, construction and pricing.

The traffic police (*trafik polis*) deals with all traffic incidents.

BANKS, CURRENCY AND CURRENCY EXCHANGE

Currency

The currency in Turkey is the *Türk Lirası* (Turkish Lira), although Euros, US dollars and occasionally sterling pounds may be accepted in some larger tourist areas. Generally you will not get a great rate of exchange for using other currencies, so stick to spending Turkish Lira as far as possible.

In the past Turkey had suffered from spiralling inflation, which meant that even ordering a meal in a restaurant could cost you millions of Lira. In 2005 the government introduced a new currency, the Yeni (new) Turkish Lira (YTL). Essentially it lopped six zeros off the old currency, with 1,000,000 old Turkish Lira being equivalent to 1 Yeni Turkish Lira. The Yeni Turkish Lira was also divided into 100 kuruş (pronounced *koo-roosh*), which makes it similar to other decimal currencies.

On 1 January 2009 the term Yeni was dropped and the currency became known again as simply the Turkish Lira (TL).

All this can lead to a certain amount of confusion with the terminology. Even today, four years after the change in currency, you may well be told that the price of something is *bir milyar* (1 million) rather than simply 1 TL, especially when shopping in local markets. Generally though it's easy enough to work out which price you should expect to pay for that head of lettuce or punnet of strawberries.

The Turkish Lira (TL) currently has coins in the following denominations: 1 kuruş, 5 kuruş, 10 kuruş, 25 kuruş, 50 kuruş and 1 TL; and notes in these denominations: 5TL, 10TL, 20TL, 50TL, 100TL and 200TL. All banknotes feature a portrait of Mustafa Kemal Atatürk (see page 41) on one side, and a depiction of another notable Turk on the other.

Banks

Turkey has a number of national banks with branches in towns and villages across the country. Bank opening hours are generally Monday-Friday 0900-1700 only, excluding any public holidays (see page 27).

Some of the more widespread and established Turkish banks are: Garanti bank, Yapı Kredi bank, HSBC bank, Akbank, Türkiye İş bank and Denizbank, but you will see many others on your travels through the country.

Foreigners are permitted to open bank accounts in Turkey as long as they can supply a residential address (a marina address will do), and have been issued with a tax number. To obtain a tax number you need to apply to the local tax office (*vergi dairesi*) and supply a copy of your passport. You do not need to have official Turkish residency to obtain a tax number. Generally it is possible to open current accounts in TL, Euro, Sterling and US$ currencies for no extra charge. Many banks also offer TL savings accounts which have extremely good interest rates. You should discuss the terms and conditions with the banks directly. Larger branches and those in tourist resorts will generally have at least one customer liaison staff member who can speak good English, although you may have to wait in line for an appointment.

Most bank branches will have at least one automatic teller machine (ATM) where you can withdraw local currency using any VISA or Mastercard credit or debit card. You will also find stand-alone ATM machines in many locations throughout towns and resorts, and in marinas. Some ATM machines will also let you withdraw cash in other currencies such as Euros and US dollars. You should be aware that all the usual fees for overseas withdrawal will apply whenever you use a card in one of these machines, which are normally greater for credit than for debit cards. Check with your card issuer for further details of these charges. Cash withdrawal is also available over the counter – you should present your debit or credit card plus your passport as proof of identity.

Currency exchange

The simplest way to obtain local currency in Turkey is through the wide network of ATM machines that are available throughout the country. This is quick and convenient, although you are likely to be subject to a daily withdrawal limit and may also have to pay a processing fee for each withdrawal.

Currency exchange is available over the counter at almost all bank branches as well as all PTT offices and dedicated currency exchange outlets that you will find in most towns and tourist resorts. The best currencies to exchange are Sterling, Euros and US dollars, and the exchange rates and commission scales should be displayed clearly for you to check before you complete the transaction. It is best to avoid changing large amounts of currency before you travel to Turkey, as you will often find that you can get a better rate by exchanging within the country than abroad.

Travellers' cheques are almost a thing of the past in these days of easy exchange. Their value of security in the case of loss or theft is offset by the more lengthy procedures to cash them and the commission costs involved. Having said that, it is possible to exchange travellers' cheques in most bank branches and many currency exchange centres.

Money transfer to and from abroad is also available; all PTT post offices are agents for the Western Union money wiring service.

Cash versus plastic

In northern Europe and many other places around the world, it is becoming increasingly common to pay for most goods and services using a credit or debit card rather than cash. Although plastic is becoming more widely accepted within Turkey, this is still overwhelmingly a cash economy.

Shopping facilities at top class marinas

Small restaurants in isolated bays are unlikely to have the facilities to take credit card payments; often they do not even have a phone line. If you are planning to spend much of your time visiting these kinds of locations then you should make sure that you have sufficient cash available, or plan your route so that you can top up the reserves as it becomes necessary.

Even in larger towns and resorts you can often negotiate some kind of discount if you are prepared to pay in cash, as this will save the retailer from having to pay the bank charges associated with taking payment on plastic.

PUBLIC HOLIDAYS

Turkey has 12 days of official public holiday each year, which is more than most countries.

In addition to the religious holidays of şeker *bayramı* and *kurban bayramı* (see page 41) the following days are also public holidays in Turkey:

1 January	New Year's Day
23 April	National Sovereignty and Children's day
19 May	Ataturk & youth celebration day
30 August	Victory Day (over invading forces after WWI)
29 October	Republic Day

You can expect many businesses and most public offices to be closed on these dates, and there will often be parades or public events in villages and town centres, as well as a lot of Turkish flags flying.

Opening hours

Most shops in Turkey tend to open from around 1000 until 2000/2100, or even later in many large towns and tourist resorts, and are likely to be open seven days a week. There are no siesta hours, so shops will stay open right through the day.

Supermarkets open for similar hours, but large branches may be open for even longer, from 0900 until 2200 or 2300 in some cases. Smaller mini-markets are also likely to be open until late in the evenings and will often remain open even on public holidays.

Office hours tend to be a more standard 0900-1800, Monday-Friday, with an hour closed for lunch (usually 1200-1300). Businesses will generally be closed at weekends and on public holidays, especially government offices.

For bank and vessel formalities office hours, see the appropriate sections on pages 26 and 16.

INFORMATION RESOURCES

Internet resources

www.goturkey.com is the tourism portal of the Turkish government's Ministry of Culture and Tourism. Information is available on all of Turkey's main tourist attractions and you can check updated visa requirements on this site.

www.kultur.gov.tr is the main website of the Ministry of Culture and Tourism, and contains information in a variety of languages.

www.allaboutturkey.com is a website published and maintained by one of Turkey's many official tour guides and is full of interesting information about the country and regions, which is presented in a personal way from a native Turk.

www.turkeytravelplanner.com is another guide's website, this time from an American travel organiser who has lived in the country for many years and has plenty of comments and suggestions for where to go and what to see.

www.noonsite.com is a global cruising sailor's resource, which brings together information on local activities, marina and technical facilities, health, communications and provisioning, and covers most of the Turkish coastal area.

www.turmepa.org.tr is the official website of the Turkish Marine Environment Protection Agency. You can find details of local initiatives to clean up coastal areas and promote environmental awareness amongst visitors and citizens. TURMEPA is also involved in implementing the Blue Card scheme along the coastline between Bodrum and Fethiye (see pages 15-16), and you can find information about the scheme plus a list of licensed waste disposal facilities on its website.

Local publications

• The Bay Express newspaper is sold throughout the region and features information on marinas, harbours and especially restaurants in the area. It is revised annually so should always be fairly up-to-date.

• The Yachtsman's Compass is a marine directory that covers the area between İzmir and Antalya. It is available free in many places and contains contact details for every type of marine service, including technical and mechanical services, fibreglass and sail repairs, charter, brokerage, marinas and tourism services.

• 101 Questions About Turkey is an interesting little book that covers just about every aspect of living in and visiting the country. It is written by an official tour guide and was inspired by the many questions he has been asked by clients over the years. You can find the book in book stores around the country, or visit the related website www.101-turkey.com

Other literature of interest

• Birds Without Wings by Louis de Bernieres. This novel from the writer of the well-known Captain Corelli's Mandolin is set in the area between İzmir and Fethiye during the time between the start of WWI and the conclusion of the Turkish War of Independence and the establishment of the Republic of Turkey. As in his other novels, de Bernieres chooses to tell his story through the personal recollections of a handful of characters and weaves these strands around the larger process of history and influential figures, particularly Mustafa Kemal Atatürk. This is a blend of comedy, history and tragedy.

• A Fez of the Heart by Jeremy Seal. This is a modern travelogue written by a long term yabancı (foreign) resident of Ankara and teacher of English. The writer follows the footsteps of Atatürk as he travels through the country searching for the now-outlawed Fez, and encountering a variety of different attitudes to himself and his quest along the way. This is enlightening, entertaining and ultimately

a serious look at modern Turkish identity and the problems within.

• Snow (Kar) by Orhan Pamuk.
Orhan Pamuk won the Nobel Prize for Literature in 2006 and is Turkey's only Nobel laureate. He is also one of the country's best-known authors and has courted his share of controversy for his willingness to address issues such as the Kurdish 'problem' and the Armenian (so-called) genocide. Snow is set in the fictional eastern town of Kars, where Islamism and secularism are colliding in the spheres of politics and culture. The main character is a poet named Ka, who becomes enamoured of a childhood friend who has found notoriety for refusing to remove her headscarf. Pamuk's published writings cover 30 years and include several other novels as well as pieces of journalism and the personal memoir İstanbul: Memories of a City.

• Kaptan June and the Dalyan Turtles by June Haimoff. This short book is a memoir from the colourful lady who organised an international movement to protect the turtle breeding grounds near the Dalyan River and ultimately succeeded in having the area proclaimed a protected area by the Turkish Ministry of the Environment. The book is full of anecdotes and local colour. The author is still a resident of Dalyan – see page 47 – and recently had a local street named after her.

Turkey and Turkish Culture

TURKISH VOCABULARY AND PRONUNCIATION

Although English is widely spoken in most tourist centres, if you can take the trouble to learn a few Turkish phrases you will find that the already hospitable Turks will welcome your efforts greatly and you will get much more out of your visit. See page 220 for a glossary of useful words and phrases.

TOURIST SITES AND ATTRACTIONS

Turkey is home to a wealth of archaeological treasures, including ancient burial sites, libraries and bath houses, and even the remains of entire cities. Many of these fabulous locations are within easy reach of the Aegean and Mediterranean coastlines and are well worth a visit if you are in the area. In fact it is this wealth of history and culture that has made the country such a popular destination and keeps visitors returning again and again to experience more of what the country has to offer. Some of the most famous attractions are listed below, but other sites are located along the coastline and are continually being discovered and preserved.

Ephesus (also known as Efes)

The ruins of this ancient city are fascinating and well preserved, and lie between the towns of İzmir and

Kuşadası on the Aegean coast of Turkey. Although the town was a major commercial port in its heyday, the ruins today are some 5km from the sea, which illustrates how much the coastline has changed in the last 2,000 years. Ongoing excavations since the mid 1800s have still uncovered only around 10% of the overall site and are today carried out under the auspices of the Ephesus Museum and Turkish Ministry of Culture and Tourism. Greater emphasis is now being placed on the preservation and restoration of structures already unearthed, which serves to bring the ancient city to life more readily for the visitor.

Ephesus is a popular day trip for visitors from nearby resorts, the city of İzmir and the cruise ship ports in İzmir and Kuşadası. If possible, visit the site early in the day or out of the main season, which will help you to avoid both the fierce summer heat and the main arrival times of the coach parties. It is well worth paying for an official tour guide to accompany you through the ruins. They are extremely knowledgeable and will bring the city to life for you in the most memorable way.

Highlights of the tour include the Celsus Library, the twin amphitheatres, the temple of Artemis and the public baths and toilets. Most visitors to the site also stop at the nearby location where it is said that the Virgin Mary spent her final days in the company of St John. This typical Roman house was converted into

The ruins at Ephesus are well preserved

a church in the 4th century AD. It was visited by Pope John-Paul II in the 1980s when it was declared a place of pilgrimage, and more recently, in 2006, by the current Pope Benedict XV1 on a visit to foster relations between the Catholic Church and Muslims in Turkey.

Pamukkale

Pamukkale literally means 'cotton castle' in Turkish, which is an apt description of the famous travertine terraces located near the town of Denizli. The terraces are formed from calcium bicarbonate, which has precipitated from the area's mineral-rich hot springs. In ancient times a Greek settlement known as Hieropolis developed on the hills behind the terraces and the inhabitants profited from the medical benefits that the waters were supposed to confer.

These days the area is protected as a UNESCO World Heritage site, but in the past the area was so commercialised that it became seriously degraded. The delicate terraces were damaged by the passage of people walking across them and bathing in them, and the waters required for re-generation were diverted towards the large hotels that had been built over the ruins of Hieropolis.

Today the hotels are gone and attempts at preservation and conservation are being made. Human traffic is now restricted to a path through the centre of the travertine terraces and bathing is permitted in

The ancient biblical city of Ephesus

Amphitheatre at Hieropolis

only a few pools to allow others the time to recover and regenerate. The reduced water flow is directed over different areas of the terraces in rotation, in an attempt to bring recovery to the whole area. It will take many years for the terraces to regain their former glory, but what is left today is still an undeniably impressive sight.

As well as walking through the travertine terraces and bathing in the warm waters of the permitted pools, visitors can also explore the nearby remains of Hieropolis, including a large amphitheatre, colonnaded streets and ruined baths. There is also an interesting museum containing various sarcophagi, statues and smaller finds from the Hieropolis excavations. For an extra fee you can take a swim in the warm mineral waters of the Pamukkale Termal. These baths are featured in many of the postcards of Pamukkale, with stone columns strewn artistically around the pools, but the bathing fees are steep and the pools can get too crowded during the high season.

Dalyan and Kaunos

The Dalyan River area is the location of several different attractions and is a popular day trip for visitors staying in nearby resorts. It is easy to visit the area by boat and the local river boat co-operative organises trips from the nearby harbour of Ekincik.

The river winds through extensive reed beds towards the village of Dalyan and Köyceğiz Lake, and is overlooked by 7,000 year old Lycian rock tombs built into the cliff faces for the ancient kings. They gaze across the river to the town of Dalyan and can be reached from there by rowboat across the river. A road winds past them to the remains of ancient Kaunos. This well preserved Greco/Roman city was once a thriving port and is now under excavation. A token entry fee will allow you access to explore the remains, which include a small amphitheatre and a ruined bath house. The settlement once covered a large area and is an interesting and atmospheric place to explore at leisure.

Further along the river you come to Köyceğiz Lake and the small town of Köyceğiz. The Sultaniye spa complex on the south-west side of the lake includes two mud baths and two thermal pools with temperatures around 40°C. The mud is supposed to have beneficial properties to the skin when caked on and allowed to set. The warm sulphurous waters are also said to have medicinal benefits for those suffering from rheumatism, arthritis and liver complaints.

The Dalyan River delta is protected from the sea by the sweeping sands of İztuzu beach, which is also a protected nesting habitat for the Caretta caretta loggerhead sea turtles. The plight of these animals was brought to international attention through the efforts

Kaunos, near Dalyan

as well as various education initiatives amongst local residents and school children.

Knidos

Knidos was an important settlement and the primary city of the Dorian hexapolis federation. The original site was close to the modern day town of Datça, but the settlement later moved to the location at the far western end of the Datça peninsula where the remains can be seen today.

It is a desolate and windswept location that feels rather like the end of the world, but it is easy to see the strategic advantage of such a location in a world ruled by seafarers and traders. The settlement's size and importance can be determined from the fact that it has two amphitheatres.

The city is also famous for being home to the sculptor Praxiteles' nude statue of Venus, which became known as the 'Aphrodite of Knidos'. The story is that the sculpture was commissioned by the inhabitants of Kos island, and Praxiteles created both a nude version and a clothed version of the goddess. The citizens of Kos chose the clothed version, but the nude version was purchased by the inhabitants of Knidos and became famed for its beauty and the fact that it was the first life-size statue of a nude female form. Although the original has been lost, several copies of it exist, including one in the Vatican museum.

Aspendos

Aspendos is located approximately 40km to the east of Antalya, in an area that used to be known as Pamphylia. The remains visible today date from Roman times, although settlement in the area is believed to go back as far as the Hittite Empire of 800 BCE. Aspendos is most famous for the large (93m diameter) Roman amphitheatre which was built during the reign of Marcus Aurelius and restored after a visit from Atatürk in the 1930s.

of the English environmentalist June Haimoff. After settling in the area in 1984 she realised that the nesting habits of the turtles were in danger of being disrupted by the large scale developments that were planned along the beach. She began campaigning to raise awareness of the issue and eventually succeeded in having the area declared a natural reserve which is safe from further development. 'Kaptan' June, as she is affectionately known, still lives in Dalyan and campaigns on environmental issues, and now has a village street named in her honour. You can read about her efforts on behalf of the turtles in the book *Kaptan June and the Dalyan Turtles* – see page 28.

In 2009 a research and rehabilitation centre was established at the eastern end of İztuzu beach. Here a team of students from Pamukkale University, under the guidance of Professor Yakup Kaska, are dedicated to rescuing injured turtles, restoring them to health and ultimately releasing them back into the sea. They are also involved in programmes to research the behaviours of the loggerhad turtles (*Caretta caretta*) and Nile Turtles (*Trionyx Triunguis*) that inhabit this area,

The ancient harbour at Knidos

The ruins at Olympos

Today this amphitheatre is host to the annual Aspendos International Opera and Ballet Festival, which is organised by the Turkish State Opera and Ballet every June/July. Unfortunately there is no official website for this festival, even though it has been running for over 10 years, but you can contact the Antalya Tourist Office for information, Tel: 0312 311 24 30, email: aspendosfestival@kultur.gov.tr, and details

are usually shown on the website www.antalyafestivals. org once the year's programmes have been finalised. Tickets can be ordered in advance and collected from offices in Antalya and Side.

All performances are held in the ancient amphitheatre and feature the Turkish state opera and ballet, as well as visiting companies from other Turkish cities and abroad. It is possible to visit Aspendos quite easily from

the larger coastal towns in the area, and if you are able to catch a performance at the amphitheatre this is not to be missed!

Olympos, Phaselis and the Chimaera

The Olympos National Park is located between Finike and Antalya, close to the town of Kemer. The small village of Olympos has become a popular destination for backpackers, many of whom stay overnight in the charming wooden cabin hostels that are found here. Little is known about the settlement here, which is thought to date back to the time of Alexander the Great, and various ruins are scattered throughout the valley around the village.

Not far from here are the remains of a Lycian port town known as Phaselis. These remains are located around three adjacent bays (Northern Harbour, Battle Harbour and Protected Harbour), and once included a grand main street, aquaduct and irrigation system, bath house and numerous sarcophagi. The town was associated with roses, as well as the production and shipping of rose oil and perfumes, and fell into decline with the emergence of other ports at Antalya and Alanya.

A legendary monster was believed to live in this area and terrorised the inhabitants for many years. The Chimaera was a fire-breathing beast with the head of a lion, body of a goat and tail of a snake, and was the son of the snake-headed wind god, Typhon, who had challenged Zeus for his position as king of the gods. The beast was eventually slain by the hero Bellerophon, who managed to lodge a lump of lead in its throat. This was melted by the monster's fiery breath and it choked to death on molten lead.

Today the Chimaera is the name given to 'eternal flames' that burn on the hillsides above the village. These are created from vents of natural methane gas, which escape from the ground and can be seen burning after dark. Trips to see this phenomenon can be organised from the villages of Olympos (approximately 7km) or nearer Çıralı. Expect to walk for around 30 minutes over rough terrain in the dark, so sturdy footwear is advisable and you should take a torch.

Xanthos, Letoon and Patara

The twin sites of Xanthos and Letoon are situated near modern Kınık, just inland of the Yediburunlar section of coastline (see page 191) and within easy reach of the harbour towns of Kaş, Kalkan and Fethiye. They are the location of some fantastic remains and were declared a UNESCO World Heritage site in 1988.

Xanthos was the capital of the Lycian federation, and was the largest and most important of its cities. Its people were fierce and warlike, but also created great architecture and administration. The remains were discovered by the British explorer Charles Fellowes in the 19th century, who took many of the finds home with him, where they can now be viewed in the British Museum's Lycian collection. Much of interest still remains, however, including a number of distinctive tombs, the Xanthian Obelisk (which helped to decipher the Lycian language), an acropolis and necropolis complex, a basilica and a well-preserved amphitheatre.

Nearby Letoon was the sacred cult centre of the Lycian federation, which was dedicated to the three national deities: Apollo, Artemis and their mother Leto. The two sites are less than 10km apart and are considered as twin sites because Letoon was administered by the municipality of Xanthos. Letoon has been under excavation for over 50 years by the French Archaeological Mission, which is in the process of restoring the important Temple of Leto. One of the most significant finds here has been the Trilingual

Stele, which contains text in Greek, Aramaic and Lycian. Along with the Xanthian Obelisk, this stele has enabled archaeologists to decipher the Lycian language and is now on display in the Fethiye museum (see page 187).

Today Patara is renowned for its long sandy beach and is a popular holiday destination, but in ancient times it was an important trading port and one of Lycia's six principal cities. The ruins have been excavated by a team of Turkish archaeologists working over several summers and include an amphitheatre, several bath houses, a lighthouse structure, a triumphal arch, a large main street, several tombs and many sarcophagi. The lighthouse structure is believed to be one of the oldest in the world, and you can also find the world's oldest road sign here, which shows the distance between Lycian cities. Patara is equally well known as the birthplace of St Nicholas, who later became identified with the figure of Santa Claus or Father Christmas.

Myra, Demre and St Nicholas

Myra was one of the principal cities of Lycia and even took the place of Xanthos as its capital for a while. Today it is mainly covered by the modern town of Demre (also called Kale), although some sites on the outskirts have been preserved and can still be visited. St Nicholas was made bishop of Myra, and his church has recently been excavated and restored in Demre town. Originally the saint was buried in this church, but in the 11th century his remains were stolen and taken to the Italian city of Bari. Despite this, the mayor of Demre is keen to capitalise on the town's relationship with one of Christianity's favourite saints and the world's most popular icons. A bronze Russian Orthodox statue of the saint has been erected near the church, and a larger one depicting Father Christmas (*Noel Baba*) stands nearby. The feast day of St Nicholas is celebrated in the town on 6 December each year.

Ruins of Myra can be seen around the outskirts of the town of Demre, and include the usual amphitheatres and baths as well as a striking necropolis of ornate temple rock tombs carved into the hillsides above the amphitheatre and near the river.

Priene, Miletus and Herakleia

These three sites are all located in the region around the Bafa Gölü Lake to the south of the Dilek peninsula. In ancient times this lake was open to the sea and known as the Gulf of Latmos, although centuries of silt deposits have extended the coastline a mile or so to the west.

Priene is situated at the northern end of the Gulf of Latmos and dates from around 350 BCE. Prior to this the settlement had been located elsewhere, but was moved due to the silting up of the harbour from the nearby river mouth. Although remains of the original settlement have yet to be located, those excavated at the later site are generally held to be amongst the best preserved ruins of an ancient Greek city that have been uncovered to date.

The town was a wealthy one, and many of its buildings were constructed from marble and have been well preserved. The settlement was laid out in a grid pattern on the hillsides, and much of the well planned water and sewage distribution systems have survived, along with temples, monuments, stairways and paved streets.

The city of Miletus was located at the southern end of the Gulf of Latmos and was one of the most powerful in the region, with around 90 colonies founded in the Mediterranean and as far away as the Black Sea. The ruins visible today centre around a magnificent amphitheatre that was designed to seat 24,000 people originally. A large baths complex and a number of public buildings have also been preserved, and you can still see the remains of the long silted-up harbour. In addition, there are the ruins of several temples, byzantine churches, a mosque and even a synagogue.

Herakleia was a much smaller settlement, which can be explored on the eastern shores of the Bafa Gölü Lake. The small village of Kapıkırı is situated in the same place today and visitors can spend the night in one of the small hotels here. The ruins are extensive but largely unrestored and include a temple, castle, collection of tombs and the ruined city walls that have all blended into the landscape surrounding the village. The area served as a refuge for Christian hermits attempting to flee the Arab invasions of the 8th century and is overlooked by the imposing mountains of Beşparmak Dağı (known as the Five-Fingered Mountain) and Mount Latmos, from which the gulf gets its name.

Cappadocia

The region of Cappadocia lies within the Central Anatolian area of Turkey and is rather outside the scope of this book. However, overnight trips to the region can be organised easily from any of the larger towns and resorts featured here, and a visit is highly recommended if you are planning to spend an extended period in the country. You will not see the like anywhere else on earth. Cappadocia once formed the heart of the Hittite Empire and its other-worldly landscapes are some of the most recognisable on earth, having long been a draw for visitors to the country.

Most tours concentrate on the attractions within the Göreme National Park, which include underground cities, bizarrely-shaped natural rock formations, ancient church and temple complexes and the distinctive 'fairy-chimney' formations. Many hotels are built into the rocks themselves and it has become popular to take hot-air balloon rides to gain a different perspective of the vast area and striking geology of the region. There are also waterfalls as well as walking and horse-riding trails to be explored if you have more time to spend here.

FLORA AND FAUNA

Turkey has a vast land mass and correspondingly lengthy coastline, so you would expect to find a diverse collection of plants and animals native to this area and you will not be disappointed. Habitats include the temperate Mediterranean coastal areas, mountainous interior, the arid eastern plains and cooler Black Sea coast.

Flora

Turkey has over 9,000 species of native wildflowers, which is almost equivalent to the rest of Europe put together. It is also the home of the wild ancestors of many agricultural crops that are harvested today, including different strains of wild wheat and barley, as well as flowering fruit and nut trees such as almond, fig, chick pea and, of course, olives. Common flowering plants such as crocuses and tulips have their origins in Turkey, and the tulip in particular is associated with İstanbul and is a national emblem of the country.

Most of the coastal landscape included in this book is home to the Red Pine, which thrives in mountainous arid locations. Unfortunately the sap of this tree is highly flammable, leaving it susceptible to the forest fires which destroy around 20,000 hectares each year. For this reason the environmental authorities impose a blanket fire ban during the summer months, which includes all beach barbecues.

An important native species is the Liquid Amber Tree, also known as the Sweetgum. Although this tree was once found all over Europe, North America and Asia, today there are only four species remaining in the world, and they can all be found growing naturally in Turkey. The tree is similar to a plane tree in size and leaf formation, and has characteristically spiky fruits that contain a number of seeds. The tree is named for its fragrant oil, also known as frankincense, which has medicinal qualities and is used in the manufacturing of soap and perfume, and sometimes for flavouring tobacco.

Fauna

Large predators such as bears, wolves and even lions were once common in Turkey, but are no longer considered indigenous species today. Smaller animals such as wild goats, wild boar, deer, pine martens and even lynx are still prevalent, although they mostly inhabit wild areas away from towns and resorts, and you are unlikely to encounter many of them (apart from goats) during a cruising visit.

Turkey is an important location in the migration routes for many migratory birds such as storks, swallows and swifts, which can be observed during the appropriate seasons as they make their way between winter and summer habitats. Eagles, hawks

and buzzards are a fairly common sight around the mountains and in the Dalyan delta, where there are cormorants, a variety of water fowl, egrets and even occasionally flamingoes.

Tortoises are fairly common and can often be found lumbering across a village street or in the woodlands behind a remote beach area.

Domestic animals

Especially in the more modern and sophisticated resorts along the coast, Turks are becoming increasingly fond of keeping animals as pets rather than just as working animals. Cats are often fed by restaurant owners keen to encourage sentimental foreign visitors to play with them and to have a drink, and dogs are displayed on leads as fashion accessories; pampered pooches for the ladies and large muscle dogs for the boys. The Kangal dog is the national breed of Turkey and is also sometimes known as the Anatolian Shepherd Dog. It is a large mastiff type that was originally bred as a livestock guardian, and the males can grow as large as 120 lbs. Well-bred Kangals are intelligent and never vicious towards humans, and they are often kept as pets even by Turks living in urban areas. The breed has been exported, and some Kangals have been successfully used to protect African livestock from cheetahs in Namibia and Kenya.

Van cats are native to the area around Lake Van in south-east Turkey. They are distinctive because of their pure white coats and differently coloured eyes (one is usually blue and the other green). The cats are also said to enjoy swimming, and not to thrive if they are taken away from their native areas on the high mountain plateaus around Van.

Sea life

Around the coast of Turkey you will see all of the marine life common to this area of the Mediterranean. Loggerhead sea turtles (*Caretta caretta*) use many of the beaches in this area as nesting locations, which sometimes brings them into conflict with those who

A *Caretta caretta* loggerhead turtle returning to the sea in Dalyan

would develop these areas (see the section on Dalyan above). They are extremely long lived and can reach almost 200 years, returning to the same beaches time and again to bring forth the new generation.

The Mediterranean Monk Seal (*Monarchus Monarchus*) is also native to the coast of Turkey, and several colonies have been observed along the coastline covered in this book. This species is highly endangered because of habitat destruction, so all breeding colonies are under close supervision. One seal in particular (named *Badem*) has found a sort of fame amongst locals and visitors to the area after being rescued and re-released in the Gökova area (see pages 102-103 for more details).

Dolphins can frequently be encountered during the summer months, and it is always a great pleasure to share their company for a while as they play in the waves generated by your boat. Rather sadly to my mind the Turkish government has recently allowed several dolphin parks to be constructed along the coast. Although ostensibly for research and therapeutic purposes, these parks are also open to tourists who wish to have a 'swim with dolphins' experience or to watch them perform. It is incredibly sad to see such beautiful, intelligent and free-spirited creatures confined to netted enclosures and forced to perform for the masses, and is infinitely preferable to interact with them from the deck of your boat as they play in their natural environment.

FOOD AND DRINK

Turkish cuisine offers a wonderful variety of dishes containing meat, fish and seasonal vegetables, all flavoured with fragrant herbs and often accompanied by fresh salad greens. Everyone has heard of döner kebab, but the genuine article cooked against a charcoal grill and served in a freshly made pitta is a million miles away from the takeaway version you will find in most British high streets.

Another famous aspect of Turkish cuisine is the *meze* (pronounced *mez-eh*), which refers to the numerous

appetiser dishes that can be eaten before a main dish or over the course of an entire evening as a meal in themselves. They are usually vegetarian or fish-based, and often take the form of dips that are eaten with freshly baked Turkish flat bread. If you don't recognise the dishes from a menu you can usually pick what looks good from a buffet display, or just order a mixed *meze* selection and try them all.

Fabulous selections of Turkish *meze* are the norm in restaurants along the coast

Seafood is plentiful along the coast, but it is not cheap and you will usually pay by the kilo in restaurants, so remember to check the cost of the fish you have ordered before it is cooked and served up to your table. If you visit Turkey during the winter or springtime then be sure to try some of the famous Black Sea anchovies (*hamsi*, pronounced *ham-see*). Usually these are served grilled with salad, but apparently there are 41 different recipes to choose from for this 'king of fish'.

Freshly caught seafood is available directly from the fishermen in some places

Another favourite for a light meal or snack is Turkish *pide* (pronounced *peed-eh*), which is similar to Italian pizza. The Turkish version is oval-shaped rather than round, with the edges rolled in to create a tasty crust. All kinds of toppings are available and it can be seasoned at the table with dried chilli flakes. The *pide* is usually served cut into strips, so is ideal for sharing with others. *Gözleme* is a pancake 'wrap' filled with potato, spinach or honey, and you will often see *gözleme* houses by the road side.

Depending on where you are in Turkey you will find a variety of different kinds of restaurants. In tourist areas you will discover plenty of places offering nondescript 'international' food, but it is always worth avoiding these and seeking out somewhere that will give you a taste of Turkey rather than of home. You should have no problem finding something for children to eat either – *pide* always goes down well, as do tender lamb chops or chicken pieces from the grill. Turkish meatballs or *köfte* (pronounced *kof-teh*) are another favourite and can be served with or without sauce.

The average Turkish restaurant will have a written menu for you to see at the table, but the staff are usually quite happy to show you into the kitchen to examine the meat, fish and *meze* selection on offer, and will make their own suggestions as to what is good.

An *Ocak Başı* (pronounced *oh-jak bash-uh*) restaurant is one that specialises in dishes prepared on an open charcoal grill or mangal. Expect a good choice of *meze* and salads to start with, as well as a variety of different kebab dishes. These are more than just pieces of meat cooked on a skewer, and are often delicately flavoured with herbs and combined with vegetables.

A *Lokantası* (pronounced *loh-kant-as-uh*) is usually a small, no-frills family run affair and can get very busy. A variety of hot oven-cooked dishes will be on display for you to pick and choose from, as well as the usual selection of *meze*, grilled meats and often a döner kebab or two. These are great for a light meal and allow you to mix and match small quantities of different dishes to give you a taste of each. Steamed rice or bulgur wheat is usually served as an accompaniment, along with bottles of water on the tables and spicy pickled chilli peppers for the brave.

If you are a lager drinker then you will quickly find yourself at home with the Turkish brewed *Efes*. This is sold everywhere and is available in bottles, cans or on tap (there is a small deposit paid on the glass bottles so recycle them if possible by returning them to another shop that stocks *Efes*). Dark brewed, low alcohol and ice brewed versions of *Efes* are also available.

Turkey has a flourishing wine-making industry and it is definitely worth taking the time to sample some of the local varieties on offer rather than expensive imports (which are available in larger supermarkets). Two very drinkable labels at a reasonable price are Kavaklidere's Angora and Doluca Wine's Villa Doluca – both are available in red and white, and Villa Doluca has a rosé as well. You will also find a good variety of more exotic and expensive wines, many of which are made from grapes grown only in Turkey.

Imported drinks in Turkey are expensive, so spirit drinkers are likely to find that their usual tipple costs rather more in Turkey than they are used to. Cheaper, locally-produced vodka and gin (spelt *cin*) are available though, so ask for these or make the most of your duty free allowances on the outward journey.

The one spirit that you will see everyone drinking, however, is the famous Turkish *rakı* (pronounced *rak-uh*). This clear aniseed-flavoured spirit is similar to Greek *ouzo* and is usually drunk in a tall glass mixed with water or sometimes over a little ice. Mixing the spirit with water causes it to turn cloudy, giving it the local name *Aslan süt*, meaning lion's milk. A large variety of brands are available – some of the most popular are *Efe Rakı* (not to be confused with *Efes* lager) and *Yeni Rakı*. The Turks believe that drinking *rakı* should be accompanied by eating food, so often a plate of *meze* or even just a bowl of nuts will be served with your drink.

SHOPPING FOR SOUVENIRS

Turkey is one big market place and offers plenty of opportunities for browsing and buying. If you are thinking of taking souvenirs home for friends, family or yourself then the following items generally represent good value and have traditional associations with the country.

Tying up your boat just outside the restaurant where you will eat is one of the pleasures of cruising in Turkey

Traditionally woven Turkish carpets and kilims make great presents and souvenirs

Carpets and kilims

Turkish carpets are one of the items most readily associated with the country, and you will find numerous outlets where you can purchase them. Carpets are larger than kilims (also known as the nomad's carpet), and both sorts can be woven from a combination of materials such as silk, cotton and wool. The difference between traditional Turkish and Persian carpets relates to the type of knot used during the weaving process. Persian carpets are woven using a single knot whilst Turkish carpets use a double knot.

Authentic carpets are handwoven and only natural dyes and materials are used in their manufacture. Each region in Turkey has its own tradition of carpet weaving, often with identifiable local patterns and designs. In several areas along the coast local artisans have joined together to form Carpet Weavers' Associations. Tours are available around their premises, where you can learn about the traditional methods used to make the fibres and dyes and watch the weaving process on traditional looms. A carpet presentation usually follows, but even if you don't buy anything it is an interesting and enjoyable experience.

Turkish Delight

This soft jelly-like confection is often known by its local name *lokum* and is widely available all over Turkey. It is thought to have been developed during the 15th century, when it gained popularity with the Sultan for its difference in texture to the hard boiled candies that were consumed at the time. Lokum comes in many different flavours such as mint, rose water, orange blossom and various types of fruit and nuts. Pre-packaged selections can be bought at supermarkets, or you can make your own choice at specialist shops. It tastes as good as it looks.

Herbs and spices

Turkey lies at the western end of the traditional spice route used by overland traders from the east. Many of these spices have been incorporated into Turkish cuisine and most bazaars and markets will have at least one specialist spice dealer where you can buy loose spices by weight or pre-packaged spice blends.

Handcrafts

Turkish artisans have long been famed for their work and there are many kinds of souvenirs of this type that are worth collecting. Keep an eye-out for the following: Samovars, coffee pots and trays made from engraved brass or copper-ware; beautifully painted ceramic items such as plates, vases and wall tiles are available in a variety of traditional designs; Meerschaum is a soft white substance collected from the Black Sea areas and often fashioned into elaborately carved pipes or other decorative objects; Hookah pipes, also known as *narghile*, are used for smoking sweet-flavoured tobaccos bubbled through water to reduce the roughness of smoking. They can be very ornate and are usually used in a social group where each smoker has his own mouthpiece.

In recent times Turkey has unfortunately become flooded with cheap counterfeit items such as 'designer' shoes, clothing, watches and pirated copies of CDs, DVDs and computer games. Although purchasing these 'genuine fakes' can seem harmless, it does have consequences for those working in the industries being copied like this. Turkish branded products are just as stylish and usually of far better quality than many of these rip-off items, and it is worth supporting those who are trying to establish their own commercial identities rather than just copying the ideas of others.

HASSLE

Competition between shops and restaurants in Turkey's main tourist resorts is stiff and these businesses have developed a variety of tactics aimed to get your attention and get you into their shops or restaurants. Most of these involve having a member of staff standing on the street nearby, ostensibly to answer queries but in reality to call out to passers-by and win

Souvenir shopping in the Turkish bazaars

their custom. 'Excuse me!', 'Are you from England? (or Holland, Germany, France etc)', 'Have you dropped something?' and other fairly inane questions are called out at random as you stroll around shopping and restaurant districts.

Generally this is all good-natured banter and only mildly irritating at worst, but the authorities in Turkey are aware that it can appear unpleasant and many of the larger resorts where this is occasionally a problem have active 'No Hassle' campaigns. They will take action against individuals and businesses involved if complaints are made. If this happens to you then try to take a note of the business or individual's name if possible, and tell them that you are going to report them for hassling. Your complaint will be logged and acted upon by the local police, and hopefully the more aggravated 'hassling' practices will be driven out for good before too long.

ÇAY VE KAHVE

Everywhere you go in Turkey you will see people drinking Turkish tea or *çay* (pronounced *chai*) out of little tulip-shaped glasses. Tea leaves are stewed in the upper part of a special double teapot that is boiled over a stove and topped up with boiling water from the lower part. A single pot can be kept going all day, and you are likely to be offered a glass in shops, offices and after a meal. Drink it like the Turks do with no milk and plenty of sugar.

Turkish coffee (*kahve*, pronounced *kah-veh*) is brewed very strong and made with the grounds still in the cup. It is drunk from small espresso mugs and is generally served sweet and black (*orta*).

THE TURKISH BATH OR HAMAM

Hamams have played an important role in Turkish culture since early Ottoman times and were used as social meeting places as well as simply for bathing purposes. The traditional hamam is formed of three interconnecting rooms and you should take clean flip flops or similar shoes for walking between the rooms. These days it is normal to wear a swimsuit whilst using the baths, although a traditional cloth wrap may be provided in some places. You should also take your own rough sponge, although you can usually buy one at the hamam if necessary.

Bathers start off in a room that is heated by hot dry air, which encourages the bather to sweat freely as in a sauna. After this you move to the main steam room, which will often be decorated with marble and may have seating areas and fountains around the wall from where you can splash water over yourself before scrubbing with your sponge. Bath attendants use the marble slab in the centre of this room to perform a variety of traditional massages, which can involve oil, soap bubbles, coarse scrubbing or a combination of the maintained and is actively pursuing entry to the EU.

Of Atatürk's many widely-quoted sayings, perhaps the most appropriate for these times is *Yurtta Sulh, Cihanda Sulh* – 'Peace at home; peace in the world.'

RAMAZAN AND BAYRAM

The dates of *bayram* (pronounced *by-ram*) and *ramazan* are amongst the most important in the Turkish cultural calendar.

Ramazan takes place during the 10th month of the Muslim year (currently September, although the exact dates are recalculated each year). During this month the observant muslim will fast during daylight hours, as well as performing various religious observances. In many Turkish towns and villages the local authorities erect public cafeterias where a fast breaking meal is served each night to local inhabitants. If you are in the country during *ramazan* then you will still be able to visit restaurants during the day, as not all Turks will be fasting during this month either. But you may find that some restaurants will close during the month (particularly in smaller more traditional villages) and it is considered impolite to eat in the street during daylight hours.

The end of *ramazan* month is celebrated in Turkey with the *şeker bayramı* (sweet festival), also known as the *Eid-ul-Fitr* in Arabic Islam. This three-day festival celebrates the end of the month of fasting and is a time when family members visit each other, old quarrels are forgiven, alms and charity are shown to others and children are given plenty of sweets!

The *kurban bayramı* (feast of the sacrifice or Arabic *Eid-ul-Adha*) is a four-day festival held towards the end of the year. It is traditional for families to slaughter an animal on the first day of the festival and distribute the meat to neighbours and to the poor during the festival.

Take time to enjoy a traditional Turkish bath at the *hamam*

three. Finally you can move into a cooler room where drinks may be available and you can relax your body back to its usual temperature.

MUSTAFA KEMAL ATATÜRK

Known as the 'Father of Turks', there is no escaping the imposing visage of Mustafa Kemal as you will see it on posters, paintings, photographs and statues in offices, restaurants, shops and homes throughout the country. Details of Atatürk's rise to prominence and ground-breaking reforms are given on page 10, and there is no denying that he was a man well ahead of his time in many ways.

Atatürk is still revered in modern Turkey 70 years after his death, with school children taught about aspects of his life and a minute's silence held every year to commemorate his death. The secular principles of 'Kemalism' formed the foundation of his government and although Islamic in its origins, the current government hopefully lays emphasis on the key concepts of democracy and debate being

Mustafa Kemal Atatürk – the father of modern Turkey

ABBREVIATIONS AND SYMBOLS

✈	Airport	🚢	Ferry terminal	PHM	Port-hand mark
⚓	Anchoring	◄●◄	Fishing boats	PA	Position approx.
⚓	Anchoring prohibited	⊖	Fishing harbour/quay	✉	Post office
	Anchoring stern/bows-to	⊠	Fish farm	☎	Public telephone
	Berthing stern/bows-to	FV(s)	Fishing vessel(s)	⇌	Railway station
	Boat hoist	⬤	Fuel berth	✗	Restaurant
	Boatyard	⚓	Harbour Master	SWM	Safe water mark
Ca	Cable(s)	♫	Holding tank pump-out		Shore power
P	Car park	✚	Hospital		Showers
⚓	Chandlery	i	Information bureau		Slipway
✚	Chemist	IDM	Isolated danger mark	SCM	South cardinal mark
⊹	Church		Launderette	SHM	Starboard-hand mark
H24	Continuous	Ldg	Leading		Supermarket
⏲	Crane	◆	Lifeboat	SS	Traffic signals
⊖	Customs office	Ⓛ	Marina	Ⓥ	Visitors' berth/buoy
	Direction of buoyage		Mooring stern/bows-to buoy	WPT⊕	Waypoint
	Flying dolphin	☿	Mosque	WCM	West cardinal mark
ECM	East cardinal mark	NCM	North cardinal mark	⛵	Yacht berthing facilities

BUOY COLOURS, LIGHTS AND FREQUENCIES

FR	Fixed red light
FG	Fixed green light
Fl	Flashing light, period of darkness longer than light. A number indicates a group of flashes, eg: Fl (2). Most lights are white unless a colour follows the number of flashes, eg: Fl (2) G. The timing of the sequence, including light and darkness, is shown by the number of seconds, eg: Fl (2) G 10s. The range of the more powerful lights is given in nautical miles (M), eg: Fl (2) G 10s 20M
L Fl	Long flash, of not less than two seconds
Oc	Occulting light, period of light longer than darkness
Iso	Isophase light, equal periods of light and darkness
Q	Quick flashing light, up to 50/60 flashes per minute
VQ	Very quick flashing, up to 120 flashes per minute
Mo	Light flashing a (dot/dash) Morse single letter sequences, eg: Mo (S)
Dir	A light, usually sectored, RWG or RG, usually giving a safe approach within the W sector. Either fixed or displaying some kind of flashing characteristic

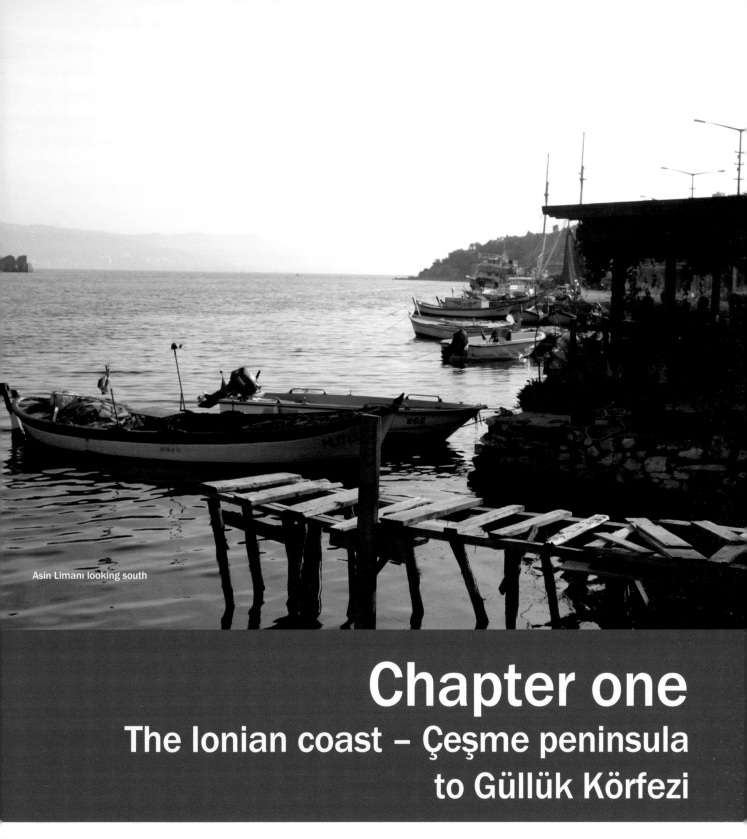

Asin Limanı looking south

Chapter one
The Ionian coast – Çeşme peninsula to Güllük Körfezi

**Charts: Turkish Hydrographic Charts: 222, 223, 224;
Turkish Hydrographic Leisure Folios: 2004;
Imray Charts: G2, G3, G28, G32, Admiralty 1087, 1095,
SC 5773, SC 5776**

The Ionian coastline stretches from the Çeşme peninsula west of the city of İzmir down to the Güllük Körfezi gulf to the east of the Bodrum peninsula. The city of İzmir itself is home to a large commercial port and NATO military base. Many of the bays and harbours surrounding the approaches are closed to navigation for military reasons, and the port is busy and without

good shelter, so this area is of little interest to visiting yachts. The peninsula extending to the west of here, however, is a popular weekend destination for city inhabitants and is the location of several harbours and marinas as well as many smaller anchorages along its southern side.

The coastline south of here is mainly exposed to the prevailing north-westerly winds, but there are several resort developments that have large yacht marinas. The Dilek Boğazı channel is the narrowest stretch of water between a Greek island (Samos) and the Turkish mainland.

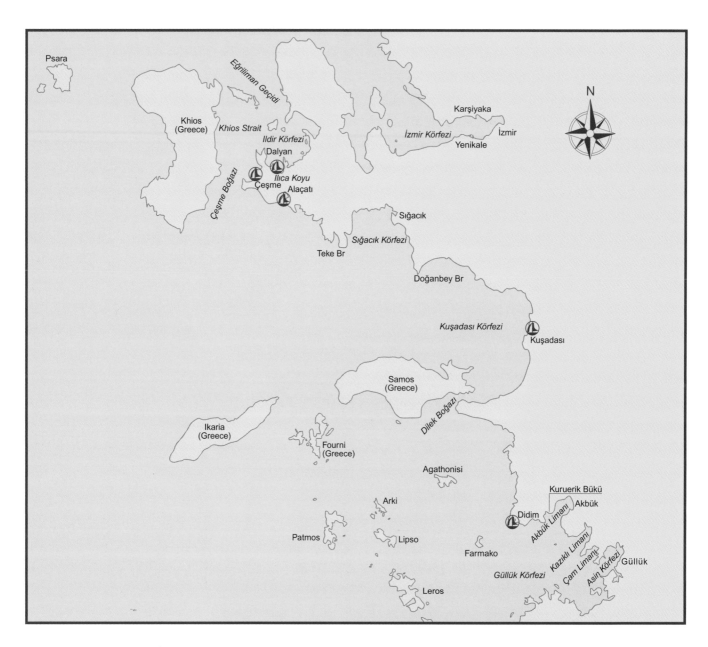

The gulf known as Güllük Körfezi extends from the bustling resort town of Altınkum and the newly developed marina in Didim down to the more peaceful fishing harbour of Güllük itself, which is slowly starting to develop its tourist potential and is also known as a commercial harbour for the transportation of the locally-found mineral bauxite. In between these are a number of sheltered bays and small villages, and this area is generally quieter ashore, with far fewer boats cruising its waters than the peninsulas of Çeşme and Bodrum to the north and south.

Island ruins on the Bafa Gölü Lake

Ilıca Koyu

Middle of the bay opposite the beach:
38°19'.84N 26°21'.80E
Just east of the entrance to Setur Marina:
38°19'.64N 26°20'.81E
Just off Ilıca Harbour: 38°18'.68N 26°21'.74E

Ilıca Koyu is a large open bay a few miles east of the town of Çeşme on the northern side of the Çeşme peninsula. It is the location of the resort town of Ilıca and its small fishing harbour, as well as the Setur Çeşme Marina, part of the Altın Yunus (Golden Dolphin) Hotel and Marina.

NAVIGATION

Charts: Turkish Hydrographic Charts: 222, 2223;
Imray Charts: G2, G28; Admiralty 1625, 1058, SC 5776

Ilıca Koyu lies between the Kalytaş Burnu and Kalem Burnu headlands and there are no dangers in the approach.

A long sandy beach rings the wide bay and is backed by the buildings of Ilıca town. The Setur Çeşme Marina complex can be easily identified to the east of Kalem Burnu, and Ilıca's small harbour is approximately 1M to the east of here. If you are approaching the town harbour from this direction then keep well clear of the shallow waters immediately to the north of the harbour wall and approach the entrance from the eastern side to avoid these.

BERTHING AND ANCHORING

The small harbour in Ilıca has a concrete quay, which is used mainly by local fishing boats, and a shallow inner harbour that is protected by a rocky mole to the north. The area within the harbour is fairly shallow, particularly on the southern side, but it is possible to anchor stern-to or bows-to against the rock wall near the entrance. The harbour is rarely used by visiting boats, which tend to berth at the nearby marina.

Ilıca fishing harbour

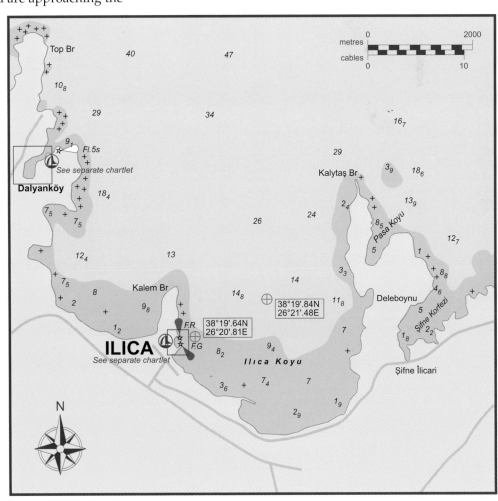

Ilıca harbour is rarely used by visiting boats

The Setur Çeşme Marina and Altın Yunus Hotel complex has all the facilities that you would expect from a 5 star resort. The marina has berthing space for 180 vessels up to 30m long and with draughts of up to 4m, and has a hard standing area for another 60 vessels ashore. All berthing is with lazylines. Many of the berths in the marina are occupied year round, although they do have some that can be allocated to visitors. It is best to call the marina in advance to check berthing availability and reserve a space, particularly during the high season. Setur Çeşme Marina can be contacted on Tel: 0232 723 14 34, Fax: 0232 723 46 20, email: cesme@seturmarinas.com, website: www.seturmarinas.com

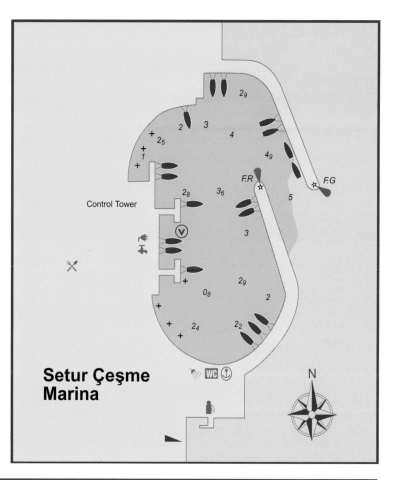

Control Tower

F.R

F.G

Setur Çeşme Marina

N

Useful information – Ilıca Koyu

FACILITIES
Water: Fresh water can be obtained in both the marina and the fishing harbour.
Electricity: At the marina.
Fuel: From the marina fuel dock.
Showers: Available at the marina.
Ice: Can be bought from the marina mini-market.
Laundry: A laundry service is provided by the Altın Yunus hotel in the marina complex.
Gas: Can be obtained in the marina.
Rubbish: Rubbish disposal facilities are in the marina and near the fishing harbour.
Telephone: Public phone boxes can be found in the marina and near the fishing harbour. Mobile phone reception here is good.
Internet: Emailing is available in the marina office.

YACHT SERVICES AND CHANDLERY
The marina has a 60 ton travel lift and hard standing area for up to 60 vessels,
with water and electricity supplies. There is a small chandler on site, and repairs and technical works of most kinds can be organised through the marina office.

PROVISIONING AND SERVICES
Grocery shops: There are several supermarkets and mini-markets within the town of Ilıca, and the marina has a small supermarket to service the needs of hotel guests and visiting yachts.
Bakery: Several bakeries and butchers can be found in the town.
Local market: Is held in Ilıca on Wednesdays.
Banks: Several bank branches and ATM machines are situated within Ilıca town, but there is none within the marina.
Pharmacy: A few pharmacies are located in the town.
Post office: There is a PTT office in Ilıca town, but the marina office

will also send and receive mail for visiting yachts and can supply stamps as well.

EATING OUT
Within the Altın Yunus complex are two bars (Neptun and Havuz bars) and also two restaurants (Baküs restaurant and Pınar Balık restaurant). Both are part of the hotel complex but are open to guests of the marina as well.

There is also a great number of restaurants within the resort of Ilıca, which can be reached by taxi from the marina.

ASHORE
All of the facilities at the Altın Yunus hotel are available to guests at the marina, so there is plenty to occupy you during your stay here. The hotel has a sports and fitness centre, indoor and outdoor swimming pools, sauna, tennis courts, hairdressers, beauty salon and a number of souvenir, clothing, photo and jewellery

shops for you to browse.

It is only a short taxi ride from the marina into Ilıca town. Although there is little to see here in the way of interesting architecture, there are plenty more shops to explore and a long sandy beach to enjoy. Daily boat tours and diving trips are available to the nearby islands and dive spots within Ildır Körfezi.

TRANSPORT
Car hire: An Avis car hire office is situated at the Altın Yunus hotel, with several other agencies based within the town.
Taxis: There is a taxi rank near the marina.
Dolmuş: Local dolmuş services operate between Çeşme and Ilıca, but do not directly pass the marina.
Air travel: The nearest airport is İzmir's Adnan Menderes airport, which is approximately 1 hour away by road.

USEFUL INFORMATION
Local tel code: İzmir area, 0232, Ilıca 723.

Dalyan harbour looking north-west

Dalyan

Harbour entrance: 38°21'.57N 26°19'.13E

Dalyan is a quiet and upmarket resort on the eastern side of the Üç Burunlar peninsula, only a few kilometres away from the town of Çeşme and the Setur Çeşme Marina. It is known as a place where wealthy Turks from İzmir keep second homes, and there are some very exclusive developments around the newly completed harbour.

NAVIGATION
Charts: Turkish Hydrographic Charts: 222, 2223; Imray Charts: G2, G28; Admiralty 1625, 1058, SC 5776

The harbour entrance faces north-east and is approximately 1M from the tip of the Top Burnu headland on the eastern side of the peninsula. Vessels approaching from the east will find no dangers, but vessels coming from the west must negotiate the rocky passage between the tip of Üç Burunlar and Toprak Adası (see page 49), or pass to the north of Toprak Adası.

The entrance to Dalyan harbour is difficult to see until close to, but can be identified by the statue of navigator Piri Reis on the port side of the entrance and, at night, the green light on the starboard side.

MOORING AND ANCHORING
Dalyan is a natural harbour that has been dredged and surrounded with a concrete quay, providing plenty of space for visiting boats to berth stern-to with an anchor. There is a harbour master here and a charge is made for overnight mooring.

It is possible to free swing at anchor off the buoyed swimming area just north of the entrance to the harbour, but shelter from the prevailing winds is not good and this should only be used as a daytime stop in calm weather.

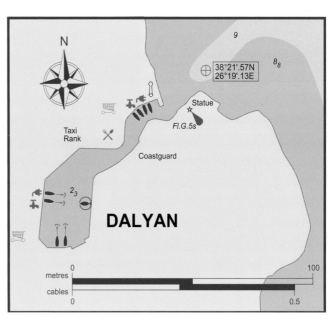

Useful information – Dalyan

FACILITIES
Water and electricity: Available in the harbour.
Ice: Is supplied at the supermarket at the south-west end of the harbour.
Rubbish: Rubbish bins are located ashore.
Telephone: There are a few public phone boxes ashore and the mobile reception here is good.

PROVISIONING AND SERVICES
Grocery shops: You will find a small supermarket at the southern end of the harbour and a mini-Tansaş in the small village centre near the harbour entrance.
Bakery: There is none near the harbour, but fresh bread is available at the supermarkets.
Butcher: Located in the main village centre, which is a fair walk away from the harbour.
Post office: There is a small PTT office in the village centre near the harbour entrance.

EATING OUT
Dalyan is known for upmarket harbour-side restaurants that specialise in serving fresh local fish. Prices are not cheap but the atmosphere is exclusive and peaceful.

ASHORE
New development has focused on the area just to the west of the harbour entrance, where most visiting yachts moor up. There are a few shops to browse around here and the area is undeniably attractive, but progress of this development is rather slow and the place can seem quite lifeless during the day. It has more atmosphere at night and during weekends and holidays when the nearby villas and estates are occupied and their inhabitants are likely to enjoy eating or drinking at some of the restaurants in the harbour.

The older part of the village is approximately 20 minutes walk away from the harbour area and is less manicured, with a bit more life.

TRANSPORT
Taxis: There is a taxi rank near the northern end of the harbour.
Dolmuş: A mini bus service operates to Çeşme.
Air travel: The nearest airport is İzmir's Adnan Menderes.

USEFUL INFORMATION
Local tel code: İzmir area, 0232, Dalyan 724.

Dalyan quayside

Dalyan fishing boats

Mermaid statue and light structure at Dalyan harbour entrance

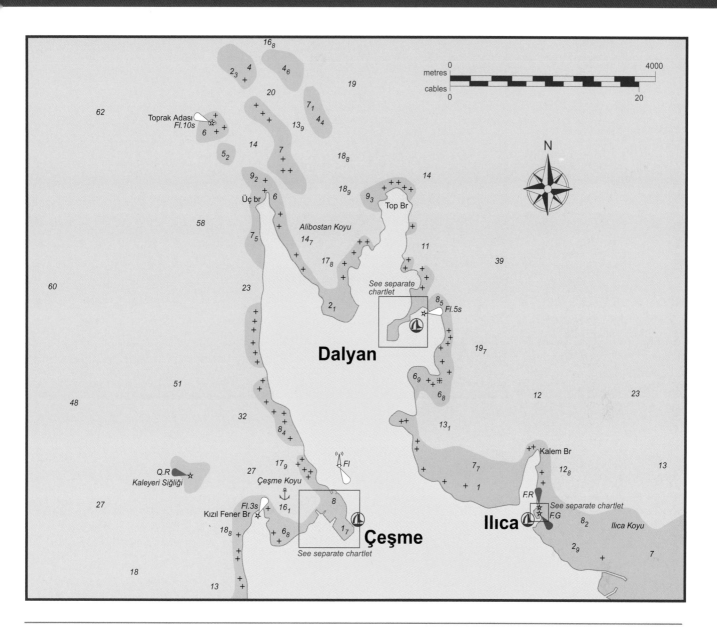

Çeşme

North-west of Toprak Adası, Üç Burunlar:
38°23'.71N 26°16'.10E
Kaleyeri shoal: 38°19'.76N 26°16'.07E
Harbour entrance: 38°19'.49N 26°17'.92E

The harbour town of Çeşme lies at the far western end of Çeşme peninsula and is a popular weekend destination for the inhabitants of İzmir, some 85km to the east. It is only 3M from the Greek island of Khios and is a port of entry to Turkey. Çeşme castle dominates the centre of the town and houses an archaeological museum of exhibits from nearby Erythrai. The word *çeşme* means fountain in Turkish, and there are many examples of these around the side streets of the town.

NAVIGATION

Charts: Turkish Hydrographic Charts: 222, 2224;
Imray Charts: G2, G28, Admiralty 1625, 1058, SC 5776

Vessels approaching from the south will round the Karaabdullah Burnu and Beyaz Burun headlands and will then see the two islands of Boğaz Adası and Süngükaya Adası. Süngükaya Asadı is the smaller of the two, is further west and is lit at night (Fl 5s). There is an area of shallow water about 9m deep between the two islands.

Vessels approaching from the north will round the Üç Burunlar headland and will have to navigate between here and the small island of Toprak Adası, which is just to the north. The waters in this area are shallow with numerous rocks, so care is needed. The simplest and safest course is to pass well clear to the north and west of Toprak Adası, which is lit at night (Fl 10s). Rocks extend to the north and west of Üç Burunlar, and there is also a rocky reef stretching north to south just to the east of Toprak Adası. It is possible to pass between the two reefs, but this should only be attempted in calm weather and in good light.

As you approach the entrance to Çeşme harbour you will see a white lighthouse structure (QR) on the Kaleyeri Sığlığı reef immediately west of the harbour. There is another light (Fl 3s) on the Kızıl Fener Burnu headland, which is immediately west of the town. The harbour entrance lies just to the east of the ferry port and is also lit on the starboard side.

BERTHING

Çeşme has a large harbour with plenty of space for visiting boats to berth, although construction of the marina is not completed yet. The marina is being developed by Camper & Nicholsons Marinas in conjunction with the Turkish company İçtaş Ports and is due to open for business in spring 2010. Eventual plans will include a large hard standing area, travel lift, shopping centre and many technical services, as well as in-water berthing for over 350 vessels. For the time being there are four floating pontoons with lazylines. The marina office is situated across the road on the northern side of the marina and can be contacted on Tel: 0232 712 99 13, Fax: 0232 712 99 14, websites: www.icport.com.tr, www.cncesmemarina.com

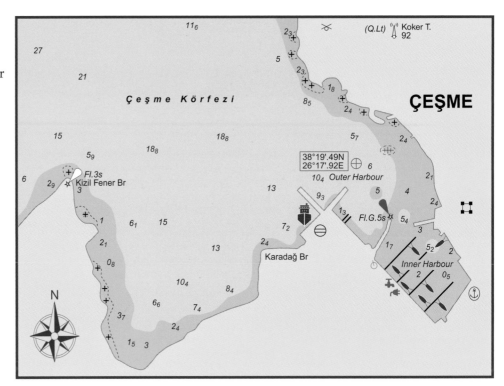

A town quay for day tripper boats runs along the northern side of the marina, with a small fishing port at the northern end of this.

FORMALITIES

The customs and immigration offices can be found in the terminal building at the ferry port. The harbour master's office and health authority buildings are at the southern end of the marina.

View across Çeşme marina from the entrance

Useful information – Çeşme

FACILITIES
Water and electricity: On the marina pontoons.
Showers: At the marina.
Fuel: Can be obtained by tanker; enquire at the marina office.
Ice: Is supplied at supermarkets in the town.
Laundry: A laundry service is available in the town.
Gas: Can be purchased in the town.
Rubbish: Rubbish disposal facilities ashore.
Telephone: There are public phone boxes throughout the town. Mobile reception here is good.
Internet: The Blue Moon internet café is along the waterfront by the town quay.

PROVISIONING AND SERVICES
Grocery shops: There are several mini-markets and supermarkets in the town, including a few close to the harbour that offer a free delivery service to your boat.
Bakery: You will find a choice of bakeries and butchers in the town centre, as well as a fishmonger along the town quay.
Local market: Held on Sundays.
Banks: A number of banks are situated in the town centre and along the town quay harbour front, including ING Bank, İş Bank and TC

Ziraat Bank. All of these have ATM machines.
Pharmacy: There are several to choose from in the town centre.
Post office: The PTT is half way along the town quay harbour front.

EATING OUT
There is a good choice of restaurants in Çeşme, predominantly located around the town square, in the main shopping street running north from here and along the waterfront between the marina and the local fishing harbour.

ASHORE
The centre of Çeşme is a pedestrian area, so is pleasant to explore on foot. There are many pretty cobbled streets and alleyways lined with shops, cafés and restaurants, and some attractive architecture remains despite the usual proliferation of concrete.

The castle area is open to the public and provides good views across the harbour and the approaches. You can also visit a museum in the northern tower showcasing archaeological finds from the excavation of nearby Erythrai. Çeşme was formerly known as Cyssus and was the harbour for this important settlement,

Çeşme pedestrian area

allowing it to maintain ties and trade with Egypt, Cyprus and other western states.

At the base of the castle walls near the harbour is a statue of Turkish admiral Cezayirli Gazi Hasan Paşa, who was a hero of the Battle of Çeşme in 1770 against the Russians.

TRANSPORT
Car hire: Several car hire companies are based in the town, many with offices in the main square and shopping street, including the following: Sultan Rent-a-Car, Tel: 0232 712 67 75, Blue Rent-a-Car, Tel: 0232 712 09 39, and Marin Motor, Tel: 0232 712 74 10.
Taxis: You will find many taxi ranks in the town, including some near the

harbour and the ferry port.
Dolmuş: Local minibus services operate to the nearby towns of Alaçatı and Ilıca.
Coach: Coaches run to İzmir, where you can get connecting services to other major towns in Turkey.
Ferry: International ferry services operate between Çeşme and the Greek island of Khios, as well as the Greek port of Piraeus and the Italian ports of Ancona and Brindisi. The ferry port is immediately to the west of the yacht harbour. Tickets can be obtained from booking offices within the ferry terminal, or from travel agents on the road to the other side of the marina. Day trips to the island of Khios can easily be arranged through any of the local travel agents' offices.
Air travel: The nearest airport is the İzmir Adnan Menderes airport to the south of the town of İzmir.

USEFUL INFORMATION
Local tel code: İzmir area, 0232, Çeşme 712.
Tourist office: This is located close to the marina on the northern side and is open Monday-Friday between 0830-1200 and 1300-1730, Tel: 0232 712 66 53.
Hospital: There is the Çeşme Devlet (state hospital) in Çeşme, and many other private and specialist hospitals in İzmir. Cesme Alper Cizgekanat State Hospital, Cesme-Izmir, Tel: 0232 712 07 77/78 0232
Local websites: www.cesme.gen.tr

Çeşme castle

Alaçatı

Outside bay entrance: 38°13'.16N 26°22'.39E
Marina entrance: 38°15'.32N 26°23'.25E

Alaçatı Marina lies at the northern end of an inlet on the southern side of Çeşme peninsula. The marina is used as a home port for many boats with owners based in İzmir, and makes a convenient stopping point for vessels travelling along the coast past here. The nearby village of Alaçatı is a chic weekend destination for well-to-do İzmir residents and is well worth visiting if you are staying overnight or longer at the marina.

NAVIGATION

Charts: Turkish Hydrographic Charts: 223, 2235; Imray Charts: G2, G3, G28; Admiralty 1057, 1058, SC 5776

Vessels approaching from either direction should make for the waypoint as the entrance to the inlet is not easy to spot until you reach it. There is a light on the Bozalan Burnu headland immediately to the east of the entrance (Fl (2) 5s). Once you are in the right area you will be able to identify the inlet by spotting the wind turbines on the hills behind.

As you approach the marina you will have to take care to avoid the numerous windsurfers and kitesurfers who are likely to be sailing from one of the shore-based sports centres lining the beach on the approach. Remember that beginners and even intermediates in these sports find it much easier to go very fast in a straight line than they do to turn around or stop, so stay well over to the eastern side of the inlet as you enter and keep your eyes open.

The entrance to the marina is lit on either side and you should observe the speed limit of 3 knots. There is a small fishing harbour immediately to the north of the marina, but this is not suitable for yachts and is for local boats only.

BERTHING

Alaçatı Marina has three floating pontoons with stern-to berthing along both sides. Additionally, there are stern-to berths all around the edge of the marina. Call ahead on VHF Ch 72 to confirm where they would like you to head for. The marina can also be contacted on Tel: 0232 716 97 60, Fax: 0232 716 61 64, email: marina@portalacati.com.tr, website: www.portalacati.com.tr

North of the marina

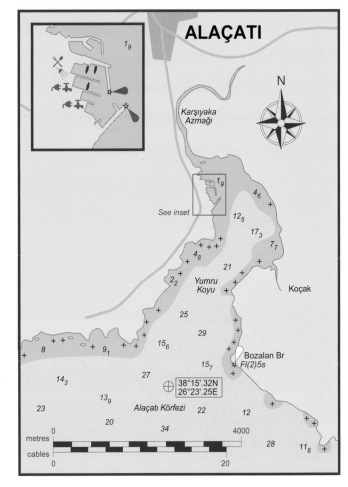

Aerial view of Alaçatı Marina and approaches

and fishing harbour is the development of Port Alaçatı. This will be a luxurious marine village that will ultimately extend most of the way up the inlet and towards Alaçatı town. Eventually it will be filled with many individual houses with private moorings, but for now they are still working on completing the first two phases of the development.

Alaçatı Marina boatyard

Useful information – Alaçatı

Alaçatı Marina

FACILITIES
Water and electricity: Available at all berths in the marina.
Fuel: There is no fuel supply as yet.
Showers: The marina has shower facilities for yachtsmen.
Ice: May be sold at markets in Alaçatı town.
Gas: May be available from the marina chandlery shop or in Alaçatı town.
Rubbish: Rubbish disposal facilities can be found in the marina.
Telephone: The mobile phone reception in the area is good. There are no public phones unless you go to Alaçatı town.
Internet: WiFi connection is available in the marina. Giza internet café in Alaçatı town has PC terminals available for use.

YACHT SERVICES AND CHANDLERY
The Yunus Marin Yat Market stocks basic chandlery items.

PROVISIONING AND SERVICES
Grocery shops: There is currently nowhere to buy provisions in the marina complex and you must travel towards Alaçatı town for this. The Port Alaçatı development will include a village-style shopping centre with provisions available

when the first phase of development is completed. There are a few markets along the road into Alaçatı town, although you will need to call a taxi or hitch a lift to get there. At least one of these, Marine Market, Tel: 0232 716 02 19, offers free yacht delivery.

The town has a large market on Saturdays where you will be able to buy everything you need very freshly.
Bakery: A bakery and a butcher can be found in Alaçatı town.
Banks: There are branches of ING Bank and Garantı Bank in Alaçatı town, both of which have ATMs.
Pharmacy: In Alaçatı town.
Post office: A PTT office is situated in Alaçatı town and is signposted from the road that leads into town from the marina.

EATING OUT
If you want to stay within the marina then you can choose from the classy Port Restaurant or the workers' lokanta, which may only be open during lunchtimes. There is one more restaurant on the hill above the marina, which offers standard Turkish food with a great view across the windsurfing beaches.

If you have the time though, it is well worth organising a taxi to take you

into Alaçatı town so that you can enjoy some of the well-regarded restaurants there. Fine dining is the key here and popular restaurants can get very busy, particularly at weekends and during holidays, so it is advisable to call ahead at these times if you do have a particular restaurant in mind. There is a good choice though, so if you have not booked but are prepared to wait or be flexible about location then you will not go hungry and are still sure to have a good meal.

There are likely to be a few changes in the restaurants here from season to season, but below are some suggestions to get you started:
O Ev Gourmet café, Tel: 0232 716 61 50, is attached to the boutique hotel of the same name. You can expect a variety of dishes that combine Turkish and European cuisines, but the prices are expensive. Cafe Agrilia, Tel: 0232 716 85 94, is a less expensive option but you may have to wait for a table as this is a very popular spot. Housed in an old tobacco warehouse, this restaurant has a lively atmosphere and good food. Picante, Tel: 0232 76 95 41, is owned by the same people that operate a similarly named restaurant in Bodrum. The menu

Useful information – Alaçatı (continued)

is described as Latin/ Borderline, which sounds alarming but is really just Tex-Mex; well done and a pleasant change if you fancy something different to the usual fare available.

Yildiz Café, Tel: 0232 76 80 90, serves traditional Turkish home-cooked food at reasonable prices.

ASHORE

Alaçatı is well known as a windsurfing and kitesurfing location, and if you want to have a go at either of these sports there are several centres along the beach where you can hire equipment and organise instruction if necessary. One of the biggest is the Alaçatı Surf Paradise Club, Tel: 0232 716 66 11, website: www.alacati. de. The bay usually hosts several competitions throughout the season and has also been featured in the PWA (Professional Windsurfing Association) World Tour, so there have been some famous names about and the wind must be good.

If you plan to spend any time in Alaçatı Marina then it is well worth taking a trip to explore the nearby town. The town is characterised by Ottoman Greek stone houses and is now under a preservation order to ensure that it retains its unique character. It is a popular holiday and weekend destination for Turkish city-dwellers and is full of interesting boutiques and stalls, as well as some excellent restaurants (see above). There is an antiques market in the centre of town and also a couple of galleries displaying work by local artists.

For a bit of fun try out the Go-Kart track along the road leading from the marina to the town.

TRANSPORT
Car hire: There are a couple of hire car companies in Alaçatı town (Hakaydin Renta-Car, Tel: 0232 716 74 55), or you can ask the marina office to arrange one for you.
Taxis: Ask at marina office.
Dolmuş: A minibus service operates between the

Alaçatı village

town and the marina and beaches during the summer only. A dolmuş service also operates to Çeşme, from where you can travel by coach to İzmir and connect there for other destinations.
Air travel: İzmir Adnan Menderes international airport is approximately 1 hour away.

USEFUL INFORMATION
Local tel code: İzmir area 0232, Alaçatı 716.
Doctor: In Alaçatı town – Dr Yilmazer, Tel: 0232 76 71 44, Dr Kavalci, Tel: 0232 716 72 25.
Dentist: In Alaçatı town. Ask at the marina office for recommendations.
Hospital: Nearest hospital is in Çeşme.
Yacht repairs/services: Ask at the marina for details of technical services available. The marina has a 100 ton travel lift and hard standing area.

Alaçatı weekly market

Sığacık Limanı

North-west of Eşek Adası: 38°12'.11N 26°46'.05E
Harbour entrance: 38°11'.74N 26°46'.90E

Sığacık is an attractive walled village with a sheltered harbour, which seems far off the beaten track despite its location near the fair sized town of Seferihisar. The harbour is situated within Sığacık Limanı bay, approximately half way between Alaçatı and Kuşadası on the southern side of the Çeşme peninsula.

NAVIGATION

Charts: Turkish Hydrographic Charts: 223, 2231; Imray Charts: G2, G3, G28, Admiralty 1057, 1058, SC 5776

Vessels approaching from the west will enter the Sığacık Körfezi around the headland of Teke Burnu, which is lit at night (Fl (3) 15s). From there the approach to Sığacık Limanı is free of dangers.

Vessels approaching from the south will round the headland of Doğanbey Burnu, and later the headland of Killik Burnu on the Teos peninsula. There are two islands lying off Doğanbey Burnu, and it is possible to pass between the larger of the two, Doğanbey Adası, and the mainland, although not the smaller island of Bölme Adası. Doğanbey Adası is lit at night (Fl (2) 5s).

The small island of Eşek Adası lies to the west of the entrance to Sığacık Limanı and is lit at night (Fl 10s).

Sığacık harbour

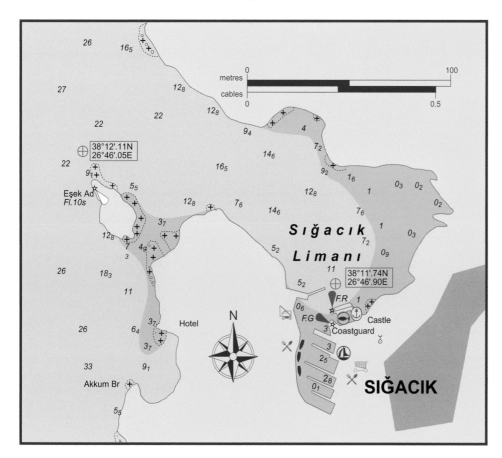

The island can be identified easily if you are approaching along the coast from the south, but is harder to see if you are coming from the west. Shallow and rocky waters extend to the north and east of the island, so you should be sure to give it a wide berth as you pass around it to enter the bay. The walled village and harbour will be visible only after you have passed well into the bay. The entrance to the fishing harbour is lit to either side, although the entrance to the main harbour is not.

BERTHING

Sığacık has a purpose-built harbour in the inlet to the west of the walled village, with a fishing harbour located just inside the entrance. The southern wall of this harbour is full of local fishing boats, but there are sufficient depths on the northern side for small yachts and power boats to anchor stern-to.

The main harbour is just to the south of this. It has several new floating pontoons and development is ongoing. Eventually these pontoons will have lazylines to allow stern-to berthing, but for now most visiting boats will tie up alongside on the western side of the harbour where there is room.

There are plans to build a travel lift and hard standing area on this side of the harbour in the future, but at the time of writing there were no facilities of this kind.

Sığacık harbour

Useful information – Sığacık Limanı

Planned development of Sığacık harbour area

that is ripe for development and is likely to become a more popular destination in the future. The walled village is attractive and timeless, and the restaurants in the harbour make good vantage points from which to watch the world go by in lovely, tranquil surroundings.

TRANSPORT
Car hire: Setur Rent-a-Car has an office on the southern side of the harbour, Tel: 0232 745 73 21.
Taxis: There is a taxi rank on the road leading into the south-east corner of the harbour.
Dolmuş: A dolmuş service operates to the nearby town of Seferihisar.

USEFUL INFORMATION
Local tel code: İzmir area, 0232, Sığacık 745.

Sığacık village walls

FACILITIES
Water and electricity: Will be installed on pontoons in the future.
Ice: Available in mini-markets near the harbour.
Rubbish: Bins ashore.
Telephone: A public phone is situated in the village and the mobile phone reception in the area is good.

PROVISIONING AND SERVICES
Grocery shops: There are several mini-markets along the road running to the south of the harbour. There is also a row of fishmongers on the road leading to the harbour from the main road.
Bakery: A bakery and a **butcher** can be found in the village.

Pharmacy: You will find one along the road at the southern end of the harbour.
Post office: A small PTT office is in the village.

EATING OUT
Sığacık is known as a fishing port, and the two restaurants in the harbour are renowned for being the place to eat fish. These are the Burç restaurant, Tel: 0232 745 73 05, and the Café Liman restaurant, Tel: 0232 745 70 11. There are some smaller and cheaper options within the village where you can get *pide* and other local dishes.

ASHORE
Sığacık is a quiet and sleepy village, but one

Kuşadası Marina and cruise ship port from the north

Kuşadası

West of Petroma reef: 37°51'.43N 27°13'.28E
Between Petroma reef and rock to the north:
37°51'.82N 27°13'.65E
Guvercin Adası light: 37°51'.85N 27°14'.81E
Marina entrance: 37°52'.08N 27°15'.63E

Kuşadası is a large resort town and busy cruise
port, located conveniently close to the ruins at
Ephesus. There is a big marina in the town, which is a
popular stopover for vessels travelling along the coast
as well as the home port for a significant number of
local boats.

NAVIGATION

Charts: Turkish Hydrographic Charts: 223, 2231;
Imray Charts: G2, G3, G3; Admiralty 1057, 1087,
SC 5776

Kuşadası town is approximately 12M north of the Dilek
Boğazı strait between the Greek island of Samos and
the Turkish Dilek Yarımadası peninsula. The buildings
of the town stretch up into the hills and along the
coast from the harbour, and can be spotted from a fair
distance away.

Vessels approaching from the north should be aware
of the Akburun Kayası reef that extends from the
northern side of the marina wall, and should give this

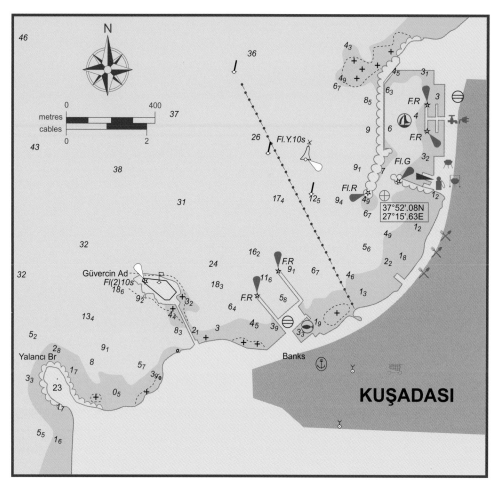

marina (Fl R 5s & Fl G 3s). A large hotel complex lies immediately to the north of the marina, which can be easily identified.

BERTHING

The Setur Kuşadası Marina has berths for 350 boats up to 70m long and with draughts of up to 5m. Berthing is stern-to with lazylines on either floating pontoons or around the marina wall.

Call the marina on VHF Ch 73 or 16 as you approach and they will send a pilot boat to guide you to a berth and give assistance with mooring if required. The marina can also be contacted on Tel: 0256 618 14 60/63, Fax: 0256 618 14 64, email: kusadasi@seturmarinas. com, website: www. seturmarinas.com

a wide berth as they head round and approach the entrance from the south.

Vessels approaching from the south will pass the Aslan Burnu and Yalancı Burnu headlands to the south of the town. They should stay well clear of the coast as they round these headlands as there are two separate reefs that extend for up to 1M off the coast here. The Yalancı Burnu Bankası (also known as Petroma reef) lies off the northern Yalancı Burnu headland, whilst the Karakeçi Bankı reef extends west of the small island of Karga Adası to the south of here. Both are dangerous to navigation and should be avoided.

As you approach the town you will see the marina at the northern end, with the cruise ship port to the south of this. A fort on the small island of Güvercin Adası is conspicuous to the south of the cruise port and is lit at night (Fl (2) 10s). There are also lights at the cruise port (FR) and the entrance to the

FORMALITIES

The marina reception office can assist with all entry and exit formalities for the usual agent's fee, but it is also possible to do the formalities yourself. The customs and immigration offices are all located in the marina near the fuel dock. The health office and harbour master are situated in the town near the cruise dock.

Aerial view of Kuşadası Marina

Kuşadası Marina and ferry port from the north

Useful information – Kuşadası

FACILITIES
Water and electricity: Available at every berth in the marina.

Fuel: The fuel berth is located just inside the entrance to the marina.

Showers: At the marina.

Ice: Is sold at the marina supermarket and others close by.

Laundry: A launderette can be found at the marina as well as in the town.

Gas: Gas bottles can be exchanged at the marina's chandlery and in the town.

Rubbish: Rubbish bins and segregated recycling bins are in the marina, while oil and bilge waste disposal facilities are in the boatyard.

Telephone: Public phone boxes in the marina and in the town. Mobile reception here is good.

Internet: An internet service is provided by the marina office and a WiFi service is available within the marina. There are plenty of other internet cafés in the town.

YACHT SERVICES AND CHANDLERY
The marina has an 80 ton travel lift and hard standing area for up to 175 boats. Water and electricity supplies are available throughout the hard standing area. You should contact the marina office to arrange any technical work on your boat. The following technical services are available from marina tenants:

Özbek Yacht Service, painting and GRP repairs, Tel: 0256 618 22 52, Mob: 0535 240 45 86.
Rubles Yachting, sail, canvas and upholstery, Mob: 0536 420 26 02.
Yacht Electric, electrics and battery service, Mob: 0535 641 76 40.
Hasan Ekşi, sails, canvas and upholstery, Mob: 0535 389 05 33.
Yakamoz Denizcilik, machinery, welding, inox and engine service, Mob: 0532 623 11 50/0535 438 03 95.
Ustaoğlu, engine

Kuşadası Marina office

Useful information – Kuşadası (continued)

and machinery work, Mob: 532 787 728.
Y&T Carpentry, teak decking, Mob: 042 552 15 61.
Manfreds Yacht Service, general service, Tel: 0256 618 1816, Mob: 0532 736 69 98.
Kayadan Yacht Service, general service, Mob: 0542 281 49 59/0537 775 26 95.
Gizmar, brokerage and maintenance, Tel: 0256 618 27 98, Mob: 0532 796 21 69, website: www.gizmar.com
Yağız Yacht Service, general service, Mob: 0532 614 82 65.

There is also a well-stocked chandlery on site: Özbek Yacht Chandlery Tel: 0256 618 18 58, Mob: 0535 240 45 86.

PROVISIONING AND SERVICES

Grocery shops: There is a Migros supermarket within walking distance of the marina and many other small mini-markets are in the town.

Bakery: You will find a selection of bakeries and butchers in the town.

Local market: Held in Kuşadası on Tuesdays and Thursdays.

Banks: All of the major Turkish banks have branches within the town centre where you can withdraw or exchange money and travellers cheques. There are also a few ATM machines close to the marina.

Pharmacy: Several pharmacies are situated throughout the town centre and close to the marina.

Post office: The PTT office is located in the town centre, a couple of streets back from the cruise dock.

EATING OUT

There are a huge number of restaurants within Kuşadası town, and although many of them are aimed at the package tourism market, there is also a good choice of more interesting options. The Istanbul Mehanesi restaurant, Tel: 0256 613 16 77, combines traditional Turkish food with traditional Turkish music in the centre of town. It may not be to everyone's taste but is certainly popular with the locals, and you may need to book in advance to ensure a table, particularly at weekends in the high season.

The Avlu lokanta restaurant is located close to the PTT office in the centre of town. It is a no frills budget option that offers excellent value for money and is popular with tourists and locals alike.

Seafood fans can visit Ali Baba's restaurant, Tel: 0256 614 15 51, near the Anatolian bazaar shopping centre. This is reputed to be one of the best fish restaurants in town, so a reservation may be required to ensure a table during the high season.

There are also several bars, cafés and restaurants within the marina, which offer a variety of cuisines and entertainments a bit closer to home. The Be-Bop restaurant and Jazz Bar provide a pleasant sound track to your meal, whilst the Orient Marine restaurant next door has live music several times a week.

ASHORE

Kuşadası is a great place to base yourself for a few days if you want to explore some of the ancient ruins and remains along this stretch of the coast. Organised tours are available from the many travel agents in the town, including overnight trips that will take in several locations in a couple of days. You can also do it yourself by hiring a car; the roads around Kuşadası are well made and reasonably well sign posted. Ephesus (see page 28) is only 17km from Kuşadası, and other interesting sites such as Pamukkale, Aphrodisias and the Dilek Peninsula National Park are within driving distance of Kuşadası.

The small Ephesus airport near Selçuk is home to the Turkish Aeronautical Association, which offers training courses in piloting, parachuting and microlight flying for the adventurous.

There is also plenty to do within Kuşadası itself. The town gets its name (meaning 'bird island') from the small Güvercin Adası (Pigeon Island) that lies just south of the cruise port. You can walk out along the causeway where you can explore the island and small fort that are situated on it. There are two *hamams* in the town, although try to avoid visiting these when the cruise liners are in as they will be packed with day trippers from these boats. You will also come across an abundance of shops of all descriptions here, but some of the sales tactics can be a bit intrusive and you may find that prices around the cruise port area are rather steeper than in other places.

TRANSPORT

Car hire: A branch of Avis car hire is situated within the marina, but you will also find a large number of local operators with offices all over town, so you can shop around for a good deal.

Taxis: A taxi rank is just outside the road entrance to the marina, with several more throughout the town. Particularly near the cruise port you will see that many of the taxis in Kuşadası are charming old-style Chevrolets rather than the usual Mercedes and Tofaş models.

Dolmuş: Local minibus services operate several times a day to the towns of Selçuk, Pamucak, Söke and Seferhisar. The main dolmuş station is in the centre of town, but buses will also pick you up as they pass by the marina entrance.

Coach: The otogar coach station is on the main road out of town, but all of the bus companies have offices in the town centre and run free shuttle buses to take you to the otogar from here.

Ferry: The ferry port is just to the south of the cruise ship dock, and there are several departures a day from here to the Greek island of Samos. Tickets must be purchased at least one day in advance and are available from several travel agencies in the town, including Meander Travel, Tel: 0256 614 38 59/73 44, website: www.meandertravel.com

Air travel: The nearest international airport is İzmir's Adnan Menderes airport, which is 80km away. A very small local airport exists near Selçuk, but is mainly used for private flights and sightseeing flights over Ephesus.

USEFUL INFORMATION

Local tel code: Aydın area, 0256, Kuşadası 614/618.

Medical: There is a state Devlet hospital, several private hospitals and a number of private outpatient clinics in Kuşadası. Kuşadası Özel Hastanesi (Private Hospital) Tel: 0256 613 16 16. Euromed Private Clinic Tel: 0256 68 25 00. A small medical clinic is based at the marina for minor injuries and prescriptions.

Local information websites: www.kusadasi.net www.infokusadasi.com www.kusadasi.biz www.kusadasi.com

Dilek Boğazı

Bayrak Adası light: 37°41'.51N 27°00'.92E
East end of channel: 37°42'.01N 27°04'.31E
West end of channel: 37°40'.69N 26°58'.60E
Su Adası and Sandal Adası anchorages:
37°38'.74N 27°00'.42E

NAVIGATION

Charts: Turkish Hydrographic Charts: 224, 2231;
Turkish Hydrographic Leisure Folio 2004: 2004_1,
2004_5; Imray Charts: G2, G3, G32; Admiralty 1526,
1095, SC 5773

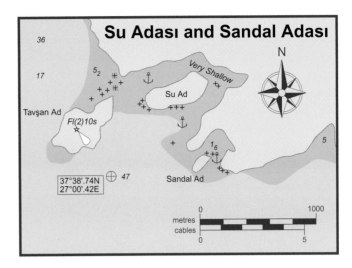

The Dilek Boğazı channel runs between the Greek
island of Samos and the Turkish Dilek Yarımadası
peninsula. It is only 1M wide at its narrowest point,
which is the closest the two countries ever get to each
other in the Aegean.

There is a light (Fl 5s) on the Turkish island of Bayrak
Adası, which is in the middle of the channel. A modern
wind farm is also conspicuous above the Greek town
of Pitagorion.

If possible it is best to pass through the channel during
the morning, when winds are lighter. As the *meltemi*
builds during the afternoon it can start to push quite a
current through the straits, although the worst of this can
be avoided by passing south of the Bayrak Adası island.
The narrowness of the channel between Samos and the
Dilek peninsula means that you can experience strong

currents in this area as the sea is squeezed through the
gap. The current generally sets in an easterly direction
and can run at up to 3 knots, especially when the
meltemi is blowing. If possible, it is best to pass through
the channel during the morning, when winds are
lighter. If you find yourself here later in the day then
you can avoid the worst of the current by staying south
of Bayrak Adası where the water is calmer.

There are two bays suitable for anchoring
immediately to the south of the Dipburnu headland.
These are located just to the east of the small islands
of Tavşan Adası, Su Adası and Sandal Adası. Tavşan
Adası is lit at night (Fl (2) 10s), but vessels should not
attempt to pass to the north of this as there are rocky
shallows between the island and the mainland.

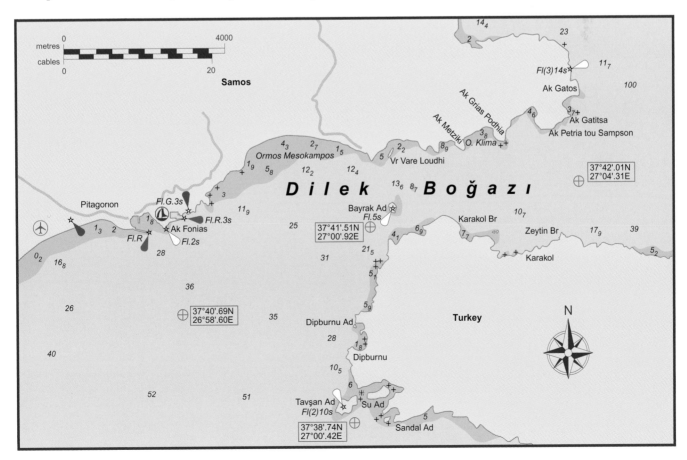

Karakuyu Koyu
(Altınkum, Didim)

Entrance to the bay anchorage: 37°21'.10N 27°17'.05E

Panayir light: 37°19'.70N 27°19'.65E

Entrance to Didim D-Marina: 37°20'.21N 27°15'.55E

Altınkum (meaning golden sands) is a busy and well-developed holiday resort that is centred around the three beaches from which the town gets its name. Although the hustle and bustle of the holiday resort may not be to everybody's taste, Altınkum is worth visiting for its proximity to the archaeological sites at Priene, Miletus and Didyma, which are all a short distance from the town and easily visited by yourself or with an excursion group. The newly-opened marina will surely add to the town's popularity with yachts cruising along this section of coast.

NAVIGATION

Charts: Turkish Hydrographic Charts: 224, 2245; Turkish Hydrographic Leisure Folio 2004: 2004_1, 2004_3, 2004_4, 2004_7; Imray Charts: G3, G32; Admiralty 1056, 1095, SC 5773

Karakuyu Koyu is a wide open bay that faces due south and is approximately 4M east of the Tekağaç Burnu headland. The island of Panayır Adası is easily identified to the south-east of the bay and is lit at night (Fl (3) 15s).

The entrance to the Karakuyu İskele harbour at Altınkum itself is obstructed by a shallow reef on the western side of the bay, so vessels should approach from the south-east and pass safely behind this area.

A large marina (see below) is now located around the Tasli Br headland, a mile or so west of the town.

BERTHING AND ANCHORING

The newly-constructed Didim D-Marina opened in 2009 and is a part of the Doğuş Marina group that also operates the Turgutreis D-Marin Marina (see pages 87-88). There are 580 in-water berths and hard standing for up to 600 yachts. Site facilities currently include a yacht club with pool and sunbathing area, tennis courts, a fuel station, boatyard cafetería, and several technical services companies that have already moved into the new boatyard. Future plans include a spa and fitness centre, shopping and commercial centre with a range of bars and restaurants, a supermarket and a cultural centre. Didim D-Marina can be contacted on VHF Ch 16/72, Tel: 0256 813 80 81, Fax: 0256 813 14 13, email: didim@dogusmarina.com.tr, www.dogusmarina.com.tr

Apart from using the marina, vessels can also anchor in around 5m of water within Karakuyu İskele off the beaches at Altınkum. Be sure to stay well clear of the new cruise port dock which has been constructed at the western end of the bay. The number of bars and restaurants that line the beaches here can make this anchorage quite noisy.

FORMALITIES

Customs and immigration formalities can currently be completed at the Didim Cruise Port in Altınkum, but from 2010 it should be possible to complete all formalities within the marina, which will be the departure point for ferries to nearby Greek islands.

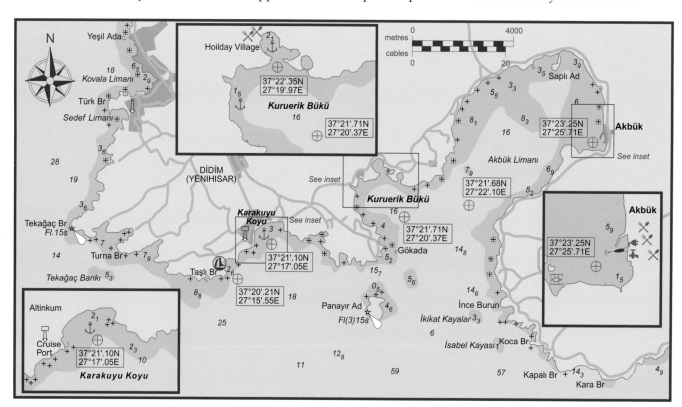

Useful information – Karakuyu Koyu

FACILITIES
Water: Available at the marina.
Electricity: Available at all berths in the marina.
Fuel: Available at the marina.
Showers: Available at the marina.
Ice: Available at supermarkets and minimarkets in the town.
Laundry: Available at the marina.
Gas: Available in the town and at the new marina.
Rubbish: Rubbish bins available in the town and segregated waste disposal facilities are available at the marina.
Telephone: Public phone boxes throughout the town, with phone cards freely available and good mobile phone reception.
Internet: Several internet cafés in the town, with internet connection and WiFi available at the marina.

YACHT SERVICES AND CHANDLERY
Didim D-Marina now has two travel lifts (400 ton and 75 ton) and can accommodate up to 600 boats on hard standing, including a covered hard standing area with two large hangars. A range of technical services are also available on site.

PROVISIONING AND SERVICES
Grocery shops: The town of Altınkum already has several large supermarkets (including Carrefour, Migros and Tansaş) and many mini-markets, but there is also scheduled to be another supermarket within the marina shopping centre when this is completed.
Bakery: Several bakeries and butchers can be found in the town.
Local market: Held on Saturdays in Altınkum.
Banks: Most Turkish banks have a branch in Altınkum where you can exchange and withdraw money. There are also ATM machines located throughout the town and along the beach, as well as one at the marina.

Pharmacy: Several are based in Altınkum.
Post office: There are two PTT offices in Altınkum; the main office is near the Migros supermarket and a smaller one is located just next to the cruise port at the western end of the town beach. A post box is situated outside the marina office.

EATING OUT
Altınkum has a large number of restaurants, bars and cafés as befits a Turkish resort of any size. Most of these are spread along the beachfront road and wind back into the town centre. They include the usual mixture of Turkish and international menus of varying quality.

There are likely to be several restaurants built within the new marina complex that will cater to guests there. The Penguen café, bar and restaurant, Tel: 0256 813 13 08, is located close to the marina and has its own beach.

The Didim Marina Yacht Club is situated within the marina complex and has a bar and *à la carte* restaurant for use of marina guests. The commercial centre will eventually be home to a number of other bars and restaurants, and there is a cafeteria style self service restaurant located within the boatyard.

ASHORE
The primary reason for visiting Altınkum is to explore the ancient ruins within the Gulf of Latmos and around the shores of Bafa Gölü lake (see page 35). Didyma is the closest of these locations and is famous for housing the ruined Temple of Apollo. Miletus and Priene are situated further to the north around the shores of the now silted up Gulf of Latmos, and were both important settlements with amphitheatres, temples and bath houses that can still be explored today. Herakleia lies on the eastern side of Bafa Gölü and is known

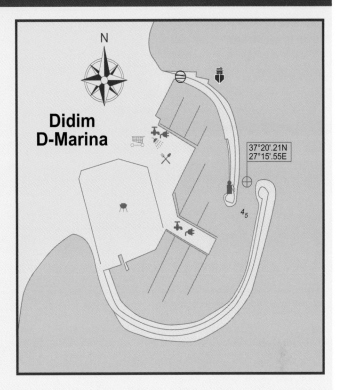

as an ancient refuge for persecuted Christians in the 8th century and as the location of the imposing Mount Latmos.

Other activities within the area include jeep safaris, water parks, horse and camel riding, diving, Turkish baths, watersports and visiting the Luna Park fairground between the town and marina development.

There are also plenty of shops to explore within the back streets and main shopping centres of Altınkum.

TRANSPORT
Car hire: There are many tour and travel agencies within Altınkum that can arrange car and vehicle hire for tourists and there is also likely to be at least one outlet in the new marina's commercial centre when this is opened.
Taxis: Taxis are readily available from a number of taxi ranks throughout Altınkum.
Dolmuş: Local minibus services operate between Altınkum and a number of outlying villages, including some services which pass close to the ruins at Didyma.

Coach: Coach services link Altınkum to İzmir, from where you can get connections to other cities and locations throughout Turkey.
Ferry: Fast catamarans operate ferry services to the Greek islands of Kos, Samos and Patmos from the newly constructed cruise port in Altınkum. These services will move to the marina in 2010. Ferry services are operated by the Yeşil Marmaris group; for more information go to www.yesilmarmaris.com
Air travel: Altınkum is accessible from either İzmir Adnan Menderes airport (160km) or from the Bodrum-Milas airport (60km).

USEFUL INFORMATION
Local tel code: Aydın area, 0256, Altınkum 813.
Didim Cruise Port: www.portdidim.com
Medical facilities: There are several private clinics within Altınkum town, but for hospital facilities you may need to travel to either Bodrum (see page 100) or Kuşadası (see page 60).
Local information websites: www.altinkum.co.uk, www.altinkum.com

Kuruerik Bükü

Entrance to main bay: 37°21'.71N 27°20'.37E
Entrance to northern cove: 37°22'.35N 27°19.97E

NAVIGATION

Charts: Turkish Hydrographic Charts: 224, 2245;
Turkish Hydrographic Leisure Folio 2004: 2004_1,
2004_3, 2004_6; Imray Charts: G3, G32; Admiralty
1056, 1095, SC 5773

This sheltered bay lies between the villages of Altınkum
and Akbük, on the western side of Akbük Limanı.
Vessels approaching from the west can pass to either
side of the island of Panayır Adası, but should leave
the smaller islet of Gökada to port in order to avoid the
rocky shallows between here and the mainland.

Vessels can free swing at anchor off the beaches
on the west of the bay, or in the smaller inlet on the
northern side. The bay is surrounded by holiday village
developments so it is no longer the peaceful anchorage
it once was, but still offers good shelter from the
prevailing winds.

Akbük Limanı

Entrance to main bay: 37°21'.68N 27°22'.10E
Just off the harbour: 37°23'.25N 27°25'.71E

NAVIGATION

Charts: Turkish Hydrographic Charts: 224, 2245;
Turkish Hydrographic Leisure Folio 2004: 2004_1,
2004_3, 2004_6; Imray Charts: G3, G32; Admiralty 1056,
1095, SC 5773

This large bay extends north-east from the island of
Panayır Adası, which lies in its entrance. There are
several shallow reefs to the east of this island, notably
the İkikat Kayalar and İsabel Kayası reefs that are 4m
and 2.4m deep respectively and are around 1.5M off
the coast.

The bay is ringed with villas and tourist developments,
but the actual village of Akbük lies in the north-east
corner of the bay and has a small harbour where vessels
can anchor stern-to amongst local fishing and day

Akbük quayside

tripper boats. Look for a small island spit extending
from the northern side of the bay, and head east of
here to find the harbour. A new wind farm has been
constructed on the hills to the west of the bay and is
conspicuous as you approach. You will also pass a
collection of fish farms on the eastern side of the bay
just before you reach the village of Akbük.

Water and electricity are available at some points
around the harbour, and there are also facilities in
the small village ashore, including two mid-sized
supermarkets (Tansaş and Bim). A butcher and
greengrocer are situated near the harbour, while the
local fishing co-operative has a stall within the harbour
where you can buy freshly caught fish directly from
the fishermen.

There are a couple of restaurants within walking
distance of the harbour, including the Castle Diner,
Deniz restaurant, Ata restaurant and Altınüç restaurant.
Dolmuş minibuses operate to the nearby towns of Söke
and Altınkum.

Akbük harbour

Kazıklı Limanı

**Entrance to bay: 37°17'.40N
27°27'.39E
Paradise Bay: 37°19'.14N
27°28'.07E
South of restaurant jetties:
37°19'.15N 27°28'.89E**

NAVIGATION

Charts: Turkish Hydrographic Charts: 224, 2246; Turkish Hydrographic Leisure Folio 2004: 2004_1, 2004_4, 2004_8; Imray Charts: G3, G32; Admiralty 1056, 1095, 1099, SC 5773

Kazıklı Limanı

This is another long bay with its entrance approximately 8M to the south-east of Akbük Limanı. There is a small inlet on the western side, known locally as Paradise Bay, which is a beautiful location suitable for lunchtime or overnight anchoring. You can identify the bay by spotting the mussel farm just off the southern headland. There will usually be several local day tripper boats visiting the bay during the daytime, but there is a good chance that you will have it all to yourself in the evening.

Towards the northern end of the bay are two small restaurants that can accommodate visiting yachts on small jetties they have constructed. In both cases there is no mooring fee levied, but it is expected that you will eat at the restaurants during your stay. The Kaptan restaurant has a wooden T-shaped jetty and the Meydan

Kaptan restaurant

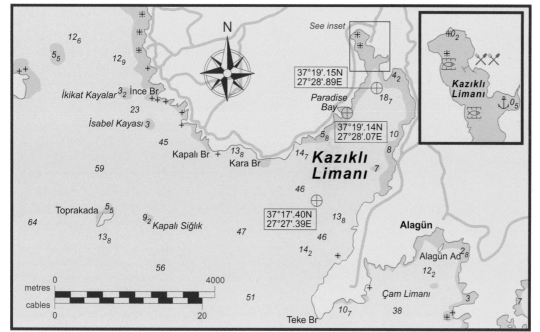

restaurant, Tel: 0532 456 8267, has a straight dock where you can tie up alongside.

There are several other coves and small inlets around this bay where you can anchor and find some shelter from the prevailing winds, although many of these are now occupied with fish farms and mussel farms, so may be less inviting than they previously were.

Çam Limanı

Centre of bay: 37°15'.38N
27°29'.67E

NAVIGATION

Charts: Turkish
Hydrographic Charts:
224, 2246; Turkish
Hydrographic Leisure
Folio 2004: 2004_1, 2004_4,
2004_9; Imray Charts: G3,
G32; Admiralty 1056, 1095,
1099, SC 5773

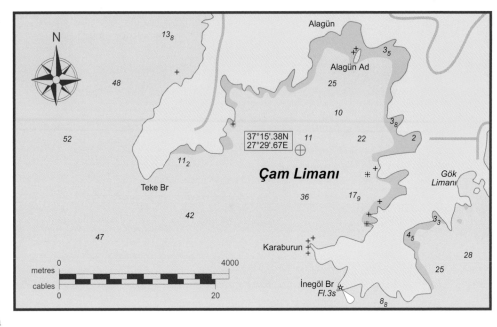

This smaller bay lies between
the headlands of Teke Burnu to the west and İnegöl
Burnu to the east. There are several small bays and
inlets along the western side that provide shelter from
the prevailing winds and are suitable for anchoring in
all but the strongest *meltemi* conditions. A very small
hamlet (Alagün) is situated at the northern end of the

bay, but little in the way of facilities can be found here.
Beware of the rocks surrounding the small Alagün
Adası islet if you venture this far into the bay. There are
also some rocks to avoid off a prominent headland on
the eastern side of the bay and a 9m shoal area just to
the north of here.

Asin Körfezi

Middle of Gök Limanı: 37°14'.92N 27°32'.20E

NAVIGATION

Charts: Turkish Hydrographic Charts: 224, 2246;
Turkish Hydrographic Leisure Folio 2004: 2004_1,
2004_4, 2004_9; Imray Charts: G3, G32; 1056, 1095, 1099,
1644; Admiralty 1056, 1095, 1099, SC 5773

The entrance to this gulf is just to the south of the
İnegöl Burnu headland, which is lit at night (Fl 3s).
The southern side of the entrance is bordered by
the İnce Burun headland, with the small Metelik Adası
islet lying just off the tip of this. There are several
usable anchorages along the northern side of the gulf,
although many of these are now occupied by fish and
mussels farms.

Asin Limanı

(İasos, Kıyıkışlacık)
South of entrance between Byzantine tower
and submerged breakwater in 10m of water:
37°16'.24N 27°35'.05E

NAVIGATION

Charts: Turkish Hydrographic Charts: 224, 2246;
Turkish Hydrographic Leisure Folio 2004: 2004_1,
2004_4, 2004_9; Imray Charts: G3, G32; 1056, 1095, 1099,
1644; Admiralty 1056, 1095, 1099, SC 5773

This is a small bay on the northern side of the Asin
Körfezi, protected to the east by a peninsula housing
the remains of the ancient fortified settlement of İasos

Byzantine tower structure in Asin Limanı

İasos fishing fleet

(see chart on page 69). The village of Kıyıkışlacık on the western side of the bay has a small fishing harbour where visiting yachts can anchor stern-to and stay overnight. A conspicuous square-shaped Byzantine fort is visible on the eastern side of the entrance, which is partially blocked by a submerged breakwater extending from the western side. Vessels should pass close to the Byzantine fort to avoid this hazard, which may or may not be marked and cannot usually be seen in choppy conditions.

Once you are through the entrance you will be able to see the village harbour and buildings on the western side of the bay, and the ruins of İasos on the hilly peninsula to the east. There are a couple of restaurants in the village that specialise in fresh locally caught fish, such as the Ceyar restaurant, Tel: 0252 537 7066, overhanging the waterfront, and the İasos Dilek

restaurant, Tel: 0252 537 73 07, just behind.

Other facilities in the village include a small mini-market where you can buy ice, fresh bread, gas bottles and phone cards in addition to basic provisions, a couple of public card phones, a taxi rank behind the village dock, a minibus stop for the dolmuş service to Milas and a small fish market at the southern end of the harbour.

The ruins of ancient İasos occupy the peninsula to the east of the village and are well worth exploring. You can cross the harbour by dinghy or walk around the northern end on foot. Be sure to wear decent shoes as the ground is rough and rocky. During high season you may be required to pay a small entrance fee, but at other times this is unlikely. You can explore the remains of an ancient fort and amphitheatre where excavation work continues each summer.

Kıyıkışlacık ruins

Kıyıkışlacık village

Güllük

West of light on headland: 37°14'.30N 27°35'.27E
To north-west of breakwater in 10m of water:
37°14'.35N 27°35'.65E

Güllük is a bauxite mining town, a boatbuilding centre and growing tourist resort, and is the largest town within the Asin Körfezi.

NAVIGATION

Charts: Turkish Hydrographic Charts: 224, 2246; Turkish Hydrographic Leisure Folio 2004: 2004_1, 2004_4, 2004_9; Imray Charts: G3, G32.1056, 1095, 1099, 1644; Admiralty 1056, 1095, 1099, SC 5773

Güllük lies on the eastern side of the Asin Körfezi gulf and is easily identified from a distance because there are usually several cargo ships at the town's commercial dock. The small yacht and fishing harbour is just to the west of here. There is a light on the headland immediately south of the town (Fl (2) 5s).

BERTHING AND ANCHORING

Visiting yachts can anchor stern-to where there is space amongst the local fishing fleet in the small harbour to the west of the commercial loading dock. This dock is used less than it previously was as there is now a new commercial facility slightly to the east of the town.

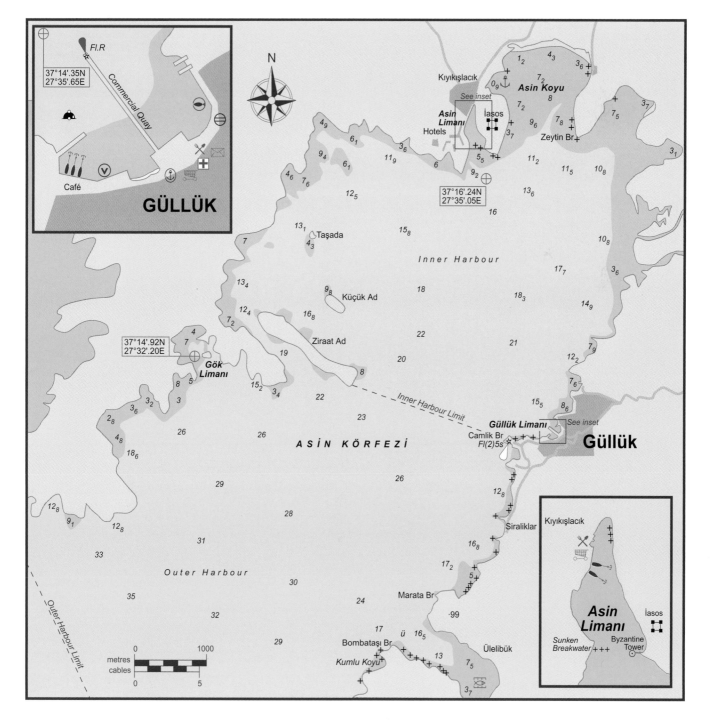

Useful information – Güllük

FACILITIES

Water: Can be obtained in the town harbour.

Ice: Is available from markets in the town.

Laundry: A laundry service is in the town.

Gas: Purchased in the town.

Rubbish: Rubbish bins are located ashore.

Telephone: Public phones are situated in the town, with phone cards sold in shops. Mobile reception here is good.

Internet: The Ayca internet café is located close to the harbour in the town centre.

PROVISIONING AND SERVICES

Grocery shops: There are several medium-sized supermarkets in the town centre, including Bim, Dia and Migros, as well as a couple of fruit and vegetable shops.

Bakery: A bakery along with a butcher and the Dönmez **fishmonger** can be found in the town centre.

Local market: Held on Thursdays in the town square.

Banks: There are several bank branches and ATM machines in the town square or close to the harbour, including Garanti Bank, Yapı Kredi Bank and Vakıf Bank.

Pharmacy: Several in the town centre.

Post office: The PTT office is located in the town centre, close to the Migros supermarket.

YACHT SERVICES AND CHANDLERY

There are a number of small boatyard facilities along the coast close to Güllük where you may be able to arrange to have your boat lifted out and stored ashore. These facilities cater mostly for local fishing boats and the construction of traditional wooden gulets, but you should be able to arrange limited engine servicing and the purchase of basic spares locally. For other items you are better off looking in Bodrum, where the industry is geared more towards pleasure boats and yachts.

EATING OUT

There are several restaurants close to the town centre or harbour in Güllük, including the Kırçın fish restaurant, Mimoza restaurant, Küçük Ev restaurant and Eski Depo restaurant.

ASHORE

Güllük is currently undergoing a fair amount of development and regeneration, including a widening and improving of the main road into the town, landscaping of the area just behind the fishing and yacht harbour, and construction of public facilities, including underground cinema, toilet and shower facilities for yachts, public swimming pool and fitness centre, and new shopping centre. These should all be located close to the town centre and yacht harbour.

TRANSPORT

Car hire: A couple of small travel agencies in Güllük can also arrange car hire, including Polat rent-a-car, which has an office in the town centre.

Taxis: A taxi rank is situated close to the harbour, Tel: 0252 255 25 07.

Dolmuş: Dolmuş services run every hour to the towns of Bodrum and Milas, departing from the town centre.

Air travel: The Bodrum-Milas airport is only about 10 minutes drive from Güllük.

USEFUL INFORMATION

Local tel code: Muğla area, 0252, Güllük 255.

Medical: There is a small medical centre near the belediye office. For hospitals see entry for Bodrum on page 100.

Local websites: www. gulluk.net

Güllük quayside

English Harbour anchorage at Değirmen Bükü

Chapter two
The Carian coast – Bodrum peninsula and the Gulf of Gökova

The Carian coastline contrasts the resort towns and sophistication of the Bodrum peninsula with the remote anchorages and sleepy hamlets of the Gökova Körfezi. Both sections of coast have their own character and environments, and are well known as part of the blue cruise routes.

The landscape here is rugged and mountainous, and although the Bodrum peninsula has been opened up by the construction of new roads, much of the coastline around the Gökova Körfezi is still hard to reach by land and remains wonderfully unspoilt and underdeveloped.

Bodrum peninsula
Charts: Turkish Hydrographic Charts: 224, 2247, 2248, 311, 3110, 3111; Turkish Hydrographic Leisure Folios: 2004, 3001; Imray Charts: G3, G32, G35; Admiralty 1055, 1099, SC 5773

The Bodrum peninsula extends between the gulfs of Güllük Körfezi to the north and Gökova Körfezi to the south. The area has long been a popular holiday destination for fashionable and wealthy Turks from İstanbul and since the 1970s has been discovered by

Aspat beach

foreign visitors, who return in increasing numbers each year.

This has resulted in the building of large numbers of private holiday villas and developments on the outskirts of more conventional villages and harbours. These modern developments are based on traditional styles, incorporating whitewashed walls and flat roofs with distinctive upturned corners. In the past the buildings were made of stone, however, whereas today they are generally poured from concrete.

Bodrum is a populous area, and its inhabitants have always been seafaring people. There is a strong tradition of wooden boatbuilding here, which continues in boatyards around İçmeler and Gümbet.

Winds are consistently strong in the summer months, reaching force 4-5 most afternoons and blowing from the north-west. This has made the area very popular with windsurfing and watersports enthusiasts.

There are a number of islands off the coast of the peninsula, both Greek and Turkish. These islands make useful landmarks for vessels navigating in this area.

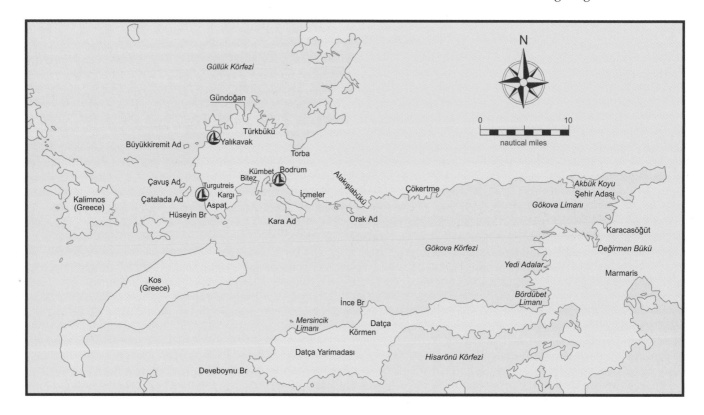

Torba

Middle of the bay: 37°05'.57N 27°28'.06E
Harbour entrance: 37°05'.22N 27°27'.35E

This large bay on the north-east side of the Bodrum peninsula has a small harbour and village, and has become an upmarket destination with plenty of charm for land-based visitors as well as those on yachts.

NAVIGATION

Charts: Turkish Hydrographic Charts: 224, 2247; Turkish Hydrographic Leisure Folio 2004: 2004_1, 2004_4, 2004_11; Imray Charts: G3, G32; Admiralty 1095, 1099, SC 5773

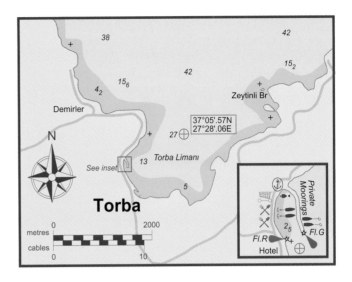

Torba Limanı is located on the southern side of Güllük Körfezi and can be identified by the two small islands of İkizadalar lying immediately to the north of the village. The harbour is on the western side of the bay and will not be seen by vessels approaching from this direction until they round the Boz Burnu headland. Vessels approaching from the east will be able to see the white buildings of the village as they near the harbour, and should watch out for the few submerged rocks lying off the shore approximately 1M to the east of the village. The harbour entrance faces to the south and is lit on either side.

BERTHING AND ANCHORING

The western side of the harbour closest to the shore is very shallow and is filled with local fishing boats.

Torba harbour

There are usually a few berths for visiting yachts on the eastern quay, backed by a rock wall. It is advisable to moor bows-to along this quay, as it is rocky and shallow close to the dock. Use an anchor as there are no lazylines. You will probably see several large yachts, gulets and motor boats berthed stern-to on the outer rock wall, but most of these are local boats with permanent laid moorings here. If the weather is calm then you can join them if you find the space. There is a fee for overnight berthing here.

Vessels wanting to anchor will be able to free swing within the bay, but should stay on the western side for the best shelter and to avoid the many buoyed swimming areas just off the beaches to the east of the harbour. Take a line ashore if you plan to stay the night, and try to tuck in behind the Boz Burnu headland.

Vessels moored bows-to

Useful information – Torba

Electricity supply box

mostly serving fresh fish and *meze* selections. Ali Gonca's restaurant, Tel: 0252 367 15 99, Mob: 0542 321 77 86, website: www.aligoncabodrum.com, is well established and convenient. The nearby Dalli restaurant, Tel: 0252 367 10 76, is known for good kebabs. There are also several upmarket hotels along the beach that all have restaurants open to the public.

FACILITIES
Water and electricity: Available in the harbour.
Ice: Can be bought from the small market near the harbour.
Rubbish: Rubbish bins are located ashore.
Telephone: Phone boxes ashore and phone cards are sold at the small markets in the village. The mobile phone reception here is good.

PROVISIONING AND SERVICES
Services are limited and include a small mini-market on the road alongside the harbour and a larger midi-Tansaş supermarket on the road out of town leading back to the main road to Bodrum.

EATING OUT
There are several restaurants around the harbour in Torba,

ASHORE
Torba village itself is quite small and is one of the only villages in the area that has no mosque. The pebbly beach can get crowded during the high season but otherwise you should be able to find space to relax here. The water is clear and perfect for swimming.

TRANSPORT
Car hire: Easily organised through any of the hotels or restaurants in the village.
Taxis: Available near the harbour.
Dolmuş: Regular dolmuş service to Bodrum town.
Air travel: Bodrum-Milas airport is less than 30 minutes by car.

USEFUL INFORMATION
Local tel code: Muğla area, 0252, Torba 367.

Torba harbour entrance

Torba beach

Traditional storehouse

The harbour at Türkbükü

Türkbükü

East of Büyük Ada: 37°08'.33N 27°24'.12E
Harbour entrance: 37°07'.73N 27°22'.79E
Anchorage: 37°07'.98N 27°22'.90E

The exclusive and fashionable resort of Türkbükü is home in the summer months to the elite of Turkish society and is regularly featured in Turkish lifestyle magazines. It is also a popular destination for holidaymakers looking for peaceful sophistication during the day and a vibrant nightlife in the evenings.

western side, separated by a small headland.

The two islands of Fener Adası and the larger Küçüktavşan Ada can be identified to the north-west of Türkbükü bay, and another island, Büyük Ada, is tucked under the northern Kesire Burun headland, opposite the village buildings of Türkbükü itself.

There are several fish pens in the area to the west of Büyük Ada, so it is best to pass to the east of here and keep well clear of these as you approach the village. The harbour is located at the southern end of the beach, to the north of the headland that separates the villages of Türkbükü and Göl Koyu.

NAVIGATION

Charts: Turkish Hydrographic Charts: 224, 2247; Turkish Hydrographic Leisure Folio 2004: 2004_1, 2004_4, 2004_12; Imray Charts: G3, G32; Admiralty 1095, 1099, SC 5773

The large double bay on the north coast of the Bodrum peninsula faces to the north-east and offers excellent shelter from the prevailing winds. There are two villages within the bay, Göl Koyu at the southern end and Türkbükü on the

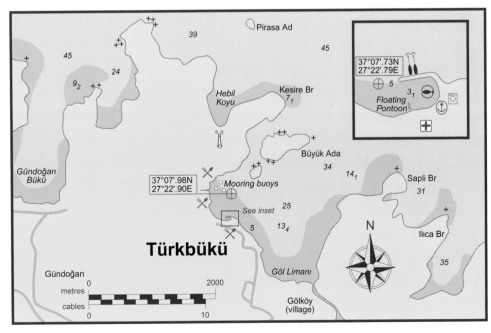

Boats at anchor in Türkbükü

BERTHING AND ANCHORING

The original fishing harbour in Türkbükü has recently been improved and enlarged, and now has room for quite a few private vessels apart from the local fishing fleet. The inner harbour is shallow and full of local boats, but there is space on the outer side of the new quay for visiting boats to berth stern-to with lazylines.

Fees are charged for overnight berthing in Türkbükü harbour, which can be paid at the harbour master's office located at the northern end of the harbour.

There is plenty of room for boats to free swing at anchor within the bay opposite the row of fashionable restaurants and bars that line the beach. It is quite deep here so you will be anchoring in around 15m of water. There are also 12 mooring buoys suitable for large private vessels, which are maintained by the restaurants ashore.

Many of the bars and restaurants along the beach have small jetties where you can tie your dinghy if going ashore from the anchorage or one of the moorings in the bay.

Useful information – Türkbükü

FACILITIES
Water and electricity: On the new dock in the harbour.
Fuel: Available by tanker. Ask the harbour master to arrange this.
Showers: Some of the restaurants and hotels near the harbour have shower facilities for yachtsmen, including Yakamoz restaurant – see below.
Ice: Sold at the small mini-markets in the village.
Laundry: Inci Camaşirhane laundry has a premises right next to the harbour and a shop front along the beach, Tel: 0252 377 59 88. The Lilyan laundry is on the road out of town from the harbour, Tel: 0252 377 64 51.
Gas: There is an İpragaz store near the harbour master's office.
Rubbish: General rubbish bins and segregated recycling bins are located ashore at the northern end of the harbour.
Telephone: Several phone boxes can be found in the village and phone cards can be purchased at the mini-markets throughout the village. Mobile phone reception here is good.
Internet: WiFi internet service is available from several of the bars and restaurants along the beachfront.

PROVISIONING AND SERVICES
Grocery shops: You will find several well-stocked mini-markets along the beachfront.
Butcher: In Göl Koyu, at the southern end of the bay.
Local market: Is held every Monday in the area near the canal and dolmuş station
Banks: There are no banks, but you will find several ATM machines in the area near the footbridge over the canal.
Pharmacy: Near the harbour.
Post office: There is a PTT office near the mosque in the neighbouring village of Göl Koyu.

EATING OUT
A good choice of restaurants in Türkbükü caters for every budget from the modest to extravagant. Yakamoz Motel and Restaurant, Tel: 0252 377 50 35, has a reasonably priced menu specialising in fresh fish and *meze* dishes. The Ship Ahoy restaurant, Tel: 0252 377 50 70, also has a good reputation and is a popular bar later in the evenings.

There are some exclusive hotels and beach clubs in the area which have high quality restaurants open to the public, with prices to match. It would be wise to pop in during the afternoon to make sure of a reservation.

ASHORE
The neighbouring villages of Türkbükü and Göl Koyu are known jointly as Göltürkbükü, and together make for an upmarket destination for foreign holidaymakers as well as young, fashionable and wealthy Turks. During the high summer season the area attracts many Turkish celebrities, who stay in the upmarket hotel resorts and beach clubs while visiting

Berthed stern-to in the harbour

Useful information – Türkbükü (continued)

Türkbükü waterfront restaurants

A good choice of places to eat, drink and stay in Türkbükü

TRANSPORT

Car hire: There are no rental companies in the village, but car hire can be arranged through some of the hotel receptions.

Taxis: A taxi rank is located near the small river at the northern end of the beach.

Dolmuş: A regular minibus service runs to Bodrum town. The bus station is behind the small footbridge at the northern end of the beach.

Air travel: The nearest airport is Bodrum-Milas, approximately 30 minutes by car.

USEFUL INFORMATION

Local tel code: Muğla area, 0252, Türkbükü 377, Göl Koyu 357.

Useful websites: www.golturkbuku.com is the local information website and contains details on the history of the area as well as comprehensive listings for all bars, hotels and restaurants here.

on their luxury sailing yachts and motorcruisers.

The trendiest bars and clubs are clustered along the northern end of the beach at Türkbükü and are packed out until the early hours of the morning. Several of these venues feature regular live music and entertainment in a variety of styles, but at the large night clubs it is Turkish pop music that dominates. Fortunately the harbour is at the other end of the beach, so there is a better chance of getting a good night's sleep.

Shopaholics will find plenty of boutique stores to browse during the daytime and early evening in between the restaurants and cafés along the beachfront. İstanbul designer fashion and jewellery shops are much in evidence, and there is a row of beachfront stalls selling souvenirs and handicrafts.

Göl Koyu village is a short walk around the bay from the harbour at Türkbükü and has a slightly more low key atmosphere than its neighbour, although it can still get quite busy during the summer.

Some ruins, which are believed to be the remains of the settlement of Madnasa, are situated around the bay. There are also some old rock tombs in the hills above Türkbükü village and more near the village of Göl Koyu.

The ruins of Madnasa

Gündoğan

North-west of Fener Adası light:
37°10'.72N 27°21'.20E
Middle of bay:
37°08'.18N 27°20'.75E
Harbour entrance:
37°07'.90N 27°20'.85E

This large attractive bay is home to a fair-sized resort village with harbour, and is also a popular centre for watersports activities.

NAVIGATION

Charts: Turkish Hydrographic Charts: 224, 2247, 2248; Turkish Hydrographic Leisure Folio 2004: 2004_1, 2004_4, 2004_12; Imray Charts: G3, G32; Admiralty 1095, 1099, SC 5773

Gündoğan beach

Gündoğan Bükü bay lies between Yalıkavak and Türkbükü on the northern side of the Bodrum peninsula. The entrance to the bay is immediately south-west of the two islands of Küçüktavşan Ada and Fener Adası (see information on Türkbükü on page 75) and is free of hazards, although you may need to make your way through a number of windsurfers, dinghy sailors and catamaran sailors enjoying the afternoon breezes as you approach the village at the southern end of the bay.

BERTHING AND ANCHORING

The best shelter is offered by the small village harbour at the eastern end of the long beach that runs along the southern end of the bay. The southern side of the harbour nearest the beach is shallow and usable only by local fishing boats and other small vessels. On the northern wall there is usually space for a few visiting boats to tie up, but it is best to berth bows-to in order to avoid rubble at the base of the quay. There may also be space to berth stern-to against the western wall of the harbour where the water is a bit deeper. In all cases you will need to use your anchor as there are no lazylines installed here.

Towards the western end of the beach is a private restaurant jetty that belongs to Boncuk Yacht Club restaurant. This T-shaped wooden jetty has space for several boats to berth stern-to with lazylines. The jetty is located just next to a mosque, so look for the minaret as you approach the beach.

It is possible to free swing at anchor off the beach, but you will need to stay a fair way out to avoid buoyed swimming areas and to anchor in 10-15m of water. You can usually expect strong breezes in the afternoons here, so it is better to head into the harbour if you are planning to stay for longer than a brief lunchtime stop.

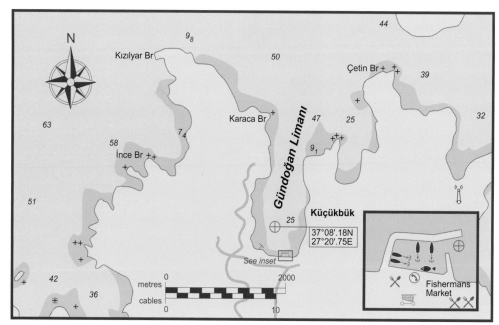

Useful information – Gündoğan

FACILITIES

Water and electricity: Available in the village harbour but not at the Boncuk Yacht Club jetty.

Showers: Some of the restaurants around the village harbour offer shower facilities and there are also some at Boncuk Yacht Club.

Ice: Is stocked at several supermarkets and mini-markets in the village.

Laundry: Can be arranged in the village.

Gas: A Milangaz shop is situated near to the harbour.

Rubbish: Rubbish bins are located in the village and close to the village harbour.

Telephone: Public phones ashore. Phone cards available from mini-markets along the beach. Mobile reception here is good.

Internet: There is an internet café located close to the village harbour and another along the beach near the mosque. Several of the restaurants offer free WiFi service.

PROVISIONING AND SERVICES

Grocery shops: A choice of small mini-markets selling basic provisions line the beach. A medium-sized Migros supermarket is situated just behind the village harbour.

Bakery: You will find a selection of bakeries and butchers in the village.

Banks: There is a cluster of ATM machines in the car park behind the village harbour and several bank branches in the main centre, a short distance back from the beach.

Pharmacy: A few in the village centre.

Post office: The PTT office is located in the main village centre, a couple of streets back from the harbour.

EATING OUT

There is a large choice of restaurants in Gündoğan, most of which are located along the long beach that stretches across the southern end of the bay. The Boncuk Yacht Club and beach restaurant, Tel: 0252 387 86 23, website: www.boncukbeach. com, is mentioned above and specialises in grilled sea food and meat with a good *meze* selection, served at tables along its wooden jetty.

Close to the harbour are a number of other beachfront restaurants, including the Yelken restaurant, Tel: 0252 387 91 34, Valentino café, Tel: 0252 387 80 95, and Terzi Mustafa'nın Yer restaurants, Tel: 0252 387 70 89.

ASHORE

The hillsides surrounding Gündoğan Büku are filled with holiday villas and developments, and the area is becoming increasingly

Gündoğan mosque

popular with foreigners wishing to own property here. Facilities in the village are developing fast to keep up with this new demand, but even so it manages to retain much of its charm as a destination. The long beach is backed with hotels, restaurants and a few small shops, whereas the main centre of the village is located a short distance back from the beach, not far from the harbour at the eastern end.

The consistent afternoon breezes have meant that Gündoğan has become known as a popular destination for windsurfers and dinghy sailors and there are a few places where you can hire equipment to use by yourself. Gravity Water Sports, Tel: 0252 387 73 22, website: www.gravity. com.tr, has windsurfing kit, sailing dinghies, catamarans and canoes available for hire at the Sail Loft Café and Bar.

TRANSPORT

Car hire: There are several rental firms in the village, including Merkez rent-a-car, Mob: 0533 747 53 28, website: www. merkezrentacar.com, which has an office near the dolmuş station.

Taxis: A taxi rank is located near the harbour, with another one based near the dolmuş station.

Dolmuş: The dolmuş station is situated at the western end of the beach and has regular services to Bodrum town.

Air travel: Bodrum-Milas airport is approximately 40 minutes form Gündoğan.

USEFUL INFORMATION

Local tel code: Muğla area, 0252, Gündoğan 387.

Gündoğan harbour

Yalıkavak Limanı

Between islands to the south-west of the bay:
37°05'.30N 27°13'.41E
Entrance to bay: 37°06'.26N 27°15'.71E
North of marina entrance: 37°06'.43N 27°17'.00E
Harbour entrance: 37°06'.52N 27°17'.54E

In recent years this attractive fishing village has developed into a thriving town and is now a popular place for visitors to purchase second homes in the Bodrum area. The relatively low-scale level of development compared with other parts of the Bodrum peninsula has meant that Yalıkavak has retained much of its charm and is well worth visiting. It is also the home of a modern marina and commercial complex that have done well to bring investment, facilities and yachts to the area without spoiling the atmosphere and environment of the village.

NAVIGATION

Charts: Turkish Hydrographic Charts: 224, 2248; Turkish Hydrographic Leisure Folio 2004: 2004_1, 2004_4, 2004_13; Imray Charts: G3, G32, G35; Admiralty 1095, 1099, SC 5773

The large bay of Yalıkavak Limanı lies to the south of the prominent headlands of İnce Burun and Küçük Burun, both approximately 4M to the west of Gündoğan Bükü. Vessels approaching from this direction should take care to avoid the hazard known as Gemitaşı, or Wreck Rock, which is just less than 1M to the north of these headlands. This rock breaks the surface by several metres and is easy to spot if you are looking out for it, making it a good landmark if passing this way in either direction.

The small islet of Çatal Adası is situated just to the south of Gemitaşı, and it is possible for most vessels to pass between the two despite the 5m shoal area that exists half way between them. Another islet called Karga Adası lies approximately 1.5M to the west of here, close to the İnce Burun headland. The waters are shallow and rocky in this area, so stand well off as you round this headland and continue south towards Yalıkavak.

Vessels approaching from the south will be able to identify the two islands of Büyükkiremit Ada and Küçükkiremit Ada, which are situated to the south-east of the entrance to Yalıkavak Limanı. It is possible to pass between these two islands, but do not attempt to go between Küçükkiremit Ada and the mainland as this area is very rocky and dangerous. A shoal area exists just to the north of these two islands, but at depths of 8m it is not dangerous for most vessels. There is a light on Büyükkiremit Ada (Fl (2) 10s).

Once you have entered the bay you will be able to see the village and harbour of Yalıkavak at the far eastern end, with the Port Bodrum Marina complex immediately west of this. Other hotels and holiday developments will be seen around the edges of the

Yalıkavak Limanı

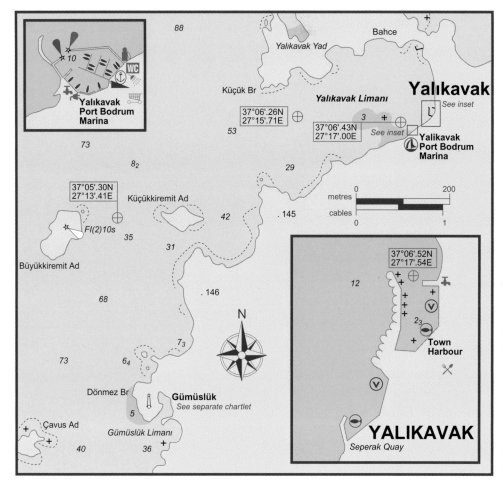

BERTHING AND ANCHORING

Yalıkavak Port Bodrum Marina has in-water berths for 450 vessels up to 65m, as well as hard standing area for 100 vessels and all the associated facilities you would expect of a modern marina complex. Advance reservations may be required in high season or for longer stays, but usually you can call the office on VHF Ch 72 on arrival and they will assign you a berth and send a pilot boat to guide you in and assist with mooring up. Berthing is stern-to or bows-to with lazylines.

The marina can also be contacted on Tel: 0252 385 38 60/311 06 00, Fax: 0252 385 32 81, email: marina@ portbodrum.com, website: www.portbodrum.com

The fishing harbour is just beyond the marina and may have space for one or two smaller yachts, although these days most visitors head straight for the marina. The harbour is rather shallow, particularly along the southern and western walls, but you may be able to fit in bows-to along the eastern side. You will need to use an anchor here.

Another option is to moor stern-to along the concrete

bay on all sides. The prevailing winds tend to curve around the headland and blow in a westerly direction right into the bay, becoming quite strong most afternoons. This has made the area popular with windsurfers and other watersports enthusiasts, but less easy for visiting yachts that are attempting to moor up, even though shelter in both the harbour and marina is good once you have negotiated the entrance and mooring procedure.

There is a shallow reef extending from the southern side of the bay between the marina and the harbour. This reef is poorly marked with only a metal stick for much of the time and can be difficult to spot in choppy afternoon conditions. To be safe it is best to enter the bay along the northern side and then head directly towards either the harbour or marina when you are ready to begin your manoeuvres for berthing.

Port Bodrum Marina in Yalıkavak

Yalıkavak village harbour

quay immediately to the west of the town harbour. You will also see a concrete T-shaped jetty here, which has sufficient depths to take vessels of an average draught. There are no lazylines in either of these places and you may be asked for an overnight berthing fee. Neither of these two locations offers particularly good shelter from the prevailing northerly winds, but they are fine during calm weather and the occasional southerly spell at the beginning and end of the summer.

There are a couple of bays along the northern side of Yalıkavak Limanı that offer good shelter from the prevailing winds and can be used as overnight anchorages. In both locations it is wise to take a line ashore for security, and the bays are fringed with holiday homes and development, so you will not be escaping from civilisation here.

Useful information – Yalıkavak Limanı

FACILITIES
Water: Can be obtained in the harbour and at every berth in Port Bodrum Marina.
Electricity: Available at all berths within the marina, but not in the harbour.
Fuel: From the fuel quay in Port Bodrum Marina.
Showers: Shower facilities can be found in Port Bodrum Marina and at Ali Baba's hotel near the harbour.
Ice: Sold at mini-markets in the village and near the marina.
Laundry: Available at Port Bodrum Marina and also at Yalıkavak Laundry, Tel: 0252 385 54 56.
Gas: Bottles can be exchanged at Port Bodrum Marina and also at one of the mini-markets close to the harbour.
Rubbish: Rubbish bins are situated near the harbour and within the marina, where segregated recycling disposal and waste oil disposal are also available.
Telephone: Several public phone boxes near the harbour and marina. Phone cards are sold at the mini-markets. Mobile reception here is good.
Internet: The Yalıkavak Internet Café is close to the harbour. Many of the restaurants here offer a WiFi service to customers, and WiFi connection is also available to guests in Port Bodrum Marina.

YACHT SERVICES AND CHANDLERY
Port Bodrum Marina has a 100 ton travel lift and hard standing space for up to 100 yachts. The following technical operations businesses have premises within the marina yard and between them can deal with most requirements, including painting and fibreglass repairs, metal work and carpentry, electrical, electronics, riggings, sail-making and upholstery:
Sound Yachts Technical Services Tel: 0252 385 37 27, Mob: 0532 407 11 17, website: www. soundyachts.net
Yalıkavak Yat Marin Technical Services Tel: 0252 311 06 14, Mob: 0542 749 16 06.
Tuncar Marine Mechanical Services Tel: 0252 385 33 79, Mob: 0532 312 37 88, website: www.tuncarmarine. com.tr
DC Electronics Raymarine agents Tel: 0252 385 26 25, Mob: 0535 845 28 65.
Kormaz Yat Interiors and Upholstery Tel: 0252 385 24 18, Mob: 0532 276 71 58, website: www. kormazyat.com
Ant Yat Market Chandlery Shop Tel: 0252 385 53 50.

PROVISIONING AND SERVICES
Grocery shops: Several mini-markets selling basic provisions are situated close to the harbour and you will find a small Migros supermarket in the marina. There are also a few large supermarkets on the outskirts of the village, including Tansaş, Migros, Bim and Dia, but you will need to take a taxi to get to these.
Bakery: You will find a bakery in the village near the harbour and

Useful information – Yalıkavak Limanı (continued)

there is also the Tartin patisserie in the marina.
Butcher: In the village near the harbour.
Local market: Is held on Thursdays.
Banks: There are several ATM machines in the village and also branches of HSBC and İş Bank.
Pharmacy: A few are located in the village.
Post office: The PTT office is near the mosque, which is behind the harbour area.

EATING OUT

There is a varied choice of restaurants in Yalıkavak, wherever you are staying on your boat. Port Bodrum Marina has a good selection within its two commercial centres, including the Yacht Club bar and restaurant with pool area, Tel: 0252 385 23 71, Mozart café restaurant, Tel: 0252 385 43 28, and the Bistro Marine restaurant, Tel: 0252 385 42 96. Around the harbour area, choices range from cheap *pide* and kebab restaurants to the popular Windmill restaurant, Tel: 0252 385 20 35, or the Cumbalı fish restaurant, Tel: 0252 385 49 96.

ASHORE

Yalıkavak has a very pleasant commercial centre in the area around the harbour, with shaded pedestrian streets and a variety of shops selling clothing, gifts, souvenirs and work by local artists. The weekly market is also a good place to buy all kinds of gifts

Yalıkavak bazaar streets

and souvenirs as well as local produce.

Port Bodrum Marina has two commercial centres with a variety of shops, including interior design, clothing, jewellers and hairdressers. There is also a modern amphitheatre that is sometimes used as an outdoor cinema or for special performances.

TRANSPORT

Car hire: Merkez Rent-a-Car, Tel: 0252 385 21 43, website: www.merkezrentacar.com
Taxis: Taxis are readily available around the village and can be ordered at the marina office.
Dolmuş: There are regular dolmuş services to Bodrum town from Yalıkavak.

A tourist helps out the local tailor

Air travel: The nearest airport is Bodrum-Milas airport, approximately 45 minutes by road.

USEFUL INFORMATION

Local tel code: Muğla area, 0252, Yalıkavak 385.
Doctor: A medical clinic is

based at the marina – ask in the marina office for details. There are also two general clinics in the area that offer **dentistry** and other services: Yalıkavak Poliklinik Tel: 0252 385 53 19; Olimpos Polklinik Tel: 0252 385 51 87.
Local information website: www.yalikavak.bel.tr

Büyükkiremit Ada

Anchorage: 37°05'.02N 27°12'.77E

NAVIGATION

Charts: Turkish Hydrographic Charts: 224, 2248; Turkish Hydrographic Leisure Folio 2004: 2004_1, 2004_4, 2004_14; Imray Charts: G3, G32, G35; Admiralty 1055, 1095, 1099, SC 5773

This island lies to the south-west of Yalıkavak Limanı and just under 1M to the west of the smaller Küçükkiremit Ada. An 8m shoal area known as Kunduz Kayası is situated between these islands, slightly to the north. Büyükkiremit Ada is lit at night (Fl (2) 10s).

A small anchorage exists about half way along the eastern side of the island. This bay offers reasonable shelter from the prevailing winds and can be used overnight in settled weather, although you should take a line ashore for extra security.

Gümüşlük

Gümüşlük Limanı

Between sunken mole and Rabbit Island:
37°03'.16N 27°13'.94E

To the south of the entrance: 37°03'.10N 27°13'.88E

Anchorage in north of bay: 37°03'.43N 27°13'.96E

The beautiful natural harbour of Gümüşlük was the location of the ancient settlement of Mindos, and today remains a peaceful hamlet offering a chance to escape the bustle of the Bodrum peninsula and enjoy some of the best seafood restaurants in the area.

NAVIGATION

Charts: Turkish Hydrographic Charts: 224, 2248; Turkish Hydrographic Leisure Folio 2004: 2004_1, 2004_4, 2004_14; Turkish Hydrographic Leisure Folio 3001: 3001_1, 3001_2; Imray Charts: G3, G32, G35; Admiralty 1055, 1095, 1099, SC 5773

Gümüşlük Limanı is on the west coast of the Bodrum peninsula, approximately 3M north of the town of Turgutreis. There are a few islands off the coastline near here that can be seen from a distance and help to identify the bay as you approach. The closest of these islands is Çavuş Adası, which is approximately 1M to the west of Gümüşlük. The smaller islands of Kardak Adaları are approximately 2.5M further west of here,

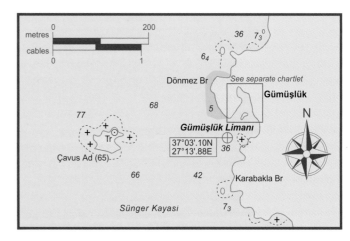

and the Greek island of Kalolimnos is another 3M to the west of these.

Gümüşlük Limanı is protected to the west by the headland of Dönmez Burun and by Tavşan Ada (Rabbit Island) to the south. This means that it is difficult to see the anchorage and small hamlet within until you are actually inside the bay. A military establishment on top of Dönmez Burun usually has a large Turkish flag flying that helps to identify the bay. A group of white villas can also be spotted to the north of the anchorage. Vessels approaching from the south should stay well clear of the shallow waters extending from Karabakla Burnu, approximately 1M south of the entrance to Gümüşlük Limanı.

You should enter the bay under power, as the winds

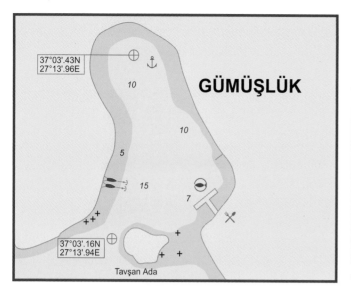

Gümüşlük fishing jetty

in this area can be confused and gusty. Pass just to the west of Tavşan Ada to stay clear of the rocky waters to the east of the island, but be careful to avoid the submerged breakwater extending from Dönmez Burun on the western side of the channel. This breakwater is visible just below the surface of the water as you pass.

ANCHORING

There are no mooring facilities within the bay, but several possibilities exist for those wishing to anchor. Most vessels head up to the northern end of the bay,

where you can either free swing at anchor or take a line ashore around the edge of the bay. Depths in this area are 5-10m.

It is also possible to anchor with a line ashore to Dönmez Burun on the western side of the bay. The Bati restaurant in the middle of the waterfront close to the village mosque maintains a few mooring buoys that can be used by visiting yachts. The restaurant staff will assist you in taking a line ashore here.

The small concrete T-jetty in the centre of the village is in shallow water and can only be used by fishing boats or small tenders.

Rabbit Island and the causeway leading out to it

Useful information – Gümüşlük Limanı

FACILITIES
Ice: May be bought at some of the small markets ashore or in one of the restaurants.
Laundry: A service is provided in the village centre above the anchorage.
Gas: Available in the village centre above the anchorage.
Rubbish: Rubbish bins in the belediye car park.
Telephone: Public phone boxes in the car park above the harbour. Good mobile phone reception.
Internet: There is a small internet café in the commercial area next to the beach and several of the restaurants, including Bati restaurant and Gümüşcafe, offer WiFi access.

PROVISIONING AND SERVICES
Grocery shops: A few mini-markets and green grocer stalls can be found amongst the beach restaurants and in the small commercial centre near Tavşan Ada.

Bakery: Bread is available from the small markets mentioned above.
Local market: Is held on Wednesdays.
Banks: There are a few ATM machines near the belediye car park, but no bank branches in the village.
Post office: A small PTT office and a pharmacy are situated in the village centre above the anchorage.

EATING OUT
Gümüşlük is the place to go if you enjoy fresh fish and seafood dishes as almost every restaurant in the village specialises in this cuisine. Most of the restaurants are located right on the seafront and display examples of the fish available in chilled cabinets so that you can choose before you sit down. It is worth taking a stroll along the beachfront before making a choice. As usual you will be paying

for seafood by the kilo, so do check the price of your meal before confirming your order to avoid any surprises at the end.
The Bati restaurant, Tel: 0252 394 30 79, Mob: 0533 563 08 42, has a raised stone terrace overlooking the harbour and has a reasonably priced menu with a combination of meat and seafood dishes. After your meal you can enjoy a glass of Turkish tea or a liqueur whilst relaxing on cushions in the 'chill-out' area.
A little further along the beach is the Gümüş café restaurant, which provides an excellent spot to enjoy a drink in the afternoon and also has a good selection of dishes available in the evenings.
The Mimoza restaurant, Tel: 0252 394 31 39, website: www.mimoza-bodrum.com, is located near the fishing jetty and is very popular amongst visiting Turks.

Gourds

ASHORE
The Carian settlement of Mindos was destroyed by a large earthquake and slid into the sea. Visitors to Gümüşlük today can snorkel over the remains in the water between the village and Tavşan Ada. This island is also known as Rabbit Island because of its population of rabbits that often come out at dusk. It is possible to wade across the partially sunken causeway that connects the island to the mainland.
The village itself is full of attractive houses and is protected from further development by order of the local authorities. A pleasant beach to the south of Rabbit Island is popular with sunbathers.

TRANSPORT
Taxis: A taxi rank is situated near the belediye car park.
Dolmuş: A dolmuş service connects the village to Bodrum town and departs from the belediye car park.

USEFUL INFORMATION
Local tel code: Muğla area, 0252, Gümüşlük 394.
Local information website: www.gumusluk.info

Gümüşlük artisans' market

Çavuş Adası
Anchorage: 37°02'.94N 27°12'.28E

NAVIGATION
Charts: Turkish Hydrographic Charts: 224, 2248; Turkish Hydrographic Leisure Folio 2004: 2004_1, 2004_4, 2004_14; Turkish Hydrographic Leisure Folio 3001:

3001_1, 3001_2; Imray Charts: G3, G32, G35; Admiralty 1055, 1095, 1099, SC 5773

This small island lies directly to the west of the entrance to Gümüşlük Limanı and has a little bight on the eastern side that can be used as a daytime anchorage in light conditions. Approach the anchorage from the south to avoid a shallow reef extending from the northern side.

Turgutreis
(Karatoprak)

South-west of marina entrance in over 10m of water:
36°59'.77N 27°15'.22E
Harbour entrance: 37°00'.32N 27°15'.36E

Turgutreis D-Marin marina entrance

The busy resort town of Turgutreis lies on the western side of the Bodrum peninsula and is the location of a large modern marina. It is the second largest town in the area, has daily ferry connections to the Greek island of Kos during the summer, and is an official port of entry to Turkey.

The town was originally known as Karatoprak, but was renamed in 1972 in honour of a 16th century naval hero, Admiral Turgut Reis, who was born in the town in 1485.

NAVIGATION

Charts: Turkish Hydrographic Charts: 224, 311, 3110; Turkish Hydrographic Leisure Folio 2004: 2004_1; Turkish Hydrographic Leisure Folio 3001: 3001_1, 3001_2; Imray Charts: G3, G35; Admiralty 1055, 1095, 1099, SC 5773

Vessels berthed in Turgutreis D-Marin marina

Several islands lie off the coast immediately west of Turgutreis and can be identified by approaching vessels. Beware of the isolated danger mark off the low-lying islet of Yassı Ada, to the south-west of the larger Çatalada. There are lights on both Topan Ada (Fl 5s) and Çatalada (Fl (4) 20s). The entrance to the marina is also lit.

Vessels approaching from the north have no dangers to avoid but should stand off slightly from the coastline as there are shallows extending immediately to the north of the town.

Vessels approaching from the south will have to round the headland of Hüseyin Burnu. The lighthouse on this point is conspicuous to passing yachts (Fl (2) 15s). Yachts should stand well off the coast as they round this point to avoid the dangerous reef known as Paşa Kayalığı, which is shown with an isolated danger mark. Another shallow reef named Bekçi Kayası lies approximately 0.5M to the south-east of here and is unmarked.

The marina is situated at the southern end of the town's stretch of beach. You will see the minarets of the town's largest mosque immediately north of the

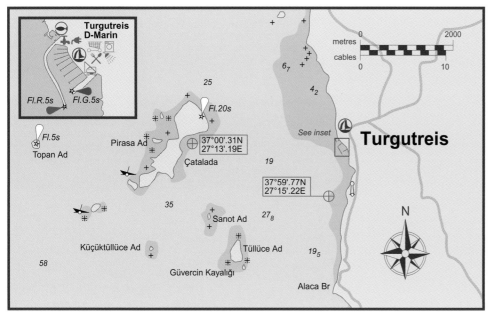

Turgutreis fishing harbour

marina and there is a walled park area to the south. A small fishing harbour can be found on the northern side of the marina.

BERTHING AND ANCHORING

Turgutreis D-Marin marina has stern-to berthing and finger pontoons for vessels up to 30m in length. It also has a 100 ton travel lift, large hard standing area and a host of technical services available for all kinds of vessels. You should call the marina office on VHF Ch 73 to request berthing instructions. The marina can also be contacted on Tel: 0252 392 92 00, Fax: 0252 382 62 00, email: info@dogusmarina.com.tr, website: www.turgutreismarina.com

The fishing harbour to the north of the marina is shallow and does not have space for visiting yachts.

FORMALITIES

All formalities can be completed in the customs area at the ferry port next to the marina.

Useful information – Turgutreis

FACILITIES

Water and electricity: Available at all berths in the marina.
Fuel: The marina has a fuel jetty next to the entrance at the southern end.
Showers: In the marina.
Ice: Can be bought at supermarkets close to the marina.
Laundry: Express Laundry at the marina, Tel: 0252 382 54 34.
Gas: Gas bottles can be exchanged in the marina.
Rubbish: Rubbish bins and segregated recycling bins are located near the marina pontoons. Disposal facilities for waste products and oil can be found in the marina boatyard.

Turgutreis D-Marin marina fuel dock

Telephone: Public phone boxes are situated around the marina shopping area and in the town. Phone cards are available from newsagents and mini-markets, and mobile phone reception in the area is good.
Internet: There are several internet cafés in the town and WiFi is available in the marina.

YACHT SERVICES AND CHANDLERY

Turgutreis D-Marin marina has a 100 ton travel lift and large hard standing area. The following companies are based in the marina and offer a wide range of services between them for all kinds of vessel:

Yacht Works Technical Services Tel: 0252 382 44 45, website: www. yachtworks.info
Tuncar Marine Mechanical Services Tel: 0252 382 29 33, website: www. tuncarmarine.com.tr
Starboat Building & Maintenance Tel: 0252 382 44 05, website: www. starboat.com.tr
Selmar Yachting Technical Services Tel: 0252 382 22 33, website: www. selmaryacht.com
Pupa Yachting Technical Services Tel: 0252 382 25 11, website: www.pupa. com.tr
Anker Marina Technical Services Tel: 0252 382 86 04, website: www. ankermarina.com
Alabora Yacht Technical Services Tel: 0252 382 75 86.
Denizci Boya Paint Specialists Tel: 0252 382 56 49.

PROVISIONING AND SERVICES

Grocery shops: You will find several large supermarkets in the Turgutreis, including MarinMar in the marina, BIM near the main mosque, and Tansaş and Migros supermarkets along the town's main street.
Bakery: There are several

bakeries and butchers in the town.
Local market: Held every Saturday in the area just north of the town's main shopping centre.
Banks: You will find several ATM machines within the marina shopping centre and more around the main mosque. There are also a number of bank branches within the town and a large exchange office near the mosque.
Pharmacy: Several in the town.
Post office: The PTT office is in the centre of town.

EATING OUT

There are quite a few restaurants within the marina shopping area, and even more within the town and along the waterfront. Most of the marina restaurants are classy affairs specialising in seafood and Mediterranean cuisine, such as the Emporio Armani Caffe, Tel: 0252 382 38 45, the Etoile de Mer seafood restaurant, Tel: 0252 382 92 20, and the Turgutreis Marina Yacht Club restaurant.

The town boasts a range of cafés, *pide* salons, kebab shops and fast food restaurants, particularly

Useful information – Turgutreis (continued)

Plenty to buy at this shop in Turgutreis bazaar area

along the street between the marina and the town and around the mosque area. Other restaurants, mainly aimed at the tourist trade, can be found along the seafront and within the bazaar area. The food here is predominantly Turkish/international, with nothing in particular to recommend most of these restaurants.

ASHORE

Turgutreis is a lively destination and always has plenty going on. The bazaar area includes all the usual types of shops; clothing, ceramics, spices and other souvenirs. There are also a number of lively bars and discos for those who enjoy going out in the evenings. During the summer months the outdoor cinema next to the marina shows blockbuster movies in the evenings.

The marina itself has a busy calendar of events during the year, as diverse as the annual International Bodrum Yacht Show, classical music festivals and offshore power boat races. Check with the marina office for upcoming events.

If you like scuba diving there are a few diving schools in the area which can provide instruction and a variety of diving trips, such as Aquanaut Diving, Mob: 0538 555 77 62, website: www.aquanautdiving.com

A short distance to the south of the marina is the attractive Sevket Sabancı Park, which is open to the public. You can explore the landscaped gardens that look out over the sea and will also find a statue of the town's namesake, Admiral Turgut Reis (*reis* means 'captain' in Turkish).

TRANSPORT

Car hire: There is a choice of car hire companies directly opposite the entrance to the marina car park, including Fulya Rent-a-Car, Tel: 0252 382 92 16, website: www.fulyarentacar.com), and Avis, Tel: 0252 382 38 51, website: www.avis.co.uk

Taxis: Several taxi ranks are situated close to the marina and within the town.

Coach: The otogar is located on the main road that leads out of town towards the Bodrum area. A number of companies have offices here, with daily departures to İstanbul, Ankara, İzmir and other large towns.

Dolmuş: The separate dolmuş station lies behind the Migros supermarket on the side of the road opposite to the main otogar. There is a regular service to Bodrum town.

Ferry: The ferry port is south of the marina and has daily departures to Kos during the summer. You can buy tickets from the Bodrum Ferryboat Association office which is on the other side of the road from the port, Tel: 0252 382 94 41, website: www.bodrumferryboat.com

Air travel: The nearest airport is Bodrum-Milas, approximately 50 minutes by taxi.

USEFUL INFORMATION

Local tel code: Muğla area, 0252, Turgutreis 382.
Turgutreis Bodrum Yacht Club: www.tbyc.org.tr
Harbour master: Tel: 0252 316 10 98.
Passport Police: Tel: 0252 316 12 15.
Customs Patrol: Tel: 0252 316 10 79.
Port Health Authorities: Tel: 0252 316 10 84.
Doctor: Tel: 0252 313 14 20.
Local information website: www.turgutreis.info

Day-trippers and gulets vying for your attention

Çatalada

Anchorage: 37°00'.31N 27°13'.19E

NAVIGATION

Charts: Turkish Hydrographic Charts: 224; Turkish Hydrographic Leisure Folio 2004: 2004_1; Turkish Hydrographic Leisure Folio 3001: 3001_1, 3001_2; Imray Charts: G3, G35; Admiralty 1055, 1095, 1099, SC 5773

This is the largest of the islands that lie immediately west of Turgutreis and has a light structure on the northern side (Fl 20s). It is possible to anchor in a bay half way along the eastern side of the island. There are hills to the north and south, and the winds can sweep across the shoulder of land connecting them directly into this bay. So the shelter is not ideal and the bay should only be used for daytime stops in fairly calm conditions.

Akyarlar Koyu
(Bitez)

Kargı Adası light: 36°57'.01N 27°18'.31E
Middle of bay: 36°57'.78N 27°17'.43E

NAVIGATION

Charts: Turkish Hydrographic Charts: 224, 311, 3110;
Turkish Hydrographic Leisure Folio 2004: 2004_1;
Turkish Hydrographic Leisure Folio 3001: 3001_1,
3001_2; Imray Charts: G3, G35; Admiralty 1055, 1095,
1099, SC 5773

Akyarlar is a mid-sized bay on the south-west tip of
the Bodrum peninsula and is home to a fast developing
resort and a small harbour.

Vessels approaching from the north-west will round
the Hüseyin Burnu headland and should take care to
avoid the Paşa Kayalığı and Bekçi Kayası shoals as
described on page 87. An underwater sewage pipe
is marked by a series of buoys extending from the
headland west of the bay.

Vessels approaching from the east should be able to
identify the small island of Kargı Adası lying off the
Kocaburun headland as they approach. It is possible
to pass either to the north or the south of this island,
which is lit at night (Fl 5s). If passing to the south then
stand off slightly to avoid shallows extending from the
southern side of the island. If passing to the north then
stay close to the island to avoid the shallows extending
from Kocaburun.

The shoreline of the bay is becoming heavily
developed, in particular with a large hotel complex
on the eastern side of the bay. There is shallow water
extending from the shore opposite this hotel, currently
indicated with a small Turkish flag.

The village and harbour are in the north-east corner of
the bay. Although the harbour is mainly occupied with
local fishing boats, there is sometimes space for a small
yacht to anchor bows-to amongst these. Otherwise
there is plenty of room to free swing at anchor in 5-
10m of water just outside the harbour. The holding
is reasonably good, but you should ensure that your
anchor is well dug in as there can be strong gusts from
the hillsides behind the harbour.

There are several small restaurants ashore, along with
a couple of mini-markets and souvenir shops. A dolmuş
service to Bodrum operates a number of times a day
and taxis are also available near the harbour.

Kargı Adası

The harbour at Akyarlar Koyu

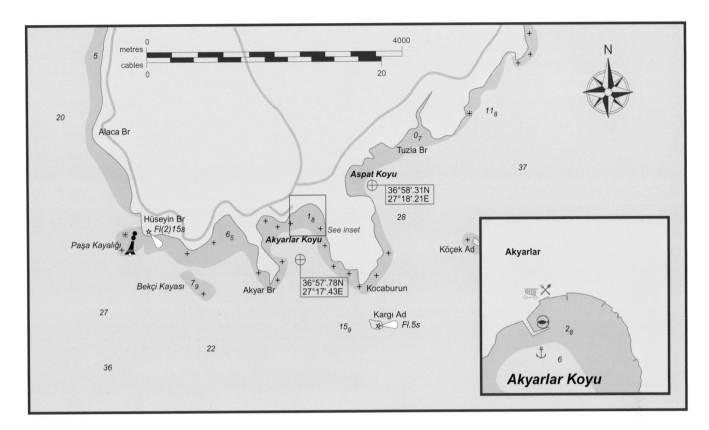

Aspat Koyu
(Karaincir Koyu)
Middle of bay: 36°58'.31N 27°18'.21E
Köçek Adası: 36°57'.77N 27°19'.35E

NAVIGATION
Charts: Turkish Hydrographic Charts: 224, 311, 3110;
Turkish Hydrographic Leisure Folio 2004: 2004_1;
Turkish Hydrographic Leisure Folio 3001: 3001_1,
3001_2; Imray Charts: G3, G35; Admiralty 1055, 1095,
1099, SC 5773

Aspat is a small hamlet with a pleasant beach and
a few restaurants and pansiyons ashore. The bay is
immediately to the east of the Kocaburun headland
and there is a conspicuous conical hill to the east of
the bay. Take care of the Köçek Adacık rock that lies
approximately ¾M to the east of the bay and breaks
the surface.

Although there are a couple of wooden jetties in
the bay, the water is too shallow for these to be used
by yachts. Instead there is plenty of room to free
swing at anchor in around 5m of water anywhere
off the beach.

Two small mini-markets are situated close to the
beach, with several restaurants ashore. At least one
of these, the Kardeşler restaurant, Tel: 0252 393 60 34,
Mob: 0532 226 35 33, website: www.kardeslermotel.
com, has a small boat that will collect you from your
yacht and bring you ashore to eat.

There can be strong gusts off the hillsides and this is
recommended as a lunchtime anchorage only.

Aspat Koyu

Kargı Koyu

Middle of anchorage: 37°00'.57N 27°20'.18E

Anchorage to east of Çelibi Adası:
37°00'.56N 27°21'.75E

NAVIGATION

Charts: Turkish Hydrographic Charts: 224, 311, 3110; Turkish Hydrographic Leisure Folio 2004: 2004_1; Turkish Hydrographic Leisure Folio 3001: 3001_1, 3001_2; Imray Charts: G3, G35; Admiralty 1055, 1095, 1099, SC 5773

This large bay lies to the west of Ağaçlı Koyu and the resort of Bitez, and is sheltered to the south by the Bağlar Burun headland. A long sandy beach runs along the northern shore, with several small villages and resorts such as Ortakent and Yahşi beach.

Although there are no harbours as such, it is possible to anchor off the beach in several places and enjoy the surroundings for a few hours before heading somewhere more sheltered for overnight. There is a selection of windsurfing and sailing centres in this area, so you can expect winds to build up quite reliably during the afternoons.

Çelebi Ada island is conspicuous in the middle of the bay, and you will often see gulets moored in the small coves on the more sheltered side of the island. These anchorages are recommended for lunchtime stops only.

Çelebi Ada

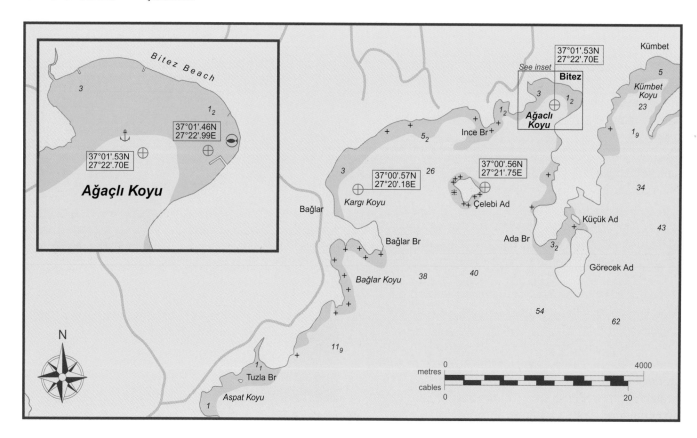

The harbour to the east of Bitez village, with the island of Çelebi Ada visible behind it

Ağaçlı Koyu
Anchorage in the bay: 37°01'.53N 27°22'.70E
Just off the harbour: 37°01'.46N 27°22'.99E

Ağaçlı Koyu lies between Kargı Koyu and Kümbet Limanı and is the location of the pleasant resort town of Bitez. Consistent cross-shore winds make this a popular spot for sailing and windsurfing, and there are several watersports centres along the beach.

NAVIGATION
Charts: Turkish Hydrographic Charts: 224, 311, 3110; Turkish Hydrographic Leisure Folio 2004: 2004_1; Turkish Hydrographic Leisure Folio 3001: 3001_1, 3001_2, 3001_6; Imray Charts: G3, G35; Admiralty 1055, 1095, 1099, SC 5773

Vessels can pass to either side of Çelebi Ada island as they approach the Bitez beach at the head of the bay. For details of anchorages around this island see page 92.

Bitez has a long beach backed with restaurants, bars and hotels. The watersports centres are mainly at the western end of the beach and you may need to watch out for other sailors if approaching during the windy afternoons.

BERTHING AND ANCHORING
A small harbour is located at the eastern end of the beach, but because it lacks any kind of protection or breakwater it is not particularly safe. Despite this, it is usually quite full and is used by visiting yachts as well as local charter boats and gulets. There are lazylines available on both the quays pointing towards the north, although beware that the southern end is very shallow and suitable only for small fishing craft.

If you are only stopping for a short while or the weather is calm then you can anchor in 5-10m in the bay off the beach.

Bitez harbour

Useful information – Ağaçlı Koyu

Bitez harbour

FACILITIES

Water: Available in the harbour.
Ice: Is sold in the town.
Laundry: Bitez laundry service, Tel: 0252 382 82 50.
Gas: Can be obtained in the town.
Rubbish: Rubbish bins and recycling bins are located near the harbour.
Telephone: There are public phones ashore and phone cards are sold at mini-markets (see below).

Mobile phone reception here is good.
Internet: Several internet cafés can be found in the village.

PROVISIONING AND SERVICES

Grocery shops: A couple of mini-markets are located near the beach, with more in the village.
Bakery: A bakery and a butcher can be found in the village.
Local market: The local market is held on Fridays.
Banks: There are several ATM machines near the mosque by the beach.
Pharmacy: One near the mosque.
Post office: A PTT office is situated in Bitez village.

EATING OUT

The whole stretch of Bitez beach is backed with hotels and restaurants, so there is a great choice of places to eat. One of the best is the small Istanbul restaurant near the mosque. This serves fantastic ottoman cuisine, such as aphrodisiac chicken, and is definitely a cut above the usual tourist fare. Other options include fairly decent Chinese and Indian restaurants, as well as the usual Turkish-International menus. You can also try the popular Lavaş ocak başı grill restaurant that is on the main road behind the beach.

ASHORE

Bitez village centre is a short distance behind the beach strip of bars, restaurants and hotels, and contains a selection of shops and travel agents.

The main reason for visiting Bitez is to enjoy the watersports, especially windsurfing and catamaran sailing. There are a few watersports centres at the western end of the beach and you may be able to hire equipment from some of these.

TRANSPORT

Car hire: Several car hire companies are in the village.
Taxis: There is a taxi rank near the harbour, with others in the village.
Dolmuş: A regular minibus service to Bodrum runs along the road behind the beach. The dolmuş station is right next to the harbour.
Local information website: www.bitezbeach.com

View from the harbour towards Bitez beach

Kümbet Limanı

(Gümbet)

Southern entry to
Aquarium anchorage:
36°59'.81N 27°22'.62E
Eastern entrance to
Aquarium anchorage: 37°00'.17N
27°23'.43E
Entrance to bay, west of headland:
37°01'.04N 27°23'.70E

NAVIGATION

Charts: Turkish Hydrographic
Charts: 224, 311, 3110, 3111;
Turkish Hydrographic
Leisure Folio 2004: 2004_1;
Turkish Hydrographic
Leisure Folio 3001: 3001_1,
3001_2, 3001_6; Imray Charts:
G3, G35; Admiralty 1055, 1095,
1099, SC 5773

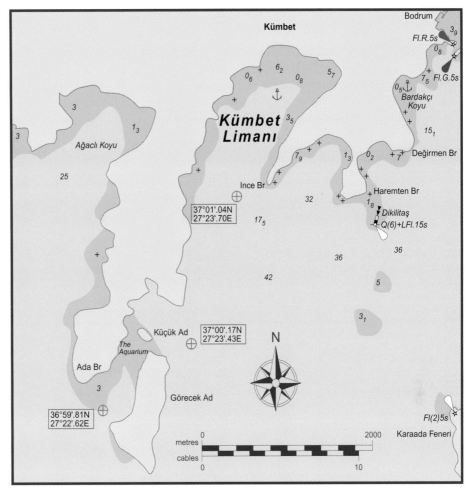

This long bay to the west of
Bodrum town has been heavily
developed as a holiday resort and
there is little to attract visiting
yachts here. However, it is possible to anchor in 5-10m
off the beach at the northern end of the bay and to find
some shelter from the prevailing winds here. Beware
of jet skis, windsurfers, pedaloes and sailing dinghies,
which may be piloted with varying degrees of skill
and awareness.

A more pleasant option is to anchor for a few hours
in the small bay formed by Görecek Ada, Küçük Ada

and the Ada Burun headland between Gümbet and
Bitez bays. This area is known locally as the Aquarium
and is popular with gulets and local day tripper boats
due to the large numbers of fish that are usually found
here. The waters are clear and ideal for snorkelling
around the rocky shoreline. If you have a dinghy you
can explore the channel between Görecek Ada and the
mainland, but this is very shallow and rocky and is not
suitable for taking any larger vessel through.

View across Gümbet Limanı

Bodrum Limanı

Dikilitaş shoal light: 37°00'.91N 27°24'.92E
Anchorage in Kale Koyu: 37°01'.86N 27°26'.10E
Just outside the harbour channel entrance:
37°01'.59N 27°25'.44E

The resort town of Bodrum is the largest in the area and is one of the major centres for yachting along this part of the coast. The modern settlement is on the site of ancient Halicarnassus and was the birth place of the Ancient Greek historian Herodotus in 484 BC. One of the most recognisable features of the town is the Castle of St Peter, which sits in the centre of the waterfront and separates the harbour area from Kale Koyu (Castle Bay) to the east.

NAVIGATION

Charts: Turkish Hydrographic Charts: 224, 311, 3110, 3111; Turkish Hydrographic Leisure Folio 2004: 2004_1; Turkish Hydrographic Leisure Folio 3001: 3001_1, 3001_2, 3001_6; Imray Charts: G3, G35; Admiralty 1055, 1095, 1099, 1644, SC 5773

The distinctive shape of Kara Ada island to the south of the town is easily identified from any direction. As you get closer to the town the sprawl of white buildings

Aerial view of Bodrum harbour, with Milta Marina on the left and the customs and ferry dock on the lower right-hand side of the picture

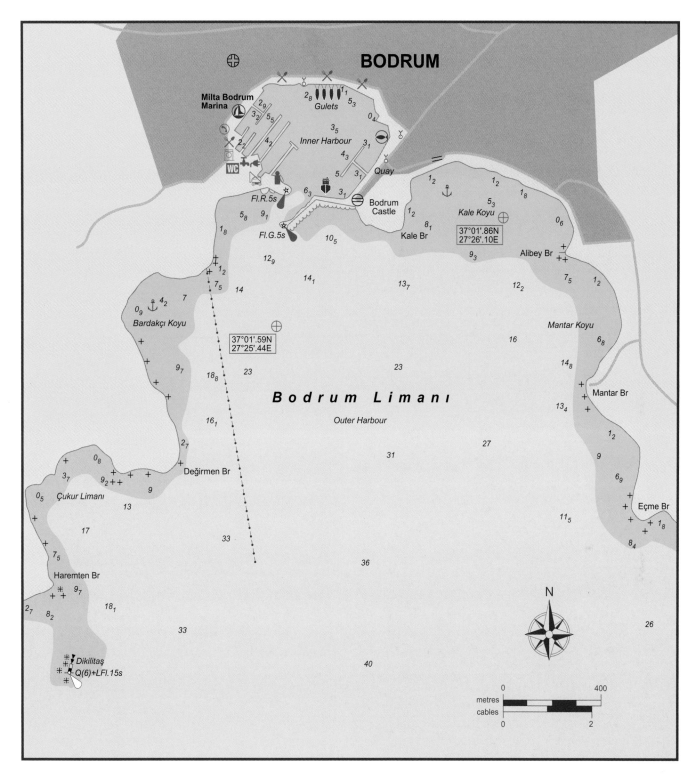

BODRUM

Milta Bodrum Marina

Gulets

Inner Harbour

Quay

Fl.R.5s

Fl.G.5s

Bodrum Castle

Kale Br

Kale Koyu

37°01'.86N 27°26'.10E

Alibey Br

37°01'.59N 27°25'.44E

Bardakçı Koyu

Mantar Koyu

B o d r u m   L i m a n ı

Outer Harbour

Mantar Br

Değirmen Br

Çukur Limanı

Eçme Br

Haremten Br

N

Dikilitaş
Q(6)+LFl.15s

0   400
metres
cables
0   2

across the hillsides can easily be seen, with the Castle of St Peter in the centre on the waterline. A long beach backed with bars and restaurants extends east of here, and the harbour is to the west of the castle.

Vessels approaching from Gümbet direction should take care to avoid the Dikilitaş Kayası reef that lies just to the south of Haremten Burnu headland, marked with a south cardinal buoy and lit at night (Q (6)+L Fl 15s). There is also a light on the northern tip of Kara Ada island (Fl (2) 5s), as well as red and green lights to either side of the harbour entrance.

The entrance to the harbour is through overlapping

Departing from Bodrum harbour

breakwaters and can be difficult to spot as you approach, although there is usually a fair amount of traffic passing through in either direction.

BERTHING AND ANCHORING

Bodrum Milta Marina occupies the western side of Bodrum's inner harbour. It has capacity for almost 500 vessels at floating berths and also has a travel lift and hard standing area. Berths are all stern-to with lazylines, and you should call the marina on VHF Ch 72/73 as you approach so they can send a pilot boat to guide you to your berth. The marina is extremely busy and advance booking is advised, particularly if you are looking for a winter berth. The marina can also be contacted on Tel: 0252 316 18 60, Fax: 0252 316 14 06, email: info@miltabodrummarina.com, website: www. miltabodrummarina.com

Most of the rest of Bodrum's harbour is occupied by fishing boats and charter gulets and is usually very full, sometimes with boats stacked two deep off the quay. At most you may be able to squeeze into a space for an hour or two to get provisions, but generally it is better to head directly to the marina.

If you prefer to anchor off then you can do so in Kale Koyu bay to the east of the castle. This bay is often full of gulets at anchor during the summer, and you will generally be able to find a space to free swing amongst them. This stretch of beach can be very noisy at night, however, as it is bordered by a long strip of restaurants, bars and night clubs that are open until early morning during the summer.

FORMALITIES

The marina reception office can assist with all entry and exit formalities for the usual agent's fee, but it is also possible to do the formalities yourself. The customs and immigration offices are at the ferry dock on the eastern

Bodrum castle, with the customs and ferry dock in the foreground

side of the harbour breakwater near the castle. The health authority and harbour master offices are close by on the town harbour quay.

Useful information – Bodrum Limanı

FACILITIES
Water and electricity: Available at all berths within the marina.
Fuel: Milta Marina fuel dock is immediately to your port side as you enter the harbour.
Showers: At Milta Marina.
Ice: Is sold at several of the mini-markets close to the marina.
Laundry: Ece Laundry and Dry Cleaning service in Milta Marina, Tel: 0252 316 24 87, Mob: 0555 512 08 25. Minik Laundry, close to the marina, Tel: 0252 316 96 80.
Gas: Can usually be

obtained at the marina.
Rubbish: There are rubbish bins in the town and at the marina. Segregated recycling bins are also available at the marina, and oil/waste disposal facilities are in the boatyard.
Telephone: Public phones can be found all through the town, including close to the marina and next to the Turk Telkom office and PTT office. Phone cards are sold in most mini-markets and newsagents, and mobile phone reception here is good.
Internet: The marina offers a WiFi connection to

visitors, as do so many of the restaurants and bars in the town. There are several internet cafés along the road from the marina into the town, with more in the centre of the town itself.

YACHT SERVICES AND CHANDLERY
Milta Marina has a 70 ton travel lift and a hard standing area close to the floating docks. Technical service operations should be arranged through the marina office, but can include painting and osmosis treatment, carpentry

and metal work, electrics and electronics, engine maintenance and service, upholstery and canvas work, outboard engine servicing and dinghy/life raft servicing.

The marina chandlery shop is Tekno Ege, Tel: 052 316 57 51.

Besides the above services, there are other businesses nearby that offer similar facilities and can oversee large projects. There are also a few more chandlery shops:
Pupa Yachting, general services, Tel: 0252 316 77 15, website: www.pupa. com.tr

Useful information – Bodrum Limanı (continued)

Milta Marina travel lift

Deniz Ticaret Odasi, chandlery, Önder Marine, electrical equipment, Tel: 0252 316 88 32.
Gino Marine, general services, Tel: 0252 316 21 66, website: www. ginogroup.com
Seagull Sails, sailmakers, Tel: 0252 316 6 11/57 26, Mob: 0532 579 35 68.

PROVISIONING AND SERVICES

Grocery shops: There is a mid-sized Carrefour supermarket in the marina shopping centre, a number of small mini-markets along the road from the marina into town and a large Tansaş supermarket behind the otogar. In nearby Konacık are several hypermarkets, including Tansaş, Migros, Dia, Carrefour and Bim.
Bakery: Several bakeries and butchers can be found in the town.
Local market: A fruit and vegetable market is held every Thursday and Friday near the dolmuş station and otogar. The market is also open on Tuesdays, but mainly sells clothing and textiles. Fishermen sell their catch every day from stalls along the harbour between the marina and the town.
Banks: Branches of several banks are situated within the town centre, including Halkbank, Finansbank, Yapı Kredi Bank and GarantıBank. All of these have 24 hour ATM machines and there are several other machines on the road between the marina and the town.
Pharmacy: There are several in the town.
Post office: The PTT office is in the centre of town on the road leading from the harbour to the otogar.

EATING OUT

There is a huge number of restaurants in Bodrum and far too many to mention here. They line the harbour all the way from the marina into the town and then out the other side along the beachfront in Kale Koyu bay, as well as being spread all through the old part of Bodrum town. The best idea is to stroll around until you spot something that takes your fancy, but here are a few suggestions to save your legs from too much walking. Starting from the marina and heading into town: The upmarket Milta Marina Yacht Club is home to the La Vela Italian Restaurant, Tel: 0252 316 12 28, which enjoys an ideal situation overlooking the marina and also offers live music several times a week during the season. The shiny new Maserati parked in the entrance to the yacht club gives an idea of the prices you are likely to encounter within.

Sünger Pizza, Tel: 0252 316 08 54, is a long established favourite with the locals and is always busy. It does fantastic pizzas for very reasonable prices and the jumbo size will feed the whole crew.

The Liman Köftecisi restaurant, Tel 0252 316 50 60, is extremely popular with locals and you may have to wait for a table at the weekend. Its specialities include all kinds of grilled meats, but in particular the köfte meatballs.

Yağhane, Tel: 025 316 27 32, is housed within an old stone olive oil factory and has a courtyard outside. The menu is Mediterranean and the atmosphere relaxed.

Caffé Piu, Tel: 0252 316 96 04, is a little further along the street and is an Italian restaurant run by real Italians. Homemade pasta dishes are their speciality, and the coffee is as good as you would expect it to be.

The Kocadon, Tel: 0252 316 37 05, website: www.kocadon.com, is an upmarket courtyard restaurant that has a fantastic atmosphere and an interesting menu offering the best in Turkish and Ottoman cuisine. A great place to celebrate the end of your holiday (or the half way point!) in style.

The daily catch

Eye-catching fruit and vegetable displays in the market

Useful information – Bodrum Limanı (continued)

The castle of St Peter in Bodrum

ASHORE

There is plenty to see and do in Bodrum, and because of the excellent network of dolmuş minibus routes you can easily visit other towns and villages on the peninsula from here. The old town itself is extremely attractive and it is enjoyable to explore the winding streets of the shopping district, which has plenty of cafés and bars where you can take a pit stop.

Nightlife is another attraction of the town, which is home to the Halikarnas night club, reputed to be the biggest (5,000 capacity) and best outdoor club in the Med. Check out its website for information on upcoming tours and residencies, www.halikarnas.com.tr. The town's bar street stretches along the beachfront to the east of the castle and caters mainly to foreign tourists. There are also some popular local bars such as the Ora bar, as well as some smaller clubs in the centre of the town.

The Castle of St Peter is the town's most prominent landmark. It was constructed in the 16th century by the Knights of St John. Fresh back from the crusades in Jerusalem, they destroyed much of Bodrum's other ancient treasure, the Mausoleum of King Mausolus, to scavenge building materials for the castle that was to serve as a place of Christian refuge. Since these times it has been used variously as a military establishment, a prison and a public bath, but is now home to the Bodrum

Museum of Underwater Archaeology. This is open to the public and exhibits include rescued glassware from a ship wrecked at Serce Limanı (page 149), the remains of which can no longer be seen today, several salvaged ancient shipwrecks, coins, jewellery and hundreds of amphorae. The museum is open from 0900-1200 and from 1400-1900 every day except Mondays. Visit the excellent website for more details – www.bodrum-museum.com

The Mausoleum mentioned above was considered to be one of the seven wonders of the ancient world, as was a tomb constructed by the Queen Artemisia II for her husband (and brother!) who gave the structure its name. The tomb structure originally supported 36 columns and a stepped pyramid roof, but none of this is visible today. The site and ruins can still be visited every day apart from Mondays.

Numerous travel agencies in the town can organise excursions and activities such as local village tours, trips to the town's two *hamams* (Turkish baths), day trips aboard typical Turkish gulets and even overnight trips to attractions such as Ephesus and Pamukkale.

The Bodrum Sailing Club (Bodrum Açıkdenz Yelken Kulübü) has a large membership and runs an active racing programme during the summer and winter months. In addition it organises the week long Bodrum Race Week at the start of November each year.

Visit its website, www.bayk.net, for more information.

Bodrum is also the host of other sailing competitions such as the Bodrum Cup International Wooden Boat Regatta, www.bodrumcup.com, and the International Women's sailing Cup held in October, www.internationalwomensailingcup.blogspot.com

TRANSPORT

Car hire: There are a number of car hire companies with offices along the road between the marina and the town, including:
Europcar Tel 0252 313 08 85, Mob: 0533 812 32 68; Onur Rent-a-Car Tel 0252 316 09 00, Mob 0535 488 43 94; Blue Rent-a-Car Tel: 0252 316 70 60, website: www.blue-rentacar.com
Taxis: A large taxi rank is situated near the mosque in the centre of town, with another one close to the marina. Contact Marina Taksi on Tel: 0252 316 21 14/16 34.
Dolmuş: The dolmuş station is located on Cevat Şakır Cadessi, leading away from the main harbour. Bodrum is a hub of dolmuş services for the entire peninsula. Buses are colour coded and have their destinations printed on roof signs. Services operate to Yalıkavak, Turgutreis, Gümüşlük, Bitez, Gündoğan and Güvercinlik, amongst others.
Coach: The otogar coach station is next to the dolmuş station. Regular coach services operate to many other cities, including İstanbul, Ankara, Marmaris, Fethiye and İzmir. You can confirm departure schedules and book tickets at the ticket offices in the otogar.
Ferry: Ferries and hydrofoils to the Greek islands of Kos, Rodos and Kalimnos depart several times a day from the ferry dock immediately to the east of the harbour entrance. Tickets can be purchased in advance from the booking offices along the ferry dock.

Bodrum Ferry Boat Association, Tel: 0252 316

08 82/313 25 09, website: www.bodrumferryboat.com
Bodrum Express Lines, Tel: 0252 316 10 87/40 67, website: www.bodrumexpresslines.com
Ferries to Datça depart daily from the other side of the harbour, with tickets available from a kiosk there or from the offices on the main ferry dock.
Air travel: Bodrum-Milas airport is approximately 30 minutes' drive from Bodrum town (32km), with daily flights from all over Europe during the summer season, as well as year round domestic services.

USEFUL INFORMATION

Local tel code: Muğla area, 0252, Bodrum 316.
Tourist information: The office is in the main town opposite the castle and is open daily from 0900-1800, Tel: 0252 316 10 91.
Medical: There are two large private hospitals and a state hospital in Bodrum, which serve the town and the rest of the peninsula. Both private hospitals offer a full range of in-patient and outpatient care and services, and are registered with major insurance companies. Universal Hospital Bodrum Tel: 0252 319 15 15, website www.uhg.com.tr Bodrum Private Hospital Tel: 0252 313 65 66. Bodrum State Hospital Tel: 0252 313 1420.

There is also at least one general clinic near the marina. The Medicare Poliklinik has a 24-hour emergency number, Tel: 0252 316 7051, website: www.medicare.com.tr, and has a pharmacy opposite.
Local information websites: There are a number of useful and informative websites that aim to give the visitor all the facts and advice they need to enjoy a stay of any length in Bodrum and the surrounding areas. The sites below all have good English translations:
www.bodrum-info.com
www.bodrumpages.com
www.bodrum-bodrum.com

İçmeler

West of Tavşan Burun:
36°59'.35N 27°28'.75E

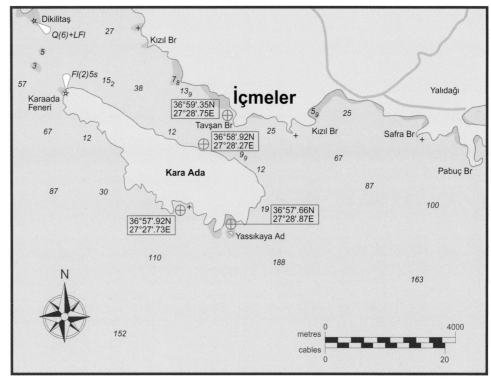

NAVIGATION

Charts: Turkish Hydrographic Charts: 224, 311, 3110, 3111; Turkish Hydrographic Leisure Folio 2004: 2004_1; Turkish Hydrographic Leisure Folio 3001: 3001_1, 3001_2, 3001_6; Imray Charts: G3, G35; Admiralty 236, 1055, 1095, 1099, SC 5773

The suburb of İçmeler is located on the coast about 4km to the east of Bodrum town, directly opposite the northern end of Kara Ada island. Although there is no village centre or harbour to speak of, it is the location of several boatyards that have dry docking and hard standing facilities as well as a full range of technical services available, usually directly through the boatyard management.

BOATYARDS

Yat Lift has a 20 ton and a 70 ton travel lift and can accommodate up to 200 yachts on its hard standing area. All technical work within the boatyard must be carried out by the yard's own staff, who can tackle most kinds of work. Contact the yard for more information on VHF Ch 69, Tel: 0252 316 7842, Fax: 0252 316 76 20, email: gunhan@yatlift.com, website: www.yatlift.com

Zetas Boatyard has hard standing space for approximately 50 boats up to 30m in length. It has water and electricity supplies ashore as well as a range of technical services available on site. Tel: 0252 316 45 32, Mob: 0542 526 73 86, email: info@zetastourism.com, website: www.zetastourism.com

Hasan Ali Usta Boatyard specialises in the construction and maintenance of wooden boats, and has a covered storage area of 15,000 square metres. Tel: 0252 316 79 40, Mob: 0532 224 43 68, Fax: 0252 313 77 59, email: info@hasanaliustaboatyard.com, website: www. hasanaliustaboatyard.com

A-Marin Boatyard has a sledge hauling system, a 40 ton travel lift and plans to build a 300 ton lift soon. It has some 15,000 square metres of covered storage space and hard standing area for up to 250 yachts. The site is home to two mini-markets, a small restaurant and about 14 technical workshops. Tel: 0252 316 17 08, Fax: 0252 313 87 66, email: info@a-marin.com.tr, website: www.a-marin.com.tr

Aegean Yacht Services accommodates vessels up to 45m in length and its technical staff can offer a full range of boatyard services. Tel: 0252 313 26 55/81 78, Mob: 0533 574 64 22, Fax: 0252 313 84 68, website: www.aegeanyacht.com

Boatyards at İçmeler

Gökova Körfezi
(The Gulf of Gökova)

Charts: Turkish Hydrographic Charts: 224, 311, 3110, 3111, 3112; Turkish Hydrographic Leisure Folios: 2004, 3001; Imray Charts: G3, G35; Admiralty 1055, 1099, SC 5773

Gökova Körfezi is bordered to the north and south by the Bodrum and Datça peninsulas. The main town in the gulf is Bodrum, which is also a point of entry into Turkey. This is the best place to provision for a trip as well as for winterising a boat and organising repairs and maintenance. It has good transport links, with an international airport approximately 30 minutes away, regular intercity coach routes and excellent local minibus services. Bodrum has the best health facilities in the area as well, with two international hospitals and several private clinics.

The waters of the gulf are surrounded by steep hills that are thickly forested with pine and contain a number of sheltered bays and anchorages. Most of these are in remote and peaceful locations, away

The sheltered anchorage at Saklı Koyu (see page 118)

from roads and settlements, although there are one or two small hamlets where you can purchase basic provisions and dine ashore in rustic local restaurants. There is also a small ferry harbour at Körmen from where a daily car ferry service operates between the Datça and Bodrum peninsulas.

Orientation in this area can be a bit tricky as the shorelines are fairly straight and it is at times hard to pick out the entrances to small bays from a distance. However, there are several landmarks that can help with pilotage. The Greek island of Kos is approximately 10M south-west of Bodrum town and its distinctive 466m peak can be seen for some distance even on hazy days. At night the lights on Ak Ammoglossa (Fl R 4s), Ak Louros (Fl (3) WR 15s) and Ak Ay Fokas (Fl 4s) can be seen and used for navigation.

Immediately south of Bodrum town is the island of Kara Ada, which has a peak of 385m that can also be seen for some distance and is helpful in locating the entrance to Bodrum town. The most obvious landmark on the northern side of the gulf is a large chimney at the Ören power station. This is approximately half way between the small hamlets of Çökertme and Akbük Koyu, so is a useful reference point if you are sailing towards either of these bays.

The southern shore of the gulf is more exposed to the prevailing winds and swell, and offers less in the way of safe harbours and anchorages. A wind farm is conspicuous on the shoulder of land that is immediately north-east of the town of Datça.

Winds in this area tend to blow strongly from the west, picking up from mid-morning to reach force 4-5 most afternoons. Stronger gusts are likely to be felt blowing off the hills along the northern side of the gulf and can also affect the anchorages on this side, so be sure that your anchor is well dug in if you are spending the night there.

If you are going to be sailing in this area then you should keep an eye-out for a local celebrity, *Badem* the

The power station at Ören

seal. She was rescued as a pup off the coast of Foca to the north of here and was released back into the wild in the Gökova area in April 2007. She now makes regular appearances along the coast and is quite bold in her interactions with humans. She is still monitored by the Turkish Mediterranean Seal Research Group that rescued her originally, and their advice to yachtsmen and locals is to keep well clear of her and avoid any direct contact. This is for the seal's benefit more than for humans, but a seal's idea of play can be rather rougher than we are used to and there have been incidents where she has bitten people who have got too friendly with her. *Badem* means 'almond' in Turkish.

Kara Ada

North-east anchorage: 36°58'.92N 27°28'.27E
Southern anchorage: 36°57'.66N 27°28'.87E
South-west anchorage: 36°57'.92N 27°27'.73E

Charts: Turkish Hydrographic Charts: 224, 311, 3110; Turkish Hydrographic Leisure Folio 2004: 2004_1; Turkish Hydrographic Leisure Folio 3001: 3001_1, 3001_2, 3001_6; Imray Charts: G3, G35; Admiralty 1055, 1095, 1099, SC 5773

Kara Ada means 'Black island' and it lies immediately to the south of Bodrum town. There are hot springs on the island, and it is a popular destination for the many day tripper boats and gulet cruises that depart from Bodrum and the surrounding resorts.

Anchorage on the northern side of Kara Ada

There are three anchorages on the island (see chart on page 101): Approximately half way along the northern side of the island are the ruins of an old hydrotherapy resort. The shelter is not particularly good here so it should only be used in calm weather.

A better anchorage is found right on the southern tip of the island and can be identified by the small islet of Yassıkaya Adası. There is a large cave here and you can snorkel right into it. Anchor in 5-10m and take a line ashore as space is limited.

Approximately 1M to the north-west of here is another anchorage where there is room for several boats to anchor in 10m with lines ashore. This bay is well protected by a headland extending from the northern side.

Anchorage on the southern tip of Kara Ada

Kargıcık Koyu

Pabuç anchorage: 36°58'.73N 27°34'.08E
Kargıcık anchorage: 36°59'.30N 27°33'.99E
Orak Adası north anchorage: 36°58'.80N 27°35'.73E
To the east of Orak Adası: 36°58'.45N 27°36'.73E

NAVIGATION

Charts: Turkish Hydrographic Charts: 224, 311;
Turkish Hydrographic Leisure Folio 2004: 2004_1;
Turkish Hydrographic Leisure Folio 3001: 3001_1,
3001_2; Imray Charts: G3, G35; Admiralty 1055, 1095,
1099, SC 5773

Kargıcık Koyu lies approximately 5M to the east of
Kara Ada, and there are several anchorages here
that offer good shelter from the prevailing winds in
attractive surroundings. Vessels approaching from
either direction should look for the island of Orak Adası
in order to identify the location. There is a light on the
southern tip of the island (Fl 10s).

Two small islands lie between here and the mainland,
but it is possible to pass to either side of these or
between them in approximately 20m of water. There are
some rather impressive private houses on these islands,
and also on Orak Adası.

The facilities in Kargıcık Koyu and Pabuç Koyu are
for guests of the holiday villages only.

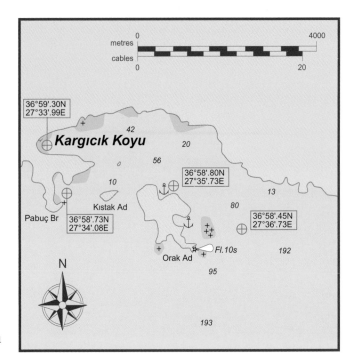

Pabuç anchorage

The hook-shaped headland of Pabuç Burnu provides
good shelter for vessels anchored behind it. A holiday
village is situated at the head of the bay, but there
is space for vessels to free swing in 5-10m. Another
smaller anchorage lies immediately to the east of here
with room for a couple of boats taking lines ashore.

Anchorage on the eastern side of Orak Adası

Kargıcık Koyu anchorage

There is another holiday resort in this bay, which has an attractive sandy beach and clear turquoise water that is ideal for swimming and snorkelling. Vessels can free swing at anchor in 5-10m here, but the wind funnels strongly off the hills so you should be sure that your anchor is well set if you plan to stay the night here.

Orak Adası anchorages

There are two anchorages on this island. On the north-east side is a small bay that houses a landing dock used for the private home ashore. You need to head right to the far end of the bay to escape the strong gusts blowing out of Kargıcık Koyu and should take a line ashore to prevent swinging. This anchorage is suitable only in settled weather and has a small beach at the southern end.

The better anchorage is on the eastern side of the island. There are rocks just breaking the surface in the middle of the bay, and you should make sure you pass to the north of these. Anchor on the northern side of the bay and take a line ashore to prevent swinging. If you are sailing between the two anchorages along the north-east side of the island then be aware of the shoal area that lies near here with depths of 5m. You will be able to spot this by the change in the colour of the water but it is otherwise unmarked.

East cardinal marker near Orak Adası

Anchorage on the eastern side of Orak Adası. Note the rocks to the left of the picture

Alakışlabükü

Anchorage: 36°59'.40N 27°39'.11E

Charts: Turkish Hydrographic Charts: 311;
Turkish Hydrographic Leisure Folio 2004: 2004_1;
Turkish Hydrographic Leisure Folio 3001: 3001_1,
3001_2; Imray Charts: G3, G35; Admiralty 1055, 1099,
SC 5773

This large bay lies approximately 3M to the east of Kargıcık Koyu and offers reasonable shelter from the prevailing winds. There are no dangers if you are approaching from the east, but if you are coming from the west then take care to avoid the rocks that extend from the Kara Burun headland. These are marked with a buoy and it is possible to pass between this headland and the island of Yıldız Adası. The best shelter is to be found in the small cove on the northern side of the bay.

Çökertme Koyu

Çökertme Koyu

Entrance to bay: 36°59'.84N 27°47'.56E

This large and well-sheltered bay on the northern side of the Gökova Körfezi is the location of a small village and is a popular stop for passing yachts.

NAVIGATION

Charts: Turkish Hydrographic Charts: 311;
Turkish Hydrographic Leisure Folio 2004: 2004_1;
Turkish Hydrographic Leisure Folio 3001: 3001_1,
3001_3; Imray Charts: G3, G35; Admiralty 1055, 1099,
SC 5773

The entrance to Çökertme is difficult to pick out from the surrounding hillsides until you are close to it. The large power station at Ören is approximately 6M to the east, and there is a cluster of white buildings above the shoreline approximately 3M to the east. When you are close in, the entrance can be identified by a group of radio masts on the headland immediately to the east. On entering the bay, you will see several buildings along the shoreline directly in front of you.

BERTHING AND ANCHORING

There are three private restaurant jetties in Çökertme belonging to Captain Ibrahim's restaurant, Rose Mary restaurant and the Çökertme restaurant. Each of these offers secure stern-to berthing with lazylines. Mooring

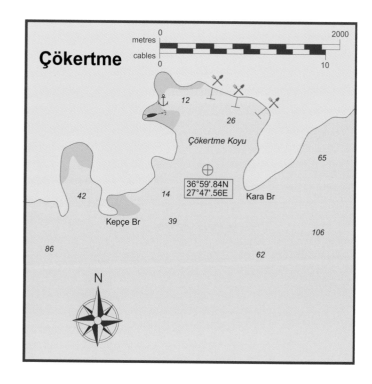

assistants will hand you the end of the lazyline from a small dinghy as you approach the jetty in reverse, so have someone at the bow ready to pull in the slack as you near the dock.

If you prefer to anchor then you can free swing in 5-10m on the western side of the bay, or take a line ashore.

Shelter in the bay is generally quite good from the prevailing winds, but it is exposed to the south and will quickly become untenable in these conditions.

Useful information – Çökertme Koyu

FACILITIES

Water and electricity: Water and electricity supplies are installed on each of the restaurant jetties.

Fuel: Available by delivery. Organised from Captain Ibrahim's and Rose Mary restaurants.

Showers: Available at all of the restaurants.

Ice: Can sometimes be bought from the small mini-market and restaurants ashore.

Laundry: Ask at the restaurants.

Rubbish: Rubbish bins can be found ashore.

Telephone: There is good mobile phone reception in the area and card phones are in each of the restaurants.

Internet: WiFi internet connection is provided by several of the restaurants.

PROVISIONING AND SERVICES

Services are limited to small mini-markets at each of the restaurants where you can buy basic provisions.

EATING OUT

The three restaurants with jetties offer similar menus of mainly Turkish village specialities, including a good selection of freshly prepared *meze* dishes and local seafood. Another restaurant, Orhan restaurant and pansiyon, offers similar choices to visitors but has no jetty, while snacks and breakfast are available from the carpet outlet's café on the beach. The contact details for the four restaurants are as follows: Captain Ibrahim's restaurant Tel: 0252 531 00 12, Mob: 0538 329 44 24. Rose Mary restaurant Tel: 0252 531 01 58, Mob: 0532 432 57 31. Çökertme Motel and Restaurant Tel: 0252 531 01 56, website: www.cokertmehotel.com Orhan restaurant and pansiyon Tel: 0252 531 00 96, Mob: 0542 587 60 92.

ASHORE

There is very little to do in Çökertme, which is a large part of its attraction. A small carpet outlet next to Orhan restaurant and pansiyon has a display showing traditional manufacturing techniques as well as a menagerie of ducks, chickens and rabbits to keep children entertained.

A rough track leads round towards the anchorage at the west of the bay, and you can walk along the road leading away from the back of the village to the east through some peaceful and ancient olive groves.

USEFUL INFORMATION

Local tel code: Muğla area, 0252, Çökertme 531.

Knick-knacks and artefacts at the Çökertme Restaurant

Rabbits at the carpet shop

Welcome to Captain Ibrahim's

Akbük Koyu

In the middle of the entrance:
37°01'.19N 28°07'.70E

This is a large and well-sheltered bay on the northern side of Gökova Körfezi, with a small village ashore.

NAVIGATION

Charts: Turkish Hydrographic Charts: 311; Turkish Hydrographic Leisure Folio 3001: 3001_1, 3001_3; Imray Charts: G3, G35; Admiralty 1055, 1099, SC 5773

The low headland of Karaburun stands out against the steep mountainous backdrop behind Akbük Koyu and helps to identify the bay, which is approximately 6M to the east of the conspicuous power station at Ören. If you are approaching from the west then keep clear of the shallow waters extending off Akbük Burnu on the east of this headland.

The bay is open to the east and will quickly become untenable in easterly/south-easterly conditions.

BERTHING AND ANCHORING

There are two restaurants with private jetties in the bay, both of which have stern-to berthing with some lazylines. The Doğa restaurant is to your left as you enter the bay, and the Altaş restaurant, Tel: 0252 529 11 46, Mob: 0536 839 53 94, is straight ahead.

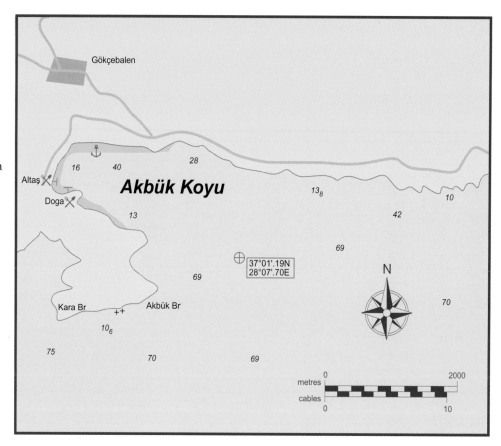

If you prefer to anchor then do so on the northern side of the bay in 5-10m. There is room to free swing but you may be more comfortable taking a line ashore if you plan to spend the night here, as there can be strong gusts off the mountains behind the bay.

The Altaş restaurant in Akbük Koyu

Useful information – Akbük Koyu

FACILITIES
Water: Available at both restaurant jetties.
Electricity: A supply is installed on the Altaş restaurant jetty.
Fuel: Can be delivered through Altaş restaurant.
Showers: Are provided at both restaurants.
Ice: Is sometimes supplied by the restaurants.
Rubbish: Rubbish bins are located ashore.

Telephone: Card phones are installed in some of the restaurants.

PROVISIONING AND SERVICES
Grocery shops: Basic provisions can sometimes be purchased from the restaurants.
Bakery: Fresh bread may be available from the restaurants in the mornings.

Şehir Adası
(Cleopatra Island)

Duck Rock: 36°59'.58N 28°11'.81E
Cleopatra anchorage: 36°59'.71N 28°12'.49E
Taş Bükü anchorage: 36°59'.25N 28°12'.59E

Şehir Adası is known locally as Cleopatra's Island because of the unusually white sand found on one of its beaches. This sand is of a different sort than is common in the area and is reputed to have been brought to the island for the enjoyment of the Egyptian queen during her visit here. Some ancient ruins of the town of Cedreae do exist, but it seems that the sand is naturally occurring rather than specially imported. Tripper boats depart regularly from Çamlı Limanı to the east of the island and it is also a popular destination for blue cruising gulets so can get rather crowded during high season. If you can visit during quieter times though, it is a beautiful and peaceful anchorage that you can happily spend some time exploring.

NAVIGATION

Charts: Turkish Hydrographic Charts: 311, 3111, 3112; Turkish Hydrographic Leisure Folio 3001: 3001_1, 3001_3, 3001_8; Imray Charts: G3, G35; Admiralty 1055, 1099, SC 5773

The light structure on Orta Adası

Şehir Adası lies at the eastern end of Gökova Körfezi, immediately to the north of the headland of Domuz Burnu. Take care of the shallows extending from this headland as you sail past.

An unlit west cardinal mark sits on top of the Ördek Kayası (Duck Rock), which lies immediately west of Şehir Adası. It is possible to pass between here and the island, but better to go around the outside and keep well clear. A sectored light on the western end of Orta Ada indicates the danger area (Fl WR 10s).

The main anchorage at Şehir Adası (Cleopatra's Island)

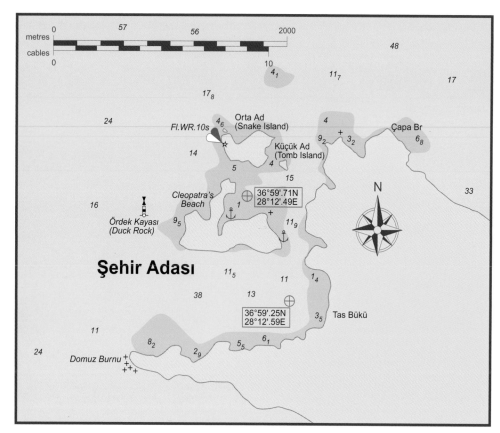

ANCHORING

The main anchorage is on the north-east side of Şehir Adası and is protected by a spit of land that extends towards Orta Adası. The wooden jetty is used by the tripper boats that bring visitors from the mainland. Yachts can free swing in 5m of water.

There are daytime anchorages in the small bay on the eastern side of the island as well as on the northern side of Domuz Burnu.

ASHORE

A track leads from the wooden jetty in the main anchorage to the white sands of Cleopatra's beach. A small restaurant serves drinks and snacks, but is only open during the day as no-one is allowed ashore after the last tripper boats depart.

It is possible to explore the ruins on the island, which include a small amphitheatre and the remains of a walled settlement on the eastern end.

There is a small restaurant in the bay to the south of Şehir Adası, although this is only open during high season.

Orta Adası (Snake Island) and the smaller Küçük Ada (Tomb Island) lie immediately north of Şehir Adası , and there is no passage between the two of these. It is possible to pass between Orta Adası and Şehir Adası, where depths are between 4 and 5m. It is also possible to travel along the coastline to the east of the islands if you want to head up into Çamlı Limanı.

The white sands of Cleopatra's beach

Karacasöğüt, looking south from the entrance into the bay

Karacasöğüt

Passage to the east of Karaca Adası island:
36°57'.68N 28°12'.23E
Entrance to bay: 36°56'.91N 28°11'.43E
Entrance to Çanak Limanı: 36°57'.09N 28°10'.36E

This landlocked bay offers excellent shelter in impressive surroundings. Densely-forested hillsides fall down to deep blue waters, which are home to a local sailing club as well as several other jetties. The small village ashore has several restaurants and is known for the purity of the natural springs that arise here.

NAVIGATION

Charts: Turkish Hydrographic Charts: 311; Turkish Hydrographic Leisure Folio 3001: 3001_1, 3001_3; Imray Charts: G3, G35; Admiralty 1055, 1099, SC 5773

The island of Karaca Adası lies immediately to the north of the entrance to the bay and can be easily identified by vessels approaching from the north or west. It is possible to pass between the island and mainland to the east; there are a few fish farms along the mainland shore here. Vessels approaching from the west will first pass the small bay of Çanak Limanı, which also holds a few fish pens.

The entrance to Karacasöğüt bay is fairly narrow, but the bay then opens out and is quite large.

BERTHING AND ANCHORING

Wooden jetties line the southern and western shores of the bay and there is space for several boats to berth stern-to to these with the lazylines provided.

The first jetty on your right-hand side as you enter the

bay is a floating dock belonging to the Gökova Sailing Club and Global Sailing, Tel: 0252 465 51 48, email: info@globalsailing.org, website: www.globalsailing. org, and is available for use by visiting yachts as well as sailing club members. Mooring fees are charged here.

After this you will see a long wooden jetty that is operated by the local belediye and is a public dock available for use by all boats. Finally you will see the T-shaped jetty of the Karacasöğüt Marina, Tel: 0252 465 53 45; Mob: 0534 798 52 13.

Although the bay is deep in the middle, there are sufficient depths for vessels to anchor in 5-10m along the shore where there is space between jetties. You will need to take a line ashore for security.

It is also possible to anchor in Çanak Limanı (sometimes called Kesr), which is immediately to the west of Karacasöğüt bay. It is a fairly small bay with good shelter, but one side of it is occupied by a fish farm so use the other side for anchoring.

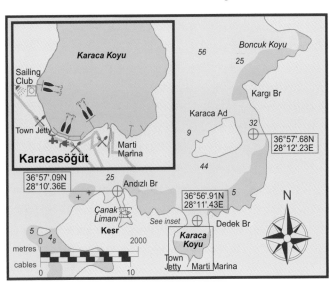

Useful information – Karacasöğüt

FACILITIES

Water and electricity: There are supplies on each of the three jetties.

Showers: Private shower facilities are available at Karacasöğüt Marina and the Global Sailing Centre. Public toilets and showers are located at the back of the car park next to the belediye jetty.

Ice and gas: May be available from some of the markets ashore.

Laundry: At the Global Sailing facility.

Rubbish: Located ashore.

Telephone: Public phones ashore and phone cards can be purchased at the Söğüt market. There is good mobile phone reception in the area.

Internet: A WiFi internet connection is provided at Karacasöğüt Marina and Global Sailing.

PROVISIONING AND SERVICES

Limited facilities consist of a couple of small markets selling basic provisions in the village and at Global Sailing.

EATING OUT

There are several restaurants ashore in Karacasöğüt as well as a small holiday village.

The Global Sailing facility on the western side of the bay has its own restaurant, the Galley Restaurant. Along the waterfront you can try the Marina restaurant, Tel: 0252 465 53 45, or the Söğüt Café, Tel: 0252 465 50 42. The Çardak restaurant is located approximately 150m along the road leading from the waterfront, Tel: 0252 465 50 52. All serve the usual Turkish fare, including fresh fish and grilled specialities.

ASHORE

The Global Sailing Centre is run by a Turkish family of sailing aficionados and circumnavigators, and has excellent facilities that are available for use by all guests, including those from visiting yachts. These comprise windsurf and dinghy hire/lessons, tennis courts and a fitness centre, a Turkish bath and sauna.

There is a pleasant beach on the eastern side of the bay and several tracks leading through the pine forests that surround the bay.

Sea kayaking trips can be organised through the reception office at Karacasöğüt Marina, with different grades of difficulty according to your level of experience.

The Global Sailing Centre jetty

TRANSPORT

Car hire: Can be arranged through Global Sailing.

Taxis: Available in the village – ask at any of the restaurants.

Dolmuş: There is a dolmuş service from Karacasöğüt to Marmaris town, which takes approximately 40 minutes. The departure times are posted at the dolmuş co-op stand in the car park area.

USEFUL INFORMATION

Local tel code: Muğla area, 0252, Karacasöğüt 465.

Medical facilities: In Marmaris – see page 168.

Yacht repairs/services: In Marmaris or Bodrum – see page 163 or 98.

The Karacasöğüt Marina jetty

Değirmen Bükü

Between Zeytinli Adası and Ayın Körfezi:
36°56'.10N 28°08'.86E
Entrance to English harbour: 36°55'.24N 28°09'.56E
Entrance to Okluk Koyu: 36°55'.10N 28°10'.06E
European Sea Sports jetty in Ayın Körfezi:
36°55'.78N 28°08'.63E

This deeply indented and heavily forested bay on the south-east side of Gökova Körfezi is popular with visiting yachts for the pleasant atmosphere and excellent shelter that it offers. Local legend has it that the English Harbour anchorage on the western side of the bay was used as a refuge for British torpedo boats during WWII.

NAVIGATION

Charts: Turkish Hydrographic Charts: 311, 3111; Turkish Hydrographic Leisure Folio 3001: 3001_1, 3001_3, 3001_8; Imray Charts: G3, G35; Admiralty 1055, 1099, SC 5773

The bay lies approximately 6M to the east of the light on Koyun Burnu (Fl (3) 10s). Vessels approaching from this direction should watch out for the Köremen Adalar group of rocks and small islets lying off the Çiçekli Burun headland, and should pass to the north of these. There are no dangers or obstructions in the approach from the east.

The entrance to Değirmen Bükü is hard to spot against the surrounding pine-clad hillsides, so the best way to find it is to follow the coastline until you are able to make out the two small islands Zeytinli Adası and Kara Ada, which lie to the north of the bay. There is safe passage to either side of both these islands, although you should be aware of the 5m shoal that exists between them.

As you enter the bay you are likely to see the masts of boats anchored in English

The mermaid statue at the entrance to Okluk Koyu

Harbour on the western side. The entrance to Okluk Koyu, the bay containing the restaurants, can be identified by a small statue of a mermaid that is sitting on a rock just off the headland.

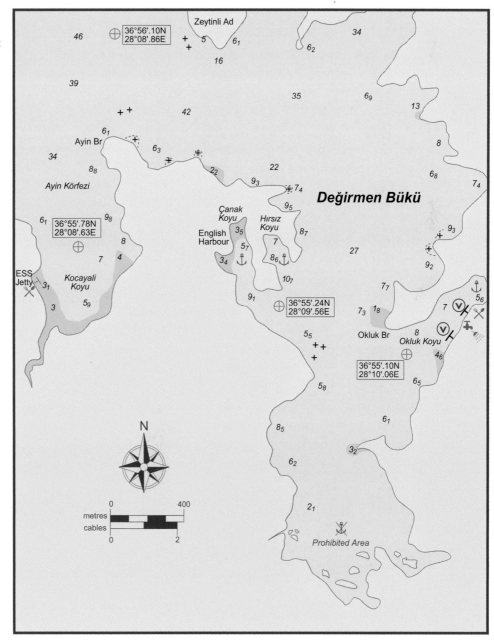

Boats at anchor and using the restaurant jetties in Okluk Koyu

BERTHING AND ANCHORING

There are two restaurants along the shore in Okluk Koyu on the eastern side of Değirmen Bükü. Both of these have wooden jetties where you can berth stern-to with either an anchor or lazyline. The restaurant staff will tell you which one to use. The prevailing wind blows onshore here, although the bay is protected from any swell, so if you are using an anchor make sure that it is dug in well with plenty of scope.

There is also another restaurant with a small jetty in a bay immediately to the west of Değirmen Bükü. This is the Defneli restaurant, which is where the European Sea Sports scuba camp is based.

If you prefer to spend the night at anchor then you have a few options: there is space at the northern end of Okluk Koyu and on the side of the bay opposite the restaurants. You will need to take a line ashore here to prevent swinging.

The English Harbour anchorage comprises Çanak Koyu and Hırsız Koyu on the western side of the bay. If you are stopping for only a few hours and have the bays to yourself, then you may have room to free swing, otherwise you will need to take a line ashore for security and to make space for other boats.

Useful information – Değirmen Bükü

FACILITIES
Water and electricity: Supplied on both restaurant jetties.
Showers: Available at both restaurants.
Ice: It may be possible to get ice from the restaurants.
Rubbish: Rubbish bins are located ashore.
Telephone: There is one public telephone ashore, and phone cards can also be purchased from the small mini-markets – see below. Mobile phone reception here is good.

PROVISIONING AND SERVICES
Grocery shops: Both restaurants have small mini-markets where you can obtain basic provisions and supplies.
Bakery: Fresh bread is delivered from the nearby village each morning.

EATING OUT
Deniz Kızı Kaptan restaurant, Tel: 0252 465 52 40, Mob: 0536 862 25 44/0536 272 80 66, is at the southern end of Okluk Koyu, while Yat Limanı restaurant, Tel: 0252 465 52 28, is at the northern end. Both have similar menus consisting of traditional meat and seafood dishes with a selection of *meze* to start with. The rustic setting and peaceful surroundings make for a good atmosphere in which to enjoy your meal.

ASHORE
There is little to do here apart from relax and soak up the environment. The pine-clad hillsides mean that the bay is very quiet, and there is only one road to and from the bay so no through traffic.

You can take your dinghy out to visit the mermaid statue that adorns the entrance to Okluk Koyu, and the clear water in the bays is ideal for swimming and snorkelling. There are a few rough tracks through the forests if you want to explore on bicycle or by foot; ask the restaurant owners for advice on where to go.

The European Sea Sports scuba-diving company is based over at the Defneli restaurant and runs scuba diving and snorkelling excursions and instruction. Visit www.europeanseasports.com for more information.

TRANSPORT
Dolmuş: There is a dolmuş minibus service to Marmaris. Check with the restaurant staff for times.

USEFUL INFORMATION
Local tel code: Muğla area, 0252, Değirmen Bükü 465.

The Deniz Kızı Kaptan restaurant

Kargılı Koyu

Entrance to bay:
36°56'.39N 28°05'.61E

NAVIGATION

Charts: Turkish Hydrographic Charts: 311;Turkish Hydrographic Leisure Folio 3001: 3001_1, 3001_3; Imray Charts: G3, G35; Admiralty 1055, 1099, SC 5773

This narrow, curving inlet lies approximately 3M to the west of Değirmen Bükü and offers good shelter in attractive surroundings. Vessels approaching from the west will be able to identify the 180m hill above Nergiz Burnu headland as they pass, and will head into the bay just before the low cliffs of Kargılı Burun.

Follow the inlet as it curves around to the west and anchor with a line ashore in 5-10m before the depths drop dramatically to less than 2m. There used to be a tiny barbecue restaurant here, with a small jetty where you could tie up your dinghy.

Tuzla Koyu

Between Koyun Burnu and Tuztutan Burnu headlands:
36°55'.79N 28°02'.15E

NAVIGATION

Charts: Turkish Hydrographic Charts: 311; Turkish Hydrographic Leisure Folio 3001: 3001_1, 3001_3; Imray Charts: G3, G35; Admiralty 1055, 1099, SC 5773

Tuzla Koyu is a long narrow bay formed between Koyun Burnu and Tuztutan Burnu a few miles north of the Yedi Adalar area. Shallow waters extend from both of these headlands so keep well clear as you round them. The reef at Karamuk Kayalığı is now marked with a north cardinal mark, so look out for this as you pass and keep well clear.

The light structure on Koyun Burnu can be seen as you approach from either direction and once you are within the bay you should be able to identify the small islet in the centre.

Although the prevailing winds do blow into the bay, there is a useful anchorage on the southern side immediately east of the Koyun Burnu headland. There

Buoy marking the Karamuk Kayalığı reef, with the light structure on Koyun Burnu visible to the left

is a double bay here that is well protected by a spit of land extending from the western side. Rocks lie to either side of the entrance, but these can be seen above the water so you should stay in the middle as you approach to keep clear of these.

Once inside the anchorage you can drop anchor in either of the bays and take a line ashore to prevent swinging. You are likely to have the place to yourself and there are no facilities ashore.

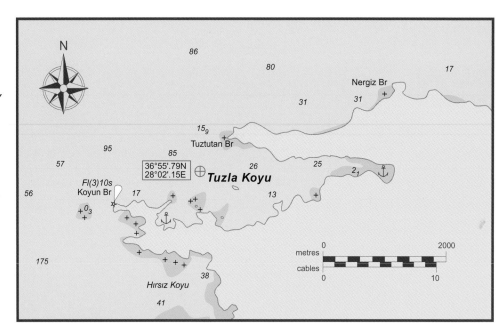

Vessel at anchor within Tuzla Koyu

Yedi Adalar

North of channel between two easternmost islands near Küfre Koyu: 36°52'.64N 28°02'.77E
Entrance to Küfre Koyu: 36°52'.75N 28°03'.27E
Entrance to Saklı Koyu: 36°52'.20N 28°02'.72E
Southern entrance to island chain:
36°51'.95N 28°00'.96E

Charts: Turkish Hydrographic Charts: 311, 3111; Turkish Hydrographic Leisure Folio 3001: 3001_1, 3001_3, 3001_7; Imray Charts: G3, G35; Admiralty 1055, 1099, 1644, SC 5773

Yedi Adalar is Turkish for Seven Islands, so unsurprisingly relates to a chain of small islands lying just off the coast between Bördübet Limanı and Tuzla Koyu. The area is inaccessible from land and so is still a completely undisturbed and natural environment. If you're looking for utter isolation then you should be sure to find at least one of the bays here completely to yourself.

The prevailing wind can push quite a chop into this area, particularly by late afternoon, and care is needed when navigating between the small islands and many rocks that break the surface in this area.

If you are approaching from the northern end around Teke Burnu you need to take care to avoid

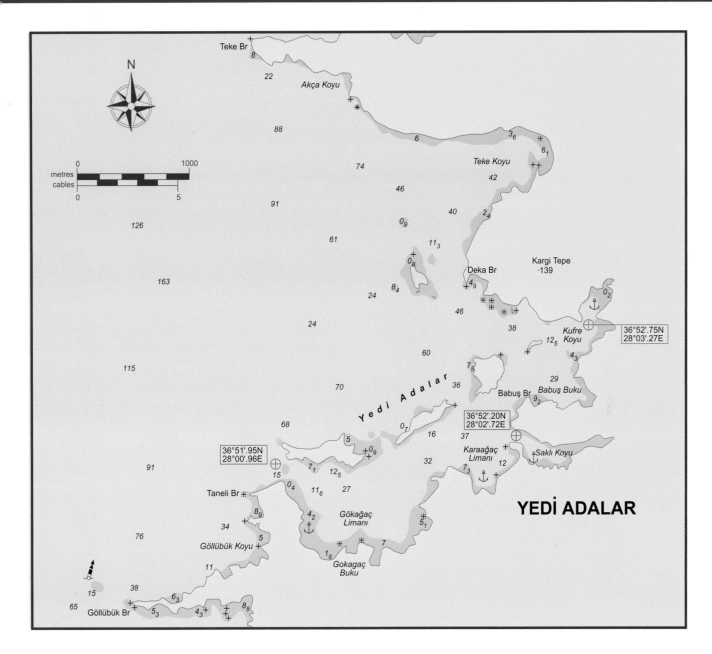

the shallow reef opposite the entrance to Teke Koyu and immediately north of the first of the seven islands that you will see. Depths here shelve to less than a metre below the surface, so you may be able to spot the reef by the change in water colour if the sea is fairly calm, although often this will not be the case. To avoid the reef area steer a course of 128°T from Teke Burnu directly towards the peak of Kargı Tepe hill to the south-east. This should keep you well clear of the shallow area and once you can see down the channel to the east of the island you can turn and start to head south towards the anchorages. Depths through this channel are over 20m for the most part, although there is a shallower area close to the island where they drop to about 10m.

Once you are past the northern island (which has two small islets just off its southern end) you should be able to see the main chain of three larger islands and one smaller one stretching from east to west along the southern end of the bay. It is possible to pass to either

side of the eastern-most smallest island in order to reach the anchorages behind.

Vessels approaching from the west will be able to access the anchorages more easily through the southern entrance between the western-most island and the headland of Taneli Burun. Depths drop to around 5m in the centre of the channel, but quickly rise again. Take care to avoid the shallows off Göllübük Burnu headland, which are indicated with a north cardinal mark.

ANCHORAGES

There are several anchorages in this area, all of which are well sheltered from the prevailing wind and swell by the chain of islands and are suitable for an overnight stay. You should take a line ashore if you plan to do this as there is little swinging room in most cases.

A number of boats can anchor in Küfre Koyu, next to the small island at the eastern end of the chain of four. For best protection head right into the northern part of the bay where there is a small beach and some low cliffs.

The Küfre Koyu anchorage

The Gökağaç anchorage

The next bay along is Babuş Bükü, which has a simple approach through the wide entrance and offers shelter at the far eastern end of the bay.

Saklı Koyu, to the south of Babuş Burnu, has a narrow entrance but immediately widens to become a fair sized bay with good shelter right behind the spit at the entrance. If you continue due east from here you will find that it narrows considerably. Keep heading into the creek, passing over a shallow bar of about 3m, and you will find that it widens slightly and gets deeper again. You can anchor anywhere here in approximately 6-8m of water and it offers the best shelter in the area.

Karaağac Limanı is the next bay along, with several small attractive coves in which to anchor. Finally Gökağaç Limanı is just to the east of Taneli Burun and also has a few possible anchorages.

Bördübet Limanı

Entrance to Amazon Creek: 36°49'.74N 28°02'.96E

Between Gökçeler Koyu and Çatı Koyu: 36°47'.77N 28°01'.15E

NAVIGATION

Charts: Turkish Hydrographic Charts: 311, 3112; Turkish Hydrographic Leisure Folio 3001: 3001_1, 3001_3, 3001_5, 3001_8; Imray Charts: G3, G35; Admiralty 1055, 1099, SC 5773

Bördübet Limanı lies just to the south of Mersincik Burnu, which has a sectored light that shows clear passage avoiding the dangers of Yedi Adalar to the north

Gökçeler Bükü and Küçük Çatı

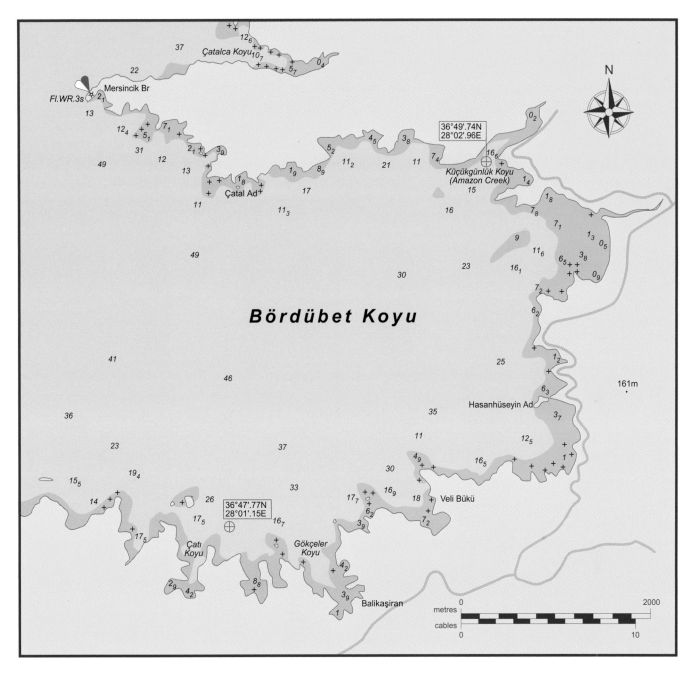

Map labels:
- 37
- 126
- Çatalca Koyu 107
- 22
- Fl.WR.3s 21 Mersincik Br
- 13
- 124 71
- 31 51
- 49 12 21 39
- 13 18
- Çatal Ad
- 11 113 17
- 52 45 38
- 112 21 11 74
- 19 89
- 02
- 36°49'.74N 28°02'.96E
- 166
- Küçükgünlük Koyu (Amazon Creek) 14
- 15
- 16
- 18 78 71
- 9 13 05
- 116 65 38
- 72 09
- 62
- 49
- 30 23 161
- Bördübet Koyu
- 41
- 46
- 25 12
- 63
- Hasanhüseyin Ad 37
- 161m
- 36
- 23
- 35 11 125
- 37
- 194
- 155
- 14
- 175
- 175
- Çatı Koyu
- 26 36°47'.77N 28°01'.15E
- 177
- 167
- Gökçeler Koyu
- 33 39
- 169 18 Veli Bükü
- 62 72
- 49
- 30 165
- 1
- 29 42
- 88
- 39 Balıkaşiran
- metres 0 ... 2000
- cables 0 ... 10

(Fl WR 3s). Apart from this there are no hazards in the approach, which is wide and open to the prevailing winds and seas.

You will find a safe anchorage in the Küçükgünlük Koyu on the north-east side of the bay. This is also known as Amazon Creek because of the Camp Amazon campsite at the head of the creek. It is possible to walk up to here from the anchorage and make use of the facilities, which include a small restaurant and bar, showers, toilets, a swimming pool and small shop. Anchor in approximately 5m with a line ashore within the creek, or in either of the small bays to either side of the entrance to the creek.

On the southern side of Bördübet Limanı are two deep bays named Gökçeler Koyu and Çatı Koyu. There are various small coves within these bays that offer shelter from the prevailing winds, and both bays are used by local fishermen who have built small jetties and

temporary shelters ashore. A number of small islets and submerged rocks are located in this area, so be vigilant as you approach and do so only in fine weather when the light is good.

Amazon Creek

Körmen

North of the outer harbour entrance:
36°46'.26N 27°37'.01E

Charts: Turkish Hydrographic Charts: 311, 3112;
Turkish Hydrographic Leisure Folio 3001: 3001_1,
3001_2, 3001_4; Imray Charts: G3, G35; Admiralty 1055,
1099, SC 5773

Körmen lies on the northern side of the Datça peninsula
towards the western end and is the departure point for
the ferry service between Datça and Bodrum.

Vessels approaching from the east can start to head
south after rounding the İnce Burun headland (lit at
night Fl (2) 5s) and the rocky harbour walls will be
visible as you approach. The prevailing winds blow
across the harbour entrance, so care is needed as you
enter here if the winds are strong.

The harbour is divided into two sections, with the
outer harbour being deeper and more suitable for
yachts and the inner harbour used mainly by local
fishing boats. On the western side of the outer harbour
is a concrete jetty with bollards to which vessels should
tie up either stern or bows-to using an anchor, taking
care to leave space for the ferry.

Water and electricity are available on the dock here,
and you will also find a small restaurant with toilet
facilities. The ferry departs for Bodrum twice a day
during the summer and tickets can be purchased in
advance from the sales office in Datça town or half an
hour prior to departure from the small ticket office
on the dock in Körmen. A shuttle bus takes ferry

passengers to and from the town of Datça, so if you
need to visit here it should be possible to ride in on this
and make the 10-minute return journey by taxi. There
are a few houses lining the road that leads away from
the harbour and you can get basic provisions from a
small mini-market close to here.

USEFUL TELEPHONE NUMBERS
Datça Ferryboat Association: Tel: 0252 712 21 43/23 23,
www.datcaferibot.com

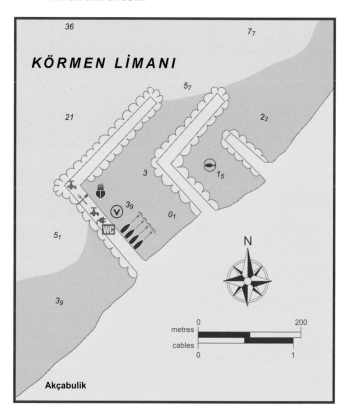

Mersincik Limanı

Middle of the bay: 36°45'.38N 27°28'.75E

NAVIGATION
Charts: Turkish Hydrographic Charts: 311;
Turkish Hydrographic Leisure Folio 3001: 3001_1,
3001_4; Imray Charts: G3, G35; Admiralty 1055, 1099,
SC 5773

This wide bay lies just to the south of the islands of
Mersincik Adası and Akçalı Adası, towards the western
end of the Datça peninsula. A small inlet immediately
under the headland on the western side of the bay
offers the best shelter here and is fairly easy to identify
to the north of a stone wall that runs along the shore.
It is also possible to free swing in the main bay. Some
swell will work its way around the headland so this
should not be considered as an overnight stop unless
in very calm weather.

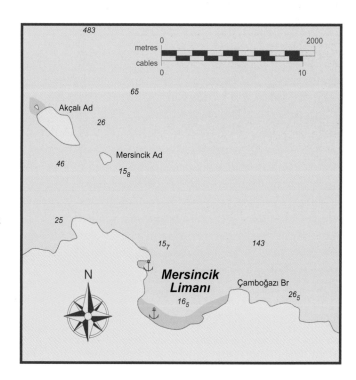

Datça town harbour

Chapter three
The Dorian coast – Hisarönü Körfezi to Marmaris

The Dorian coastline includes the bays and harbours of the Hisarönü Körfezi and Bozburun peninsula, and extends as far as the natural harbour and yachting centre of Marmaris. The region is characterised by thick pine forests that extend down steep hillsides to the water's edge, and the coastline is deeply indented to provide countless sheltered bays and anchorages. Tourism is relatively low-key in most of this region, being concentrated in the resort areas immediately surrounding Marmaris.

Hisarönü Körfezi
(The Hisarönü Gulf)

Charts: Turkish Hydrographic Charts: 311, 3112, 3113; Turkish Hydrographic Leisure Folios: 3001; Imray Charts: G3, G35; Admiralty 1055, 1099, SC 5773

The Hisarönü Körfezi is bordered to the north by the Datça peninsula, to the south-east by the Bozburun

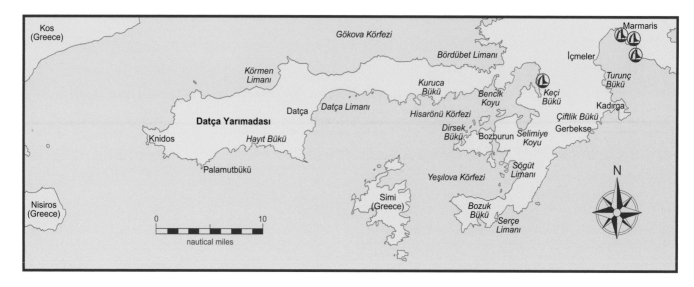

peninsula and to the south-west by the Greek island of Simi. The smaller Yeşilova Körfezi is tucked into the western side of the Bozburun peninsula. This is one of the greenest and loveliest sailing areas in Turkey, popular with yachtsmen from all over the world. The Datça peninsula is also sometimes referred to as Reşadiye peninsula, in honour of the Ottoman Sultan Mehmet V Reşad, or as the Dorian peninsula. The Dorian Greeks came here from the Peloponnese in

Boats at anchor in Kurucabükü

1000 BC and had over 50 settlements in the area with a population of more than 70,000. Knidos was the most important city in the area at that time. Originally this city was located close to modern day Datça, but in around 360 BC it moved to the western tip of the peninsula where its ruins can be seen today.

These days the town of Datça is the largest in this area and is also a port of entry for vessels clearing into or out of Turkey. There are good health care and provisioning facilities in Datça, and regular bus services connect with the rest of the country via the large resort town of Marmaris. However, the main yachting centre in the area is Keçi Bükü, also known as Orhaniye, in the far eastern end of the gulf. Nestling in a large bay under the pine forests, there is a well-appointed marina here that is only 30 minutes by road from the large resort town and yachting centre of Marmaris (see page 160 for more details of Marmaris). Dalaman airport can be reached in less than 2 hours by taxi from Orhaniye.

Apart from the rocky and barren western end of the Datça peninsula, the shores of Hisarönü Körfezi are mostly bordered by steep slopes clad in thick pine forests, and the area is pleasantly green for much of the year. The cruising area is one of the best along the Turkish coastline, with settlements varying from tiny hamlets to fair-sized towns, as well as any number of isolated anchorages that may have a single restaurant ashore or may be completely deserted.

Vessels sailing in the gulf will be able to make out the Greek island of Simi from most locations and can use this to help navigate the area. Other notable landmarks include the modern wind farm visible on the hills to the north-east of Datça town, the bay of Yeşilova Körfezi, which can be seen on the mainland opposite Simi island, and the oddly-shaped rocky island of Dişlice Adası in the entrance to Bencik Limanı on the northern side of the gulf.

The prevailing winds funnel through the gulf from the west and tend to pick up during the day to reach force 3-4 most afternoons.

Knidos

North-west of old harbour:
36°41'.49N 27°21'.96E
Middle of harbour entrance:
36°41'.05N 27°22'.56E

At the far western end of the
Datça peninsula, the ancient
harbour of Knidos presents
an impressive first sight of
Turkey to travellers arriving
from the Greek Islands
and is still in use today by
visitors heading to the well
preserved ruins.

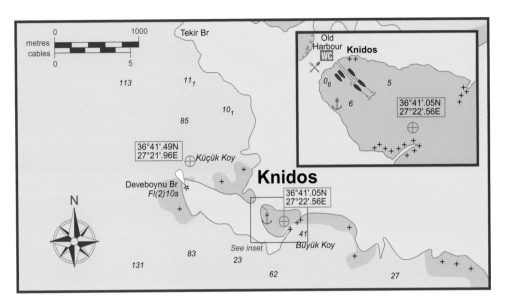

NAVIGATION
Charts: Turkish Hydrographic Charts: 311; Turkish
Hydrographic Leisure Folio 3001: 3001_1, 3001_4;
Imray Charts: G3, G35; Admiralty 1055, 1099, SC 5773

The Deveboynu Burnu headland immediately to the
west of the Knidos harbour makes a conspicuous
landmark for vessels approaching from the north and
west. The white lighthouse on top of the headland is
lit at night (Fl (2) 10s). Vessels approaching from the

south-east should be able to spot the harbour entrance
after they round Koca Burun to the south-east.

A narrow isthmus creates two harbours at Knidos;
Küçük Koy to the north and Büyük Koy to the south.
Küçük Koy is heavily silted up these days and can no
longer be used by anything larger than a small tender
or fishing boat. Büyük Koy is where visiting yachts
and gulets are able to find shelter whilst their crew and
guests explore the ruins ashore.

The entrance to the harbour is bordered by two

Büyük Koy harbour at Knidos. Note the submerged breakwater on the right-hand side of the photo

The jetty in Büyük Koy at Knidos

breakwaters; the northern one is partially submerged and can be difficult to spot if the water is choppy. Stay fairly close to the end of the southern breakwater to ensure that you pass safely between them.

BERTHING AND ANCHORING

A long T-shaped pontoon is available for visiting boats to tie up. Large boats and gulets can anchor stern-to on the T-section at the end, whilst others can tie-up side-to along either side.

Many visitors prefer to put down an anchor, and there is plenty of space either to free swing or to take a line ashore around the edge of the bay.

Useful information – Knidos

FACILITIES
Water and electricity: Available on the dock.
Ice: Ask at the restaurant.
Rubbish: Rubbish bins are located ashore.
Telephone: There is a card phone at the restaurant. Good mobile phone reception within the area.

PROVISIONING AND SERVICES
Services are very limited. Basic provisions are available from a small market at the Knidos restaurant and bread can be bought at the restaurant each morning. There are no banks, pharmacies or post offices in the area.

EATING OUT
The Aphrodite Knidos restaurant, Tel: 0252 726 1215, Mob: 0532 605 9067, is right next to the jetty and serves a variety

Ruins at Knidos

of *meze*, grilled and oven dishes and fresh fish.

ASHORE
The entrance fee to explore the ruins is 5TL per person and you can pay at a small kiosk ashore between 0830-1930. Signposts throughout the site explain what you are looking at in both Turkish and English language. Guide books are also available to purchase at the restaurant market and more information about the site can be found on page 31. Highlights include the two amphitheatres, the ancient harbour and the paved main street.

Palamutbükü

East of the harbour entrance in over 10m of water:
36°40'.13N 27°30'.36E
Southern tip of Palamutbükü Adası:
36°39'.05N 27°30'.51E

Palamut village is named after the bonito fish that are sometimes caught here by local fishermen. Although not well known amongst western tourists, the village has become a popular destination for Turkish visitors wanting to enjoy the long beach, clear waters and peaceful surroundings. It is a useful alternative to Knidos, which can get very full in the season, particularly if the *meltemi* is blowing hard. The purpose-built harbour at the western end of the beach provides shelter for those arriving by sea, and shore-based visitors are accommodated in the village's small guest houses and pensions.

NAVIGATION
Charts: Turkish Hydrographic Charts: 311, 3112; Turkish Hydrographic Leisure Folio 3001: 3001_1, 3001_4; Imray Charts: G3, G35; Admiralty 1055, 1099, SC 5773

The wide entrance to the bay has no dangers and the harbour is easily spotted at the western end of the long beach. Winds tend to blow from a westerly direction and can pick up strongly in the afternoon, creating a swell that breaks on the shingly beach, so keep well off this as you approach the harbour entrance. The island of Palamutbükü Adası is easy to identify to the south-east of the harbour. Beware of shallow waters (less than 10m) off the southern and western shores of the island.

The harbour entrance is rather narrow and you should stay close to the outer breakwater to avoid loose rocks that have tumbled from the mole extending from the beach. Depths within the harbour are 2.5-3m.

If the wind picks up from the south then it can create a swell that works directly towards the harbour entrance. Entry, therefore, should not be attempted in these conditions.

BERTHING AND ANCHORING
Visiting yachts can berth stern or bows-to with an anchor on the eastern and western sides of the harbour. There are no lazylines here. Fishing boats tend to occupy the shallow water berths nearest the beach.

In calm conditions it

Palamutbükü harbour looking towards the entrance

is possible to anchor off the beach for a lunchtime stop, but wind and swell usually pick up during the afternoon, turning this into a lee shore, so staying longer than this is not recommended.

Fees are charged for overnight mooring in the harbour, as well as for electricity and water usage. The harbour master's office is located just next to the harbour at the western end.

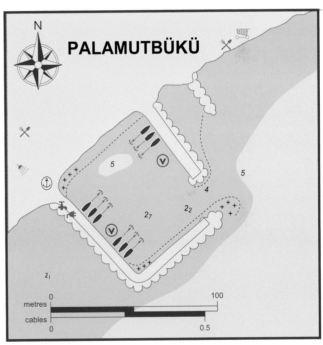

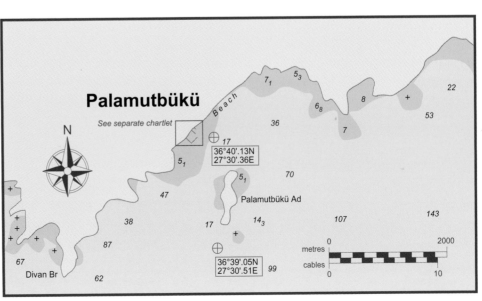

Useful information – Palamutbükü

FACILITIES
Water and electricity: Are available on the western side of the harbour.
Showers: Several restaurants near the harbour have shower and toilet facilities that can be used by visiting yacht crews. There may be a small charge for this.
Ice: Try the larger supermarkets on the outskirts of town.
Laundry: Can be dealt with via all of the restaurants mentioned below.
Rubbish: Rubbish bins are located on the eastern side of the harbour.
Telephone: There is a public phone box near the harbour and phone cards are sold at the markets in the village. Mobile phone reception here is good.
Internet: WiFi connection is available at several restaurants near the harbour.

PROVISIONING AND SERVICES
Grocery shops: You will find several small mini-markets close to the harbour and along the beach road.
Bakery: Bread can be bought at mini-markets in the village.
Butcher: Butchers, greengrocers and fishmonger shops are all located towards the eastern end of the village.
Local market: Is held on Sundays up from the beach behind the Ceylan Hotel and Restaurant.

There are no banks, post offices or pharmacies within the area.

EATING OUT
A good number of restaurants and cafés have sprung up to cater for visitors to Palamut, many of which are attached to a small hotel or guesthouse. All of the restaurants serve traditional Turkish dishes with a few international and children's options. Freshly caught fish is a local speciality – make sure that you try the Palamut (bonito) when it is in season.

The Merhaba Taverna, Tel: 0252 725 51 47, website: www.merhabapalamutbuku.com, has recently moved to a new location and offers a selection of Greek starters in addition to the usual Turkish ones.

Visit the local day tripper destinations

The Adamik restaurant and café, Tel: 0252 725 50 54, website: www.adamikrestaurant.com, is run by the owners of a bar with the same name in Bodrum and is located right next to the harbour, with facilities for yachts as well as good food.

The Dolphin restaurant, Tel: 0252 725 50 75, Mob: 0532 737 81 65, is also conveniently situated near the harbour and is run by a friendly owner who is fluent in several languages.

Other restaurants and cafés line the road that runs along the beach.

Palamutbükü businesses

ASHORE
Other than the enjoyment of eating out, there is little in the way of nightlife in Palamut village, as most visitors come here for the peaceful atmosphere and beautiful surroundings.

Although the beach is stony rather than sandy, it stretches around the bay for a good distance so there is always an uncrowded area in which to sit. The water is crystal clear so is excellent for swimming and snorkelling.

TRANSPORT
Car hire: This can be organised through some of the local restaurants.
Taxis: Ask at any of the restaurants.
Dolmuş: Regular service to Datça town.

Palamutbükü harbour

Hayıt Bükü

**(Ova Bükü,
Mesudiye Koyu)**
Middle of the bay
south of the shoal:
36°40'.91N 27°34'.52E

The sheltered bay
of Hayıt Bükü lies
approximately 4M to the
east of Palamutbükü and
10M to the west of Datça
town. It is a popular spot
for visiting yachts and a
number of restaurants have
sprung up to cater for them.

NAVIGATION

Charts: Turkish Hydrographic Charts: 311, 3112;
Turkish Hydrographic Leisure Folio 3001:
3001_1, 3001_4; Imray Charts: G3, G35; Admiralty
1055, 1099, SC 5773

The entrance to the bay is straightforward, but
yachts should be aware of a shallow area extending
south from the middle of the beach. The headland of
Adatepe Burnu lies just to the south-west of the bay
and a radio pylon on the northern side of the bay
provides a good landmark.

BERTHING AND ANCHORING

A wooden pontoon on the western side of the bay has
space for about 10 boats berthed stern-to with anchors.
There are no lazylines here. Although the pontoon was
originally built by Ogün of Ogün's Place restaurant, it is
now operated by the local belediye council and a small
fee is collected from visiting yachts.

It is also possible to anchor off the beach on the eastern
side of the bay, but shelter from the prevailing winds and
meltemi is not as good here as at the pontoon, which is
protected by the Adatepe Burnu headland.

Hayıt Bükü jetty

Useful information – Hayıt Bükü

FACILITIES

Water and electricity: Are installed on the dock.

Showers: Are provided by several restaurants ashore, including Ogun's Place right next to the jetty.

Ice: Is sometimes available from some of the mini-markets or restaurants ashore.

Laundry: Ask at Ogun's Place.

Rubbish: Rubbish bins are located near the jetty entrance.

Telephone: A public phone box is situated near the beach, and phone cards can be bought at the mini-market nearby. Mobile reception here is good.

Internet: WiFi and internet services are available from several restaurants ashore, including Ogun's Place and the Ortan restaurant and pansiyon.

PROVISIONING AND SERVICES

Services are limited in Hayıt Bükü. Basic provisions can be purchased from the Oztuk mini-market at the end of the wooden jetty.

EATING OUT

There are a few restaurants ashore where you can get mainly traditional Turkish dishes. Several of these are attached to small guest houses or pansiyon hotels for shore-based visitors to Hayıt Bükü. One of the busiest of these restaurants is Ogun's Place, located right next to the boat jetty. This is run by Ogun and his sister Semra and was one of the first restaurants in the area to trade especially for visiting yachts. As well as traditional Turkish food they offer a number of specialty dishes, including the unusual choice of spicy wild boar.

Ogun's Place can be contacted on Tel: 0252 728 00 23, Mob: 0536 572 15 07, website: www.ogunplace.com. Alternatively, try Ortam restaurant and pansiyon, Tel: 0252 728 02 28

Local businesses

ASHORE

Sun beds and umbrellas line the narrow beach close to the jetty, but there is more space further along at the quieter eastern end of the beach. The water is very clear and good for swimming and snorkelling. If you feel more active you can hire mountain bikes from Ogun's Place to explore the surrounding hillsides. A short walk over the headland to the west of the bay will bring you to another beach at Mesudiye Koyu. You can organise trips to Datça or Knidos from here if you do not have time to make the journey by boat.

The beach at Hayıt Bükü

Datça town harbour

Datça

Uzunca Adası light: 36°43'.58N 27°42'.87E
South of harbour entrance: 36°43'.29N 27°41'.31E
North bay anchorage: 36°43'.51N 27°41'.34E

The picturesque town and harbour of Datça is located towards the western end of the peninsula that bears its name. As well as offering a range of services and facilities that may not be available in some of the smaller villages nearby, Datça is also a port of entry where vessels entering or leaving Turkish waters can complete the necessary formalities.

NAVIGATION

Charts: Turkish Hydrographic Charts: 311, 3112; Turkish Hydrographic Leisure Folio 3001: 3001_1, 3001_4, 3001_7; Imray Charts: G3, G35; Admiralty 1055, 1099, 1644, SC 5773

The town of Datça nestles in an eastward-facing bay approximately two-thirds of the way along the southern side of the Datça peninsula. Vessels approaching from the east will be able to make out the white town buildings extending up the hillsides around the harbour, but vessels approaching from the west will not be able to see these until they are almost in the town. The light (Fl (3)15s) on the İnce Burun headland to the south of the town gives a good indication to vessels approaching from this

direction as to when they should alter course to head up towards the harbour. Vessels approaching from the east should stay clear of the small island of Uzunca Ada, which lies immediately east of the bay. This is lit at night (Fl R 3s).

The bay is divided in two by a small island connected to the mainland by a causeway. The main harbour and anchorage lie to the south of this, but the northern bay can also be used for anchoring.

BERTHING AND ANCHORING

The northern bay is the location of a popular beach, and approaching vessels should take care to avoid swimmers. The area adjacent to the island causeway is shallow and is accessible only for tenders, but there is plenty of room to anchor in 5-10m in the middle of the bay.

The town harbour lies on the southern side of the island and causeway. A wooden jetty has been installed around the harbour and the depth now allows most vessels to berth stern-to with an anchor along here. The prevailing winds can gust quite strongly off the hills and tend to blow across the beams of vessels using this dock. To prevent problems, ensure that you drop your anchor far enough out so that you will be able to get it well dug in as you take up the slack to prevent being blown sideways by the gusts. There is a mooring fee for using this harbour.

A concrete mole extends off the small island and encloses the northern end of the harbour, most of which

Datça harbour, with the customs dock in the background

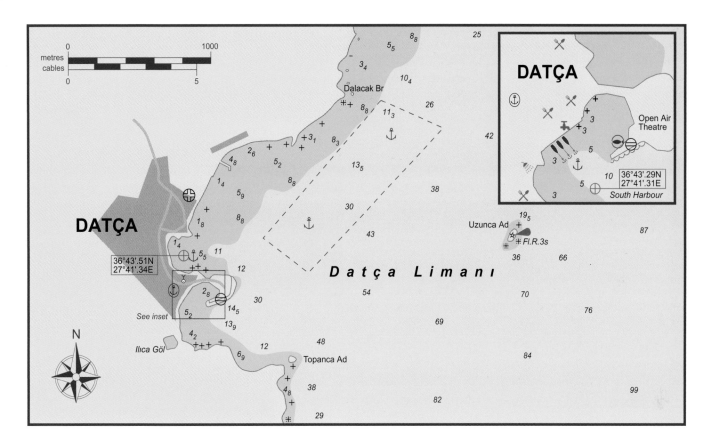

is too shallow for use by yachts and is occupied by small sports and fishing boats. The end of the concrete mole is used as a secure customs area.

The southern end of this bay can also be used for anchoring, but be careful to avoid the buoyed swimming area that extends from the beach.

FORMALITIES

The Customs and harbour master offices are located on the concrete dock at the northern end of the harbour, and all entrance and exit formalities can be completed here.

There are several yachting agencies in town that will take care of the necessary paperwork for a fee.

Useful information – Datça

FACILITIES

Water and electricity: Available from pedestals around the harbour.
Fuel: A fuel truck can be arranged through local yachting agencies.
Showers: Are provided by some restaurants and there are also public showers next to the amphitheatre.
Ice: Blocks and cubes can be bought at various supermarkets around the harbour.
Laundry: A launderette is situated near the amphitheatre.
Gas: Available from supermarkets and through yachting agencies.
Rubbish: Rubbish bins are located through the town and close to the harbour.
Telephone: Phone boxes are situated in the town,

with phone cards sold at supermarkets and kiosks. Mobile phone reception here is good.
Internet: Several internet cafés can be found in the town and WiFi is available at bars around the harbour.

PROVISIONING AND SERVICES

Grocery shops: There are numerous small to mid-sized supermarkets in the town where you can buy provisions, and many of these will be happy to deliver directly to your boat if you are purchasing a large amount. Alternatively, you can take a taxi to the large Migros supermarket just out of town on the road to Marmaris.
Bakery: Several bakeries can be found in the town,

Datça quayside

including the rather good Nokta bakery in the town centre.
Butcher: A few butchers are situated in the town centre.
Banks: Banks, with ATM machines, are located throughout the town.
Pharmacy: Several in the town.

Post office: The PTT office is in the town centre, a short walk from the harbour.

EATING OUT

There is no shortage of places to eat in Datça, with the best choice of bars, cafés and restaurants found

Useful information – Datça (continued)

around the harbour area. Seafood is of course a speciality, and some of the restaurants have upstairs terraces that overlook the harbour. One of these is the Culinarium restaurant, Tel: 0252 712 97 70, which has an interesting menu featuring specialities such as homemade ravioli.

If views are your thing then take a short taxi ride to the aptly named Panorama restaurant, Tel: 0252 712 00 44, website: www. panoramadatca.com, where you can eat good food and listen to live music on some nights whilst looking across the whole bay from the hills behind the harbour.

ASHORE

Datça is a fairly small town and has a pleasant, slightly sleepy atmosphere during the day. A number of discos and bars are located near the harbour, which can be busy and noisy during the summer until midnight or so. There are plenty of shops around which to browse close to the harbour, and two popular beaches nearby.

The amphitheatre next to the harbour is used quite regularly for musical performances. Posters advertising upcoming events are usually put up outside the amphitheatre and through the town.

Datça is the perfect place to use as a base for visiting Knidos if time constraints do not allow you to make the trip by boat. Hire a car and head out of the town in the Marmaris direction, then turn left towards the Bodrum ferry departure point at Körmen and follow the signposts to Knidos from here. The journey takes about half an hour and, although very twisty, the road is generally pretty good. You will drive through spectacular mountain scenery and pass through several small villages where honey and almond production is still a mainstay of agriculture and modern life is conspicuous by its absence.

TRANSPORT

Car hire: There are several small car and scooter hire firms in the town.

Windmills near Datça

Taxi: Taxi ranks are plentiful and located close to the harbour and throughout the town.
Coach: The otogar is situated just off the main road to Marmaris, near the big Migros supermarket. The bus companies run a shuttle service to the otogar from their ticket offices in the town centre. Most bus lines run directly to Marmaris, where you can change for other buses to İstanbul, Antalya or elsewhere.

Dolmuş: Regular services run between Datça and many of the surrounding villages to the east and west. Destinations are posted on the bus.
Ferry: A daily ferry service operates from Körmen harbour (see page 120) to Bodrum. Tickets can be purchased from the Bodrum Ferryboat Association office in town near the mosque, and a bus service runs to the ferry port half an hour before departure.

Datça

Kuruca Bükü

Anchorage: 36°45'.17N
27°53'.86E

This sheltered anchorage lies to the east of a large holiday village where the facilities are available to visiting yachts as well as land-based guests. Immediately to the west of here is another bay named Çiftlik Limanı. Anchoring is not permitted in this bay.

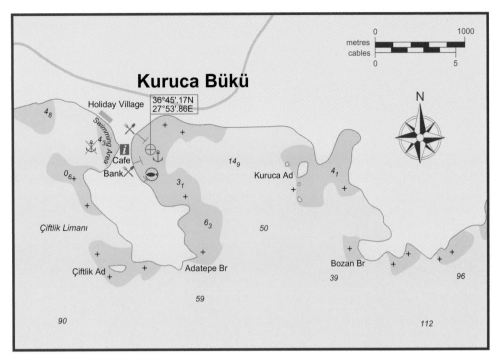

NAVIGATION

Charts: Turkish Hydrographic Charts: 311; Turkish Hydrographic Leisure Folio 3001: 3001_1, 3001_4, 3001_5; Imray Charts: G3, G35; Admiralty 1055, 1099, SC 5773

Kuruca Bükü lies approximately half way between the town of Datça and the inlet of Bencik Limanı on the northern side of Hisarönü Körfezi. The bay is easily identified by the hill on Adatepe Burnu, which divides it from Çiftlik Limanı to the west. The buildings of the holiday village can be seen along the shoreline of Çiftlik Limanı by vessels approaching from the west, but on the other side they are blended amongst the pine trees and are less visible.

There are few rocks and a small islet called Çiftlik Adası around the southern and western sides of Adatepe Burnu. As you head towards the anchorage on the eastern side you will pass an old stone tower on the east of the headland, and will also see a few small jetties extending from the beach.

ANCHORING

No docking facilities exist in this bay, but there is plenty of space to free swing at anchor in 5-10m off the long beach. If going ashore then you can tie your dinghy to one of the small jetties.

The anchorage at Kuruca Bükü

Useful information – Kuruca Bükü

Swimming jetty at Kuruca Bükü

FACILITIES
Showers: Toilet and shower facilities are provided at the campsite at the northern end of the beach as well as at the restaurant at the southern end.
Ice: May be available from the small supermarket in Çiftlik Limanı.
Rubbish: Rubbish bins are located in the campsite area.
Telephone: There are some public phones ashore and cards are sold in the small market. Mobile reception here is good.
Internet: WiFi is available at the large restaurant at the southern end of Kuruca Bükü beach and also the Vido a la Kart restaurant in Çiftlik Limanı.

PROVISIONING AND SERVICES
Grocery shops: A small market is situated within the holiday village.
Bakery: None, but bread is available from the market.
Banks: There is an İşbank branch with ATM facility near the main site office in Çiftlik Limanı.

Pharmacy: In the holiday village centre.

EATING OUT
There are two beach restaurants on the Kuruca Bükü side of the isthmus. On the Çiftlik Limanı side is the Café Mosyo and the Vido a la Kart restaurant.

ASHORE
The two bays of Çiftlik Limanı and Kuruca Bükü are separated by a sandy isthmus that leads to the hilly Adatepe Burnu headland. Most of the holiday village facilities are located on the Çiftlik Limanı side of the isthmus and can be reached easily by a five minute walk from the beach at Kuruca Bükü.

TRANSPORT
Car hire/taxis: Ask at the holiday village site office.
Dolmuş: There is a regular service to Datça. Departure times are posted in the bus station at the campsite.

Site office at the holiday village

Bencik Koyu

North-east of Dişlice Adası: 36°46'.02N 28°02'.18E

NAVIGATION

Charts: Turkish Hydrographic Charts: 311, 3113;
Turkish Hydrographic Leisure Folio 3001: 3001_1,
3001_5, 3001_9; Imray Charts: G3, G35; Admiralty 1055,
1099, SC 5773

Bencik Koyu is a narrow inlet on the north-east of
Hisarönü Körfezi. At the entrance to the bay it is easy
to identify the striking rocky island of Dişlice Adası.
It is possible to pass on both sides of this island, but
if using the western channel then stay in the middle
to avoid rocky waters to either side. A large hotel
building is conspicuous on the Kara Burun headland
to the east of this island, and you should take care
to avoid a shallow area immediately south of this
headland. The shoal waters are indicated with a
south cardinal mark.

It is not permitted to land on the eastern side of the
bay, so you should anchor with a line ashore on the
northern side at the very head of the bay. Holding
and shelter are very good here, although there are no
facilities for yachtsmen ashore.

According to the ancient Greek historian Herodotus,
the people of Knidos planned to excavate a defensive
canal between Bencik Koyu and the Gökova Körfezi,
some 800m to the north. The hard rock meant that

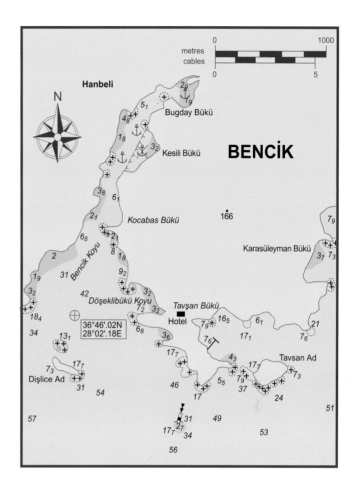

progress was very slow; even the Persian invasion of
the 6th century BC could not spur them to complete
the task and they were eventually forced to surrender.

Keçi Bükü

(Orhaniye)

Entrance to bay: 36°46'.51N 28°07'.10E
Martı Marina entrance: 36°46'.24N 28°07'.72E
West of Kızkumu beach: 36°45'.51N 28°07'.76E

This large beautiful bay is home to an established
marina, yacht charter fleets, several restaurants with
private jetties and a peaceful anchorage, so there is no
wonder that it is a much-visited destination. Fortunately
there is plenty of space so it rarely feels crowded, which
only adds to its appeal. Good road links mean it is only
about half an hour from Marmaris by car, enabling you
to take advantage of facilities there during the day and
return to a more peaceful location in the evening.

NAVIGATION

Charts: Turkish Hydrographic Charts: 311, 3113;
Turkish Hydrographic Leisure Folio 3001: 3001_1,
3001_5, 3001_9; Imray Charts: G3, G35; Admiralty 1055,
1099, SC 5773

Restaurant jetties in Keçi Bükü

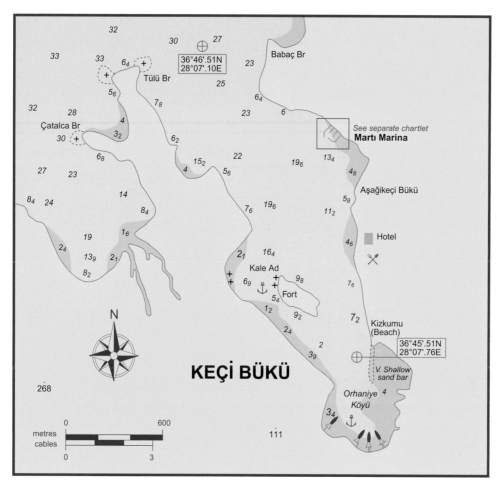

Map labels: 32 · 33 · 33 · 30 · 27 · 36°46'.51N 28°07'.10E · Babaç Br · 23 · 6₄ · Tülü Br · 25 · 5₆ · 7₈ · 6₄ · 32 · 28 · 4 · 6 · Çatalca Br · 3₂ · 6₂ · 23 · See separate chartlet · **Martı Marina** · 30 · 6₈ · 15₂ · 22 · 19₆ · 13₄ · 4₈ · 27 · 23 · 4 · 5₆ · Aşağikeçi Bükü · 8₄ · 24 · 14 · 8₄ · 5₈ · 11₂ · Hotel · 19 · 1₆ · 7₆ · 19₆ · 4₆ · 24 · 13₉ · 2₁ · 2₁ · 16₄ · 7₆ · 8₂ · Kale Ad · 9₈ · N · 6₉ · ⚓ · Fort · 5₄ · 9₂ · 7₂ · Kizkumu (Beach) · 1₂ · 36°45'.51N 28°07'.76E · 2₄ · 2 · **KEÇİ BÜKÜ** · 3₉ · V. Shallow sand bar · 268 · Orhaniye Köyü · 4 · 3₄ · ⚓ · metres · cables · 0 · 600 · 0 · 3 · 111

Two large waterside hotels are visible on the headland just to the west of the entrance to Keçi Bükü, and as you round this point the masts of boats moored at Martı Marina should start to become visible.

As you head south into the bay you will pass the marina to port, and to starboard you will see a small island with the remains of a Byzantine fort. When you reach the head of the bay you should take care to avoid the very shallow sand bar that stretches most of the way across. The depths shelve sharply as you approach this, and the deep water is indicated by a line of small buoys. These are not lit so a night approach any further than Marti Marina is not recommended.

Martı Marina

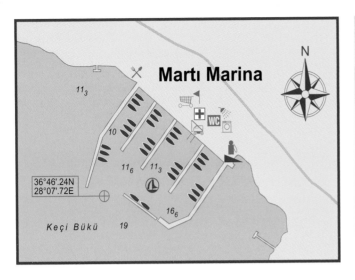

Kız Kumu beach restaurant

BERTHING AND ANCHORING

At the end of the bay are several restaurants with private jetties for the use of their customers. Berthing is stern-to with lazylines and is free for customers.

Martı Marina is a well-equipped facility that has been awarded a Blue Flag for environmental standards. Both stern-to and alongside berthing are available and lazylines are installed on the five floating pontoons. Advance booking is advisable, particularly if you plan an extended stay, and you should call the marina ahead of your arrival on VHF Ch 16 or 73 so that staff there can give berthing instructions and offer assistance if necessary. Marti Marina can also be contacted on Tel: (0252) 487 10 63/64/65/67, Mob: 0533 746 75 99, Fax: (0252) 487 10 66, website:www.martimarina.com

If you prefer to anchor off then you can do so on the western side of the small island in the bay. It is possible to enter this anchorage from both the north and the south but be aware that the depths decrease sharply to around 3m in the middle, so it is best to go out the way you came in. This anchorage is suitable for overnight as well as daytime stops, and there is usually room to free swing. If it is busy you may need to take a line ashore.

You may also see some boats anchored behind the sand bar, although this is advisable only for shallow draught vessels. To reach this spot you should go around the southern end of the bar near to the Palmiye jetty and then make your way up the inside, keeping a close eye on the depth.

Useful information – Keçi Bükü (Orhaniye)

FACILITIES

Water and electricity: Are available at all of the restaurant jetties and at all berths in Martı Marina.

Fuel: Can be obtained from the fuel dock at Martı Marina.

Showers: Toilet and shower facilities at Martı Marina, plus all of the restaurants with jetties.

Ice: Can usually be bought at the supermarket in Martı Marina and may be available from some of the restaurants in the bay.

Laundry: Facilities provided at Martı Marina and also at some of the restaurants in the bay.

Gas: Gas bottles can be exchanged at Martı Marina.

Rubbish: Rubbish bins in Martı Marina are segregated for recycling and there are special places to dispose of oil waste. Rubbish bins are also situated at each of the restaurant jetties.

Telephone: Public phones are available at Martı Marina and also in the car park at İskele restaurant. Phone cards can be purchased in the marina shop and at the mini-market near İskele restaurant. The mobile phone reception is good.

Internet: Martı Marina has an internet terminal in the marina office and WiFi available throughout the marina.

YACHT SERVICES AND CHANDLERY

Martı Marina has a 60 ton travel lift but only limited space for hard standing. Boatyard services are offered by several of the marina's tenants, including Yachting Line technical services and Gino Marine.

There is a small chandlery located within the marina's mini-market shop.

The Orhaniye Marine Market is situated along the road at the southern end of the bay and has a range of chandlery items either in stock or available to order. The staff speak good English here and will do their best to source anything you require.

PROVISIONING AND SERVICES

Grocery shops: There is a small mini-market between İskele and Kadır restaurants at the head of the bay, where you can buy basic provisions and supplies, including ice. A better choice can be found at the Martı Marina supermarket.

Bakery: None, but bread is available from the mini-market and restaurants in the bay as well as from the supermarket in Martı Marina.

Butcher: None, but some frozen meat can be bought at the Martı Marina supermarket.

Local market: Is held on Saturdays along the road at the southern end of the bay.

Post office: There is no post office, but the marina reception is happy to hold mail for guests or to send and receive faxes.

There are no banks or pharmacies nearby.

Free facilities at local restaurants

Useful information – Keçi Bükü (Orhaniye – continued)

İskele restaurant

EATING OUT
If you are staying at Martı Marina then you have a choice of eating at the marina restaurant, which has lovely views across the marina from its upstairs seating area, or at either of the restaurants next door. Club Mistral Restaurant has a selection of Thai and Far Eastern dishes to choose from as well as the more usual menu offerings. Fanari Restaurant specialises in freshly caught fish.

ASHORE
The Kız Kumu beach bar at the top of the sand spit is popular with visitors from Marmaris and other nearby resorts, who tend to flash through as a stop on a daily tour around the area. If you have a bit more time to spare, it is quite fun to walk out into the bay along the sand spit. The water does not really get above knee height but it is advisable to wear some shoes as the sand is sharp and uncomfortable to walk on. The bar also offers sun loungers and nearby are stalls selling clothing and souvenirs.

If you take your dinghy over to the small island in the bay you can climb up to explore the Byzantine ruins on top. More ruins can be found in the hills behind the village of Orhaniye, which is approximately 2km inland from the bay.

If you want to use this area as a base from which to explore the surrounding region, then you can arrange to hire a car or scooter from Alien Travel at Martı Marina. Nearby sites of interest include the waterfalls and Carpet Village at Turgutköy, and the charming hillside village of Bayır. The scenery along the Hisarönü peninsula is fantastic, and although the roads can be twisty, they are good enough to make exploring the area a pleasurable rather than a stressful experience.

Alien Travel can also organise a range of tours to take you further afield if you want to, including trips to Ephesus, Pamukkale and Rhodes. For something a little more local contact the local Carpet Weavers' Association to join one of its special tours. You will learn all about the various processes of manufacturing the natural yarns and dyes and see how the different types of carpet are woven and knotted by hand on traditional looms.

Club Mistral is located just next to Martı Marina and guests are welcome to make use of all its facilities, which include sunbathing decks, a pool and an excellent restaurant that often has live music in the evenings. Although it can get a bit crowded at the weekends, during the week this is a beautiful place to enjoy a change of pace for the day.

TRANSPORT
Car hire: Alien Travel, Tel: 0252 487 13 88, Mob: 0532 739 16 06, Fax: 0252 487 10 04, website: www.alientourism. com, has an office in Martı Marina and can rent cars and mopeds by the day as well as organise excursions and airport transfers.
Taxis: Ask at the marina reception or any of the restaurants in the bay.
Dolmuş: A regular service operates between Keçi Bükü and Marmaris and continues around the peninsula to Bozburun, Selimiye and Soğut.
Air travel: The nearest airport is Dalaman International, approximately 2 hours away by taxi.

USEFUL INFORMATION
Yachting Line Technical Services: Tel/Fax: 0252 487 11 30; Mob: 0533 324 21 92; website: www. yachtingline.com
Gino Group Brokerage and Technical Services: Tel: 0252 487 14 06; Fax: 0252 487 14 07; website: www.ginogroup.com
Club Mistral: Tel: 0252 487 13 66/71; Fax: 0252 487 10 66; website: www.mistral-marmaris.com
Turgutkoy Carpet Weavers' Association: Tel: 0252 486 81 37/27; Fax: 0252 486 80 94.
Orhaniye Marine Market: Tel: 0252 487 11 74; website: www. orhaniyemarine.com

Kadır restaurant

Selimiye Koyu looking to the north

Selimiye Koyu

Entrance to bay: 36°44'.14N 28°04'.99E
North of the harbour: 36°42'.60N 28°05'.61E

The small hamlet of Selimiye sits at the bottom of a large double bay located between Orhaniye and Bozburun on the Hisarönü peninsula. Like other villages nearby, Selimiye is home to a local wooden ship-building tradition and you may spot the odd half-finished vessel in small boatyards close to the shore. The town quay has been refurbished in the last couple of years and with the good choice of restaurants it makes this a popular spot for yachts.

NAVIGATION

Charts: Turkish Hydrographic Charts: 311, 3113; Turkish Hydrographic Leisure Folio 3001: 3001_1,

3001_5, 3001_9; Imray Charts: G3, G35; Admiralty 1055, 1099, SC 5773

The entrance to both Selimiye Koyu and Delikliyol Koyu faces to the west. Vessels approaching from this direction should try to identify the larger island of Kameriye Adası to the west of the entrance and the

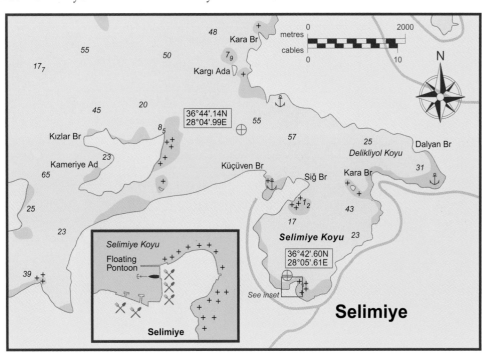

smaller one of Kargı Adası to the north. The entrance
to the two bays is deep and free of dangers. Delikliyol
Koyu lies to the north of the Kara Burun headland,
whilst Selimiye Koyu heads off to the south.

A small headland divides Selimiye Koyu in two, with
the town quay and village buildings lying to the west
and a couple of private jetties to the east. Stay towards
the centre of the bay as you approach the village to
avoid the shallow areas close to the shore on either side.
In particular there is a shoal area of less than 2m just to
the south of the Sığ Burun headland on the west side of
the entrance to Selimiye Koyu. This is indicated by an
isolated danger mark.

BERTHING AND ANCHORING

A new floating wooden pontoon with lazylines has
been installed to the north of the town harbour,
increasing the amount of berthing space available in
this popular port. The wooden walkway extends along
the eastern side of the harbour, and you will need to

The new jetty in Selimiye

Selimiye restaurant jetty

northern side of Sığ Burun, to the west of the entrance
to Selimiye Koyu. In calm weather it is possible to
anchor at the far end of Delikliyol Koyu, but usually
this is exposed to the prevailing winds and swell.

use your anchor to go stern-to here. Both of these areas
are looked after by the local belediye and there is a
small fee for berthing here, which includes the use of
electricity and water points as well as rubbish disposal.

On the southern side of the harbour are a few
restaurants with private jetties, some of which
have lazylines. They do not charge a fee but you
will be expected to make use of the restaurant facilities
if you stay here.

On the eastern side of the bay are a few more private
jetties belonging to a couple of restaurants and a spa
resort. These are mainly used for sunbathing and as
dinghy docks, and do not seem suitable for overnight
berthing, but it may be okay to tie up for a few hours
over lunch in fine weather.

There is a small bay where you can anchor on the

The local boat-building industry is alive and well

Useful information – Selimiye Koyu

FACILITIES

Water and electricity: Are installed on the town dock and some restaurant docks.

Showers: Available in some restaurants around the harbour.

Ice: Can be bought at the village markets.

Laundry: Some of the restaurants such as Aurora, see below, offer a laundry service.

Gas: Try some of the small markets in the village.

Rubbish: Rubbish bins along the quay.

Telephone: Phone boxes are located around the harbour and cards are available from village markets. Mobile reception here is good.

Internet: WiFi is provided in a few of the restaurants.

PROVISIONING AND SERVICES

There are a few small mini-markets around the town quay providing basic provisions. The only other service is a bakery on the south side of the harbour.

EATING OUT

For such a small village Selimiye certainly has a wide choice of restaurants, many of which have a good reputation amongst local Turks who will drive out from Marmaris and beyond all through the year to visit here. Fresh fish is the speciality in most of the restaurants and several of them also offer a variety of *meze* starters.

The well-established Sardunya restaurant, Tel: 0252 446 40 03, is open year round and has a very good reputation. Aurora, Tel: 0252 446 40 97, is a more recent arrival and has an excellent choice of *mezes*. It also has a shady courtyard dining area where you can keep cool during the heat of the summer. Both of these are on the southern side of the harbour and have their own jetties.

Osman's Place, Mob: 0537 225 01 00, website: www.osmansplaceselimiye.com, is right next to the new floating pontoon and is long-established with the sailing community. Osman is the owner of the restaurant and is famous for his set of gold teeth.

There are plenty of other attractive looking restaurants around the harbour, and if you walk out to the headland to the east you will find a couple more here in an unbeatable location, surrounded by water on three sides. The far eastern side of the bay is probably a bit further than most people will want to walk for a meal, but if you make it this far both the Vakana Beach Hotel and Deniz restaurants have long jetties extending into the bay and beach-front dining.

ASHORE

The village of Selimiye is little more than a road running around the bay with a cluster of buildings encircling the harbour. But the surrounding area is beautiful and many of the restaurant owners and locals will be happy to help you explore it. Osman (of the gold teeth) can help organise trips to visit the nearby carpet village, waterfalls and hillside village of Bayır.

TRANSPORT

Dolmuş: The service from Marmaris to Bozburun passes through Selimiye in both directions.

Air travel: The nearest airport is Dalaman, approximately 2½ hours away.

USEFUL INFORMATION

Local tel code: Muğla area, 0252, Selimiye 446.

Medical: Doctors, dentists and hospitals can all be found in both Marmaris and Datça.

Selimiye restaurant

Kocabahçe Bükü

Entrance to bay: 36°42'.23N 28°00'.73E

NAVIGATION

Charts: Turkish Hydrographic Charts: 311, 3113;Turkish Hydrographic Leisure Folio 3001: 3001_1, 3001_5; Imray Charts: G3, G35; Admiralty 1055, 1099, SC 5773

This small bay lies approximately 1.5M to the east of Dirsek Bükü, immediately south of the channel between Koca Ada and Uzun Adası. The Sailor's Paradise restaurant, Mob: 0536 717 17 72, has a small T-shaped jetty with lazylines and several mooring buoys on either side of the bay. Staff at the restaurant will help you to tie up against their dock, or will take a line ashore for you if you anchor or use their moorings. They can also pick you up from your boat and bring you ashore for dinner if asked. Toilets are available ashore, but there is no water or electricity on the dock.

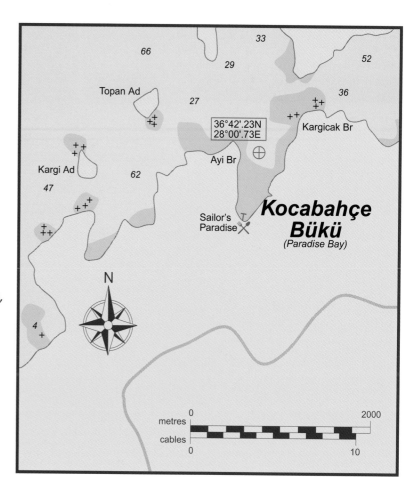

Dirsek Bükü

Entrance to bay: 36°41'.46N 27°58'.89E

NAVIGATION

Charts: Turkish Hydrographic Charts: 311, 3113; Turkish Hydrographic Leisure Folio 3001: 3001_1, 3001_5; Imray Charts: G3, G35; Admiralty 1055, 1099, SC 5773

Dirsek is a deep bay on the north-east of the Atabol Burnu headland. It is not particularly easy to spot the entrance against the hilly background, but it lies to the south-west of Kargı Adası, which is the westernmost of the chain of islands between Dirsek and Selimiye.

The Dirsek restaurant, Mob: 0532 394 00 01, has a small jetty in the south-west end of the bay where yachts can berth stern-to using lazylines, and also has a few mooring buoys. Those preferring to anchor can do so in the two small coves to the east of the restaurant jetty, and should take a line ashore if staying for the night. The bay offers good shelter from the prevailing winds and is a very peaceful and attractive location with no access by road. Toilets are available at the restaurant, which also sells fresh bread in the mornings. There are no water or electricity supplies here for boats.

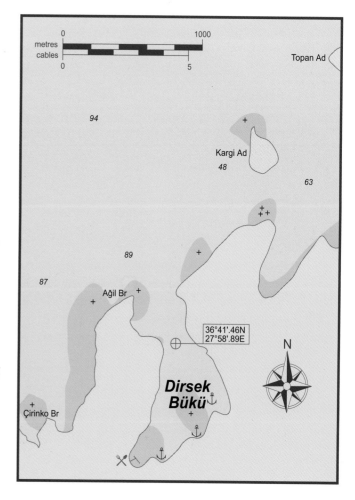

Bozburun

Entrance to Yeşilova Körfezi:
36°38'.64N 27°59'.18E
Between Kızıl Ada and Zeytin
Adası: 36°39'.11N 28°02'.91E
Entrance to Bozburun bay:
36°40'.51N 28°02'.63E
Harbour entrance: 36°41'.32N
28°02'.50E

The small town of
Bozburun is the largest on
the Bozburun peninsula
and combines a sleepy
atmosphere with a good
range of facilities for visiting
yachts. It is a well-protected
harbour and there are plenty
of attractive anchorages in
the surrounding area.

NAVIGATION

Charts: Turkish
Hydrographic Charts: 311,
3113; Turkish Hydrographic
Leisure Folio 3001: 3001_1,
3001_5, 3001_10; Imray Charts: G3, G35;
Admiralty 236, 1055, 1099, SC 5773

The approach to Bozburun is through Yeşilova Körfezi.
Vessels coming from the north will have to round the

headland of Atabol Burnu. The Atabol Kayası
is a shallow reef lying south-west of the headland.
It is marked with an isolated danger mark that is lit
at night (Fl (2) 5s). It is possible to pass between
the rock and the headland, but this should only be

Bozburun harbour

Bozburun mosque and quay

pass to either side of the small islet called Yeşil Ada, which lies to the south of Bozburun harbour.

The entrance to Bozburun harbour is lit on either side. The mosque is conspicuous to starboard as you approach the entrance.

BERTHING AND ANCHORING

A long concrete quay runs along the eastern side of the bay as you approach the harbour. There may be space to berth stern-to along here with an anchor, although it is usually busy with gulets and there is better shelter to be found within the harbour.

The harbour is quite large and has room for yachts to tie up stern-to with an anchor along the east and west sides, as well as side-to along the northern quay.

A couple of hotels along the eastern shore as you approach Bozburun have small jetties for yachts to anchor at.

Those preferring to anchor can do so in 5-10m of water off the beach to the west of the harbour, or there are a few anchorages in the approach to the town harbour. A small bay on the eastern side of Kızıl Ada has space for several boats to anchor with a line ashore. It is also possible to anchor between Kızıl Ada and Kiseli Adası, where you will find protection from the rocky shoals that lie to the west of here. Another sheltered bight in the mainland exists just north of Kiseli Adası.

attempted in calm conditions when you can see the reef that you are trying to avoid. Otherwise it is safer to stay further out and ensure that you pass to the outside of the danger area.

The approach to Bozburun town itself is from the south past the island of Kızıl Ada. Although you may see what looks like clear passage to the north of this island between it and the mainland and the smaller island of Kiseli Adası, do not try to approach the town through this gap as it is shallow and rocky and can become dangerous to boats with the *meltemi* winds pushing rough water across it. Beware also of shallow waters extending to the west of Zeytin Adası. You can

Useful information – Bozburun

FACILITIES
Water and electricity: Are installed on the town dock.
Fuel: Available by fuel tanker. There is an unused fuel station at the north-west end of the harbour.
Showers: Available at several restaurants ashore.
Ice: Sold at supermarkets in the town.
Laundry: A service is offered at Akvaryum restaurant, near the harbour.
Gas: Available from supermarkets ashore.
Rubbish: Rubbish bins are located ashore.
Telephone: Public phones in the town and phone cards can be bought from markets and kiosks. Mobile reception here is good.
Internet: There is an internet café near the mosque. WiFi connection is provided by many of the restaurants.

YACHT SERVICES AND CHANDLERY
Ilhan Ticaret near the mosque stocks some

yacht spares, Tel: 0252 456 24 45. Bozburun is an important centre for the local ship-building industry, and there is a large yard in the bay to the south-east of the town, opposite Kızıl Ada.

PROVISIONING AND SERVICES
Grocery shops: There are several supermarkets in the town that offer a provisioning service to boats.
Bakery: Bread is available from the supermarkets in the town and also from the Ocean pastry shop near the mosque.
Butcher: Several can be found in the town.
Pharmacy: A few are situated in the town.
Post office: The PTT office is next to the mosque.

EATING OUT
There are several restaurants in Bozburun, both close to the harbour

and along the eastern side of the bay. Menus are mainly of traditional Turkish dishes.
Akvaryum restaurant, Tel: 0252 456 20 62, Mob: 0546 23 45 65, is right next to the harbour and offers various services to visiting yachts. Aphrodite hotel and restaurant, Tel: 0252 456 22 68, website: www. hotelaphrodite.com, is along the eastern shore as you approach the harbour and has a small jetty for yachts to use. Sabrina's Haus, Tel: 0252 456 20 45, Mob: 0549 310 66 77, website: www.sabrinashaus. com, is a small restaurant and boutique hotel that is renowned for excellent food and atmosphere. It is located along the eastern side of the bay as you approach the harbour. Call ahead to book a table for the evening and someone will come to collect you by boat from the harbour.

ASHORE
Bozburun has a laid back atmosphere that is in stark contrast with some of the larger resort towns in this area. There are several carpet and souvenir shops in the town where you can browse freely with no pressure to buy.

TRANSPORT
Taxis: Available in the town or ask at one of the restaurants.
Dolmuş: Services to Marmaris depart from the harbour several times a day.

USEFUL INFORMATION
Local tel code: Muğla area, 0252, Bozburun, 456.
Medical: The nearest medical facilities are in Marmaris.

Söğüt Limanı

Middle of bay: 36°38'.87N
28°04'.77E

Söğüt Limanı is a large bay
within Yeşilova Körfezi,
lying to the south-east of
Bozburun. The surrounding
pine-clad hillsides shelve
steeply into deep blue
waters, making for a striking
location. The village of
Söğüt is nestled in the hills
a kilometre or so away from
the sea and there is a large
gulet-building yard in the
bay just to the west of where
the two restaurant jetties
are located.

Söğüt Limanı

NAVIGATION

Charts: Turkish Hydrographic Charts: 311, 3113;
Turkish Hydrographic Leisure Folio 3001: 3001_1,
3001_5, 3001_10; Imray Charts: G3, G35; Admiralty 236,
1055, 1099, SC 5773

Vessels entering Söğüt Limanı should do so directly
from the south, leaving Söğüt Adası to port. Do not

Traditional boat-building in Söğüt

attempt to pass between
Söğüt Adası and the
mainland as this passage
is shallow and rocky.
Apart from this the
approach to the harbour
is free of dangers.

BERTHING AND ANCHORING

There are two private
restaurant jetties in Söğüt
Limanı, with local fishing
boats lining the area in
between. Berthing is free
provided you use the
restaurant facilities.

If you prefer to anchor
then you can do so on the
western side of the bay in
a small cove. It is advisable
to take a line ashore here if
you plan to spend the night.

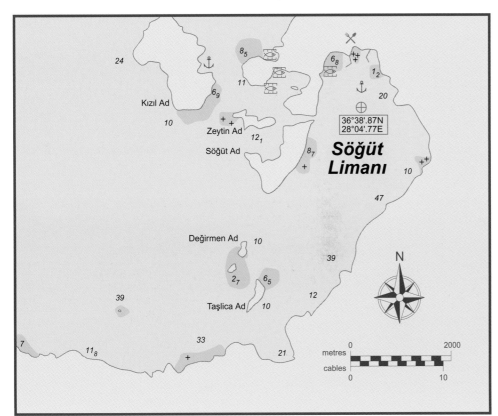

Useful information – Söğüt Limanı

A mini-market near the harbour

FACILITIES
Water and electricity: Available on the Aşkın restaurant pontoon.
Showers: Available at both restaurants – see below.
Ice: May be sold at either of the mini-markets or at the restaurants.
Rubbish: Bins are ashore.
Telephone: None, but the mobile phone reception here is good.

PROVISIONING AND SERVICES
Grocery shops: There is a small mini-market next to the Aşkın restaurant. The Uçan supermarket is located approximately 200m along the only road leading away from the shore. Here you can get everything from blocks of ice to Turkish carpets.
Bakery: Available from the two mini-markets near the harbour.
Local market: If you are in the bay on a Monday and fancy a walk, there is a weekly market in the centre of Söğüt village.
Pharmacy: You will find a pharmacy and a post office only in Söğüt village.

EATING OUT
There are two restaurants at the harbour in Söğüt Limanı. Aşkın restaurant, Tel: 0252 496 50 47/93, website: www.askinmotel.com, is the more established of the two and also has a small pansiyon hotel on the beach next door. The Captain's Table restaurant, Tel: 0252 496 50 78, is run by Sahli and his family, and is just along the beach from Aşkın.

ASHORE
Take your dinghy across to explore some ancient ruins in the cove on the western side of the bay. Alternatively, you can take a walk up to the village centre (about 45 minutes to an hour), which is in the hills behind the harbour. You will find a mosque, a couple of restaurants and a small shop here. Many of the buildings around this area are attractively built in a traditional stone construction.

TRANSPORT
Taxis: Ask at either of the restaurants.
Bus: A dolmuş service operates between Söğüt village and Marmaris, but you will have a long walk up to the village to catch the bus.

Söğüt restaurant

Dramatic scenery around Söğüt

Söğüt fishing boats

Bozuk Bükü

Entrance to bay: 36°33'.80N 28°01'.23E

Bozuk Bükü lies at the southern tip of the Bozburun peninsula and is the location of the ancient fortified settlement of Loryma. Excavations in the area are on going and remnants of the 3,000 year old Dorian settlement surround the bay, which is overlooked by the impressive and remarkably well-preserved citadel that sits atop the headland commanding the entrance to the bay. There is no access to the area by road, and it has a timeless quality, remote and isolated, even though these days it has some amenities for visiting yachts.

NAVIGATION

Charts: Turkish Hydrographic Charts: 311; Turkish Hydrographic Leisure Folio 3001: 3001_1, 3001_5; Imray Charts: G3, G35; Admiralty 236, 1055, 1099, SC 5773

The twin islets of Çatal Adaları lie just to the east of the entrance to Bozuk Bükü. Yachts approaching from this direction may pass between the two islets, staying closer to the northernmost one, but should not attempt to pass between the islands and the mainland as this passage is very shallow and full of surfacing rocks.

An isolated rock lies just off the tip of the eastern side of the entrance to the bay. Be sure to give this a wide berth as depths shelve sharply in this area. The bay can be easily identified by the remains of the ancient citadel which overlook the entrance from the western headland.

View from the citadel towards the restaurants in the bay

If you prefer to swing on your own anchor then there is plenty of room to do this in the middle of the bay in 10-15m of water. Another option is to anchor in the north-west corner of the bay and take a line ashore to prevent swinging.

BERTHING AND ANCHORING

There are now three restaurants in the bay, each with private jetties and mooring buoys available for their customers. The restaurant staff will assist you in either picking up one of their moorings and taking a line ashore, or in berthing on their jetty using a lazyline.

Despite the prevailing north-westerly winds, an occasional surge can penetrate into the bay, so you should make sure that your lazyline is well secured and that the boat is pulled a good boarding plank's length away from the dock when you tie up.

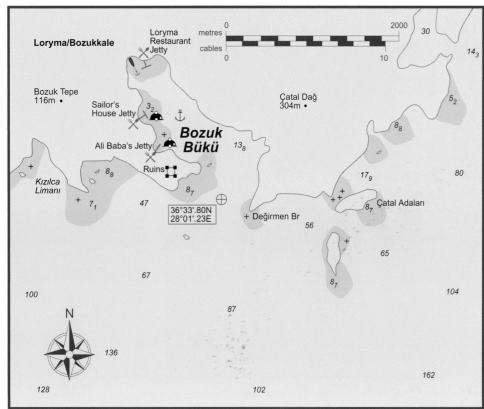

Useful information – Bozuk Bükü

A friendly donkey

The citadel

Traditional bread oven

FACILITIES

With no access by road, Bozuk Bükü feels very remote and has facilities to match. All electricity comes from generators, so there is none spare for yachts to use and water is similarly limited. Although the restaurant owners would probably agree to take rubbish off your boat for you, there are no disposal facilities here so it must be transported elsewhere for collection. It is better to keep it with you for an extra day and dispose of it yourself.

PROVISIONING AND SERVICES

None, but basics such as bread and milk may be available from the restaurants.

EATING OUT

There are three restaurants in Bozuk Bükü, each offering simply prepared yet delicious Turkish food in a rustic setting. You won't get a gourmet menu or wide variety of dishes, but you can still expect to have a great meal in unbeatable surroundings.

Ali Baba's restaurant, Mob: 0536 423 51 76, has a prime position on the western side of the bay directly beneath the citadel. It is easy to miss when you arrive in the bay, but the small dock here probably offers the best shelter of the three available. The location is also the most convenient for walking up to explore the ruins above.

In the next cove along the bay is the Sailor's House restaurant, Mob: 0536 448 63 39, which is also known as Coban Ali's. This is run by the energetic Mustafa and has the largest jetty of the three in the bay. It is a slightly longer walk across to the citadel from here, but Mustafa will be quite happy to either guide you around the headland over rocky tracks or to run you across by boat.

The Loryma restaurant, Mob: 0538 743 29 35, occupies the small beach at the head of the bay and is surrounded by ruined remains of the ancient settlement. It is a long trek to the citadel from here, but the restaurant owners can arrange to take you around by boat and there is plenty to explore closer to hand.

ASHORE

The big attraction in Bozuk Bükü is exploring the remains of ancient Loryma, either up at the hilltop citadel or close to the beaches on the western and northern sides of the bay. The ground is rough and rocky and there are no paths, so you will need a decent pair of shoes for walking. The best time to do this is in the early evening, when the sun is starting to lose its heat and the evening breezes pick up. You may also meet a few goats and donkeys wandering around the hillsides.

The water in the bay is crystal clear and great for swimming and snorkelling. With no nearby towns to provide light pollution, the sky is magnificent for star gazing at night time.

Serçe Limanı

Entrance to bay: 36°34'.59N 28°03'.12E

Charts: Turkish Hydrographic Charts: 311;
Turkish Hydrographic Leisure Folio 3001: 3001_1,
3001_5; Imray Charts: G3, G35; Admiralty 236, 1055,
1099, SC 5773

Serçe Limanı is a very sheltered bay lying approximately
2M to the east of Bozuk Bükü. Yachts approaching
from the west should take care to avoid the shallows
between Çatal Adaları and the mainland as described
on page 147.

The entrance to the bay is sometimes quite hard to
pick out, especially if you are approaching from the
west, but it can be recognised by steep cliffs on the
southern side of the gap. The water is shallower
around this southern side, so it is best to stay north as
you enter the bay.

Once through the entrance you have the choice of
turning to either the north or south. At both ends of the
bay are small restaurants that maintain mooring buoys
for their customers. Restaurant staff will be on hand to
pass you the mooring line and then take a rope ashore
to prevent you swinging in the limited space available.

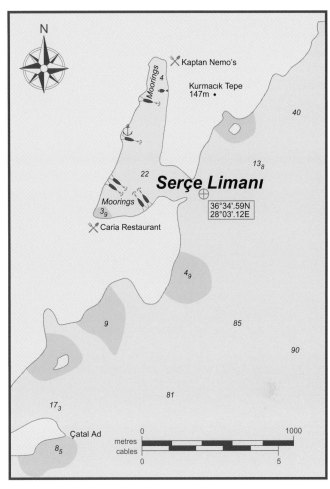

View from Serçe Limanı looking out through the entrance

If you prefer to use your own anchor then there is
space to do so in a few coves and indents around the
edge of the bay. You should drop your anchor in 5-10m
of water and take a line ashore. As the prevailing winds
are funnelled through the bay from the north this is
particularly important if you plan to stay overnight.
Apart from this the bay offers excellent shelter in all but
strong southerly conditions, which can push a swell
through the narrow entrance.

The two restaurants are Caria restaurant in the
southern part of the bay and Kaptan Nemo's, Mob: 0533
213 08 02, in the northern part. This second restaurant
is well established and is usually rather busier than
Caria as there is also road access to this part of the bay

(although not to the southern end). Both restaurants
serve village style Turkish dishes and a *meze* selection.
There are usually several local fishing boats moored in
the shallows near Kaptan Nemo's, so you can be sure
that the catch of the day is fresh!

Little is available in terms of provisions and services
in Serçe Limanı, but the stunning surroundings and
tranquil atmosphere more than make up for that.

Mooring assistance is always available!

Gerbekse
Entrance to bay: 36°42'.19N 28°13'.97E

Charts: Turkish Hydrographic Charts: 311;
Turkish Hydrographic Leisure Folio 3001: 3001_1,
3001_5; Imray Charts: G3, G35, G36; Admiralty 236,
1055, 1099, SC 5773

Ruins on the shoreline

Gerbekse anchorage

This beautiful bay lies approximately 1M to the west
of Çiftlik Adası and is a great place to visit for a swim
during the day or take shelter for an overnight stay.
It is a popular daytime stop for gulets and day cruises
from Marmaris but in the evening you have a good
chance of getting the place to yourself.

The bay is protected to the west and south
by a low headland, and the entrance to the bay
faces directly towards the gap between Çiftlik
Adası and the mainland, so is fairly easy to
spot if you are coming from this direction.

Head into the bay and drop
anchor in 5-10m of water.
There should be plenty of
room to swing if you are just
stopping for a few hours
during the day, although it
is best to take a line ashore
and dig the anchor well in
for security if you plan on
spending the night here.

The water is crystal clear
and excellent for snorkelling,
with plenty of fish to look at.
If you venture ashore you
can explore some ruined
buildings, including an old
church that is supposed to
grant a blessing of fertility
on those who visit it (so be
warned!). An enterprising
lad from nearby Çiftlik often
comes around to the bay in
his small boat and makes
himself useful to visiting
gulets and day tripper boats
by offering to take their lines
ashore when they anchor.

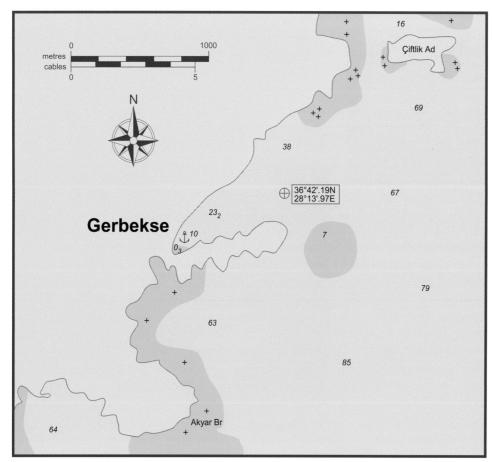

Çiftlik Bükü

Southern entrance: 36°42'.56N 28°14'.53E
Eastern entrance: 36°42'.85N 28°14'.93E

This attractive bay lies to the south of Marmaris and approximately 2.5M south-west of the Kadırga Burnu headland. A privately-owned island, Çiftlik Adası is situated in the entrance to the bay, and private dwellings can be glimpsed amongst the trees and shrubs as you sail past.

NAVIGATION
Charts: Turkish Hydrographic Charts: 311, 312, 3121; Turkish Hydrographic Leisure Folio 3001: 3001_1, 3001_5; Imray Charts: G3, G35, G36; Admiralty 236, 1054, 1055, 1099, SC 5773

It can be quite hard to spot the entrance to Çiftlik Bükü, particularly if you are approaching from the west. As you approach the waypoints the large building of the

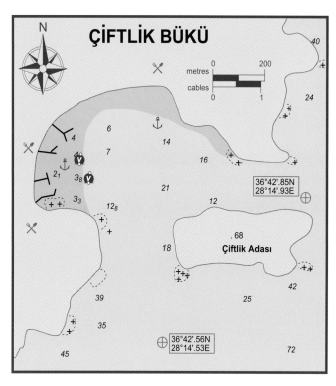

Çiftlik restaurant jetties

Green Platan hotel should become visible in the bay behind Çiftlik Adası. It is possible to pass to either side of the island as you enter the bay.

BERTHING AND ANCHORING
There are several private jetties in the bay, each belonging to one of the restaurants ashore. Visiting yachts are welcome to tie up and staff run to the end of their jetties, slapping their lazylines on the water to call you in as you approach. They are also ready to help you tie up appropriately when you arrive. Berthing is generally free provided you eat in the restaurant and use its facilities.

If you prefer to swing free at anchor there is good shelter under the northern side of the bay, but keep clear of the buoyed powerboat corridor and swimming area off the Green Platan hotel beach. There can be strong gusts off the surrounding hillsides, so make sure that your anchor is dug in well.

Çiftlik Adası

Useful information – Çiftlik Bükü

Deniz restaurant in Çiftlik

Chill out in a hammock at Mehmet's Place

FACILITIES
Fresh water and **electricity** are available to boats berthed on any of the restaurant jetties and there are **rubbish** bins ashore. **Toilets** and hot **showers** are also available at the restaurants for their customers. **WiFi** and **internet** services are provided at Alarga Sail Yacht Club (see below), Deniz restaurant, Tel: 0252 485 70 92, Mob: 0536 243 35 79, Rafet Baba restaurant, Tel: 0252 485 71 37, Mob: 0533 566 60 69, and the Green Platan hotel (see below).

PROVISIONING AND SERVICES
Basic provisions are available from small **mini-markets** at the Rafet Baba and Deniz restaurants on the beach. For fun shopping there is a clothing and souvenir boutique just by the creek behind the beach near the Deniz restaurant.

EATING OUT
Çiftlik Bükü offers a good choice of places to eat as there are two hotels and three separate restaurants here. Mehmet's Place, Deniz Restaurant and Rafet Baba are all family run affairs

and provide simple food in relaxed surroundings very close to the water. *Meze* selections and fresh seafood are the specialities, and some of the restaurants have large fish tanks from which you can choose your dinner. The Marin restaurant at the Green Platan hotel (see below) is open to visitors from outside and offers a variety of international dishes as well as the usual Turkish menu.

ASHORE
The Alarga Sail Yacht Club and Boutique Hotel, Tel: 0252 485 72 55, website: www.alargasail.com, at the southern end of the bay, has recently reopened under new management after being closed for two years. Guests using their docking facilities are also welcome to use the attractive hotel pool, bar and restaurant areas. They plan to have live music at least once a week, but it is a little noisy if you moor too close.

At the other end of the bay is the Green Platan Club Hotel and Spa, Tel: 0252 485 70 31, website: www. platanhtels.com, which offers a full range of spa and massage treatments as well as having a *hamam* and sauna. Although the hotel complex is an all-inclusive resort patrolled by security guards, non-guests are welcome to use the facilities for a fee. Besides the spa and thalassotherapy centre (spa treatments involving seawater or other ocean related substances), there is a ladies' hairdresser and men's barber, swimming pools with three water slides, a children's play area and night-time disco and bars. Watersports are available from its beach, including waterskiing, ringos and banana rides.

USEFUL INFORMATION
Medical: There is a doctor available at the Green Platan Hotel.
Su-Na Wellness Centre: website: www.sunsahealth. com (at Green Platan Hotel).

Mehmet and his garden

Kadırga Limanı

Kadırga anchorage: 36°44'.03N 28°17'.80E

Off Kadırga point: 36°43'.71N 28°18'.30E

Charts: Turkish Hydrographic Charts: 311, 312, 3121; Turkish Hydrographic Leisure Folio 3001: 3001_1, 3001_5; Imray Charts: G3, G35, G36; Admiralty 236, 1054, 1055, 1099, SC 5773

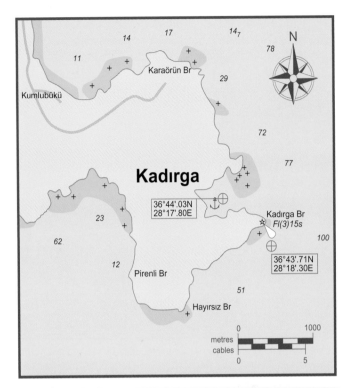

Kadırga Limanı is an indented bay located immediately north of Kadırga Burnu. This headland can be easily recognised by the conspicuous light structure on it (Fl (3) 15s).

Winds are often confused around the headland, which acts as a shield for vessels passing very close in but can accelerate winds either from the north or west towards yachts sailing further out.

A submerged rock is visible on the northern side of the entrance to the bay. Keep a sharp look-out for it and give it a wide berth as you enter or leave from this direction.

Once you are inside the bay you can usually find a sheltered spot from whichever direction the wind is blowing. Because of its proximity to Marmaris, Kadırga is very popular with the daily cruises, gulets and private boats that are based there. However, although it can get a bit crowded, you can always find some space and it is a convenient place to stop for a break on the way in or out of Marmaris. In the evenings it is much quieter after most of the boats have returned to harbour. The water here is clean and clear, and there are plenty of rocks around the edge of the bay to provide interesting snorkelling. Keep your eye-out for the ice-cream man in his modified speed boat.

Anyone for ice-cream?

The light structure on Kadırga Burnu

Kumlubükü Maris Beach Hotel jetty and moorings

Kumlubükü

Middle of bay: 36°45'.17N 28°16'.34E

Kumlubükü, meaning sandy bay, is rather a misnomer as the beach is actually fairly stony with some coarse grey sand at the northern end. Don't let that put you off, however, as it is a delightful spot located conveniently close to Marmaris. This makes it a popular destination for day trippers and equally well suited for those looking for a short leg on the first or last day of a cruise starting in Marmaris.

NAVIGATION

Charts: Turkish Hydrographic Charts: 311, 312, 3121; Turkish Hydrographic Leisure Folio 3001: 3001_1, 3001_5, 3001_11; Imray Charts: G3, G35, G36; Admiralty 236, 1054, 1055, 1099, SC 5773

The wide entrance to the bay poses no dangers and the large buildings of a private resort can clearly be seen towards the northern side of the bay as you draw near. The depths shelve gently towards the beach, allowing you to approach safely from any direction.

The bay is open to the north, which means that prevailing winds can sometimes push a swell into here causing it to become uncomfortable. The Yacht Club jetty at the southern end of the bay probably gets the worst of this, but the lazylines seem to be quite secure as long as you pull them up tight when berthing. The cliffs on the northern side of the bay offer best protection from this swell, which usually dies down during the night.

BERTHING AND ANCHORING

As well as a number of small private jetties, there are several restaurants in the bay which provide berthing facilities for visiting boats.

Kumlubükü

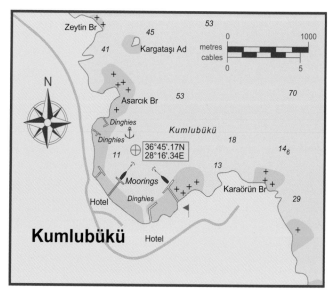

Kumlubükü Yacht Club, at the southern end of the bay, has a large T-shaped jetty with lazyline berths along the end as well as a couple of alongside berths closer to the shore. The jetty is quite high so take care when berthing.

Just north of this is the Maris Beach Restaurant, which has a smaller jetty and several mooring buoys available to visitors.

In the northern side of the bay is another large jetty opposite the Villa Florya Hotel and Restaurant, and just up from here are several moorings laid by the Dedem Restaurant.

Apart from a buoyed watersports lane immediately opposite the Villa Florya Hotel, it is possible to anchor in 5-10m of water anywhere along the beach and there is plenty of room to free swing. If you are planning to stay overnight, it is best to tuck right up behind the cliffs at the northern end of the bay as this offers the best protection from any swell that works its way in.

Kumlubükü Yacht Club jetty

Useful information – Kumlubükü

Relax in style

FACILITIES
Fresh water and 220v **electricity** are provided from pedestals on both the Yacht Club and Villa Florya jetties. **Shower** and **toilet** facilities are available to customers at any of the restaurants along the beach.

All of the restaurants have **rubbish disposal** facilities and there are a few bins located about half way along the beach as well.

PROVISIONING AND SERVICES
There are no shops in Kumlubükü, so you will need to visit one of the towns around Marmaris for any provisioning or spares.

EATING OUT
There are several small hotels along the beach at Kumlubükü, and non-guests are welcome to use the hotel restaurants if they wish. Most serve a selection of Turkish and International dishes, with the notable exception of the Kumlubükü Yacht Club, Tel: 0252 476 72 42/59, website: www.kumlubukuyachtclub.com, which offers a full Chinese menu prepared on site by a Chinese chef. It can be more expensive than others but also makes a welcome break from the fairly similar menus that you will find in most places, particularly for sailors nearing the end of their trip in Marmaris.

ASHORE
Although the beach may not be particularly striking, most of the beach restaurants have rows of sun beds which can be used by guests who want to relax in the sun. The water is crystal clear and is ideal for swimming, diving and snorkelling, although there is not much to see on the bottom. Some of the restaurants also have swimming pools that guests can use.

If you feel more active then watersports, including jetski hire, banana and ringo rides, waterskiing and pedalo hire, are available from the jetties at Marbükü restaurant and the Villa Florya Hotel.

During the daytime the bay is a popular spot for the day tripper boats operating from Marmaris, İçmeler and Turunç. The watersports craft collect clients directly from these boats and will come over to your boat if you call them. An enterprising local has also fitted a freezer into his small motorboat and will call on boats at anchor to sell them ice-creams and cold drinks.

Sizzling succulents

Turunç Bükü

Middle of bay: 36°46'.53N 28°15'.16E

The village of Turunç is situated in a bay immediately south of the entrance to Marmaris Limanı. In recent years the road connecting the village to Marmaris has been improved and the village has become more popular as a holiday destination with foreign tourists, but it still manages to remain largely unspoilt. The village has a small harbour where visiting boats can moor during the day or overnight.

NAVIGATION

Charts: Turkish Hydrographic Charts: 311, 312, 3121; Turkish Hydrographic Leisure Folio 3001: 3001_1, 3001_5, 3001_11; Imray Charts: G3, G35, G36; Admiralty 236, 1054, 1055, 1099, 1644, SC 5773

The bay of Turunç Bükü lies approximately 2M south of the entrance to Marmaris Limanı, and the approach is straightforward and free of dangers. The village buildings extend up the hillsides from the harbour and are visible as you approach, along with the minaret of the village mosque, which is conspicuous in the centre of the beach. A funicular railway servicing one of the hotels can be seen on the northern hillside.

There is a line of yellow marker buoys extending from the beach on the northern side of the bay, indicating an underwater cable. If you are approaching from the south then keep clear of the rock lying just off the headland at the southern end of the bay. The first bay past this headland is the location of a hotel complex with buoyed swimming area. The village harbour is just to the north of here.

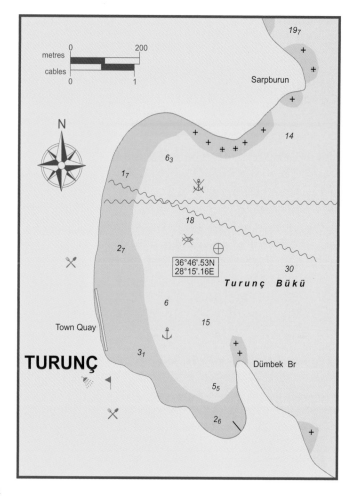

BERTHING AND ANCHORING

The harbour has space for quite a few boats to anchor stern-to. Most of the quay is occupied with local fishing boats and day tripper boats, but there is usually space for several visiting boats to anchor in between the local ones. The quay is quite exposed to winds blowing from the north out of Marmaris Limanı, but this breeze usually dies off by the early evening and is not a problem overnight.

It is also possible to anchor in the bay, but be sure to leave space for day tripper boats returning to the village quay, and stay clear of buoyed swimming areas and the yellow marker buoys in the northern part of the bay.

Turunç Yacht Club restaurant

Yellow special marker buoys in the northern part of the bay

Turunç village

Useful information – Turunç Bükü

FACILITIES
Water: Available on the dock.
Ice: From mini-markets in the village.
Gas: Available from mini-markets and the Aygaz shop in the village.
Rubbish: Rubbish bins behind the village quay.
Telephone: Public phone boxes and phone cards available in the village. Good mobile phone reception.
Internet: The Turunç Internet Café is located on the village's main street.

YACHT SERVICES AND CHANDLERY
Available in Marmaris, see page 163.

PROVISIONING AND SERVICES
Grocery shops: There is a Dia supermarket and a couple of other mini-markets in the village where you can buy basic provisions and fresh bread.

Local market: Held on Mondays.
Banks: There are no bank branches in the village, but there are a few ATM machines where you can withdraw currency, including one right on the village quay.
Pharmacy: In the main street of the village.
Post office: A small PTT office is just off the main street at the northern end.

EATING OUT
There are several restaurants in Turunç, mostly along the seafront or in the village main street, which serve Turkish and international cuisine in very agreeable surroundings. A number of restaurants are situated close to the harbour, including a Chinese restaurant, Çardak restaurant and Körfez restaurant. The Turunç Yacht Club restaurant, which is located above the harbour, has a pool and

pleasant gardens, and offers wonderful views across the harbour and village.

ASHORE
There is not a great deal to see or do whilst you are in Turunç, which is a large part of the attraction for many of the visitors who hope to escape the hustle and crowds in other resorts such as Marmaris and Bodrum. If you are visiting by boat then you do not need to make use of the water taxi services, although this can be a nice solution if you are collecting or depositing crew and prefer to stay away from the hectic atmosphere of Marmaris.

Various excursions, such as jeep safaris and horse riding, can be organised through travel agencies in Turunç, and there is also a local company that specialises in eco-tourism and outdoor activities, including kayaking, rafting

and scuba-diving, Tel: 0252 476 76 06, website: www.ecoraft.com

TRANSPORT
Car hire: Car rental is available through some of the estate and travel agencies in the village.
Taxis: There is a taxi rank just behind the main street in the village.
Dolmuş: Several services each day to Marmaris centre and İçmeler.
Ferry: None, but water taxis are available during the summer months from the town quay to İçmeler and Marmaris.
Air travel: The nearest airport is Dalaman.

USEFUL INFORMATION
Local tel code: Muğla area, 0252, Turunç 476.
Medical: See Marmaris, page 168.

İçmeler

Middle of bay: 36°48'.27N 28°14'.20E

İçmeler is located on the western side of Marmaris Limanı. As a resort it has developed separately from its larger neighbour and is the site of higher-end hotels and apartments compared with the mass appeal of Marmaris. Although the resort has evolved quickly in the last few years, the old part of the village still exists and has retained some of its charm. The resort has a less frenetic atmosphere than neighbouring Marmaris and tends to attract a different kind of visitor.

NAVIGATION

Charts: Turkish Hydrographic Charts: 311, 312, 3121; Turkish Hydrographic Leisure Folio 3001: 3001_1, 3001_5, 3001_11; Imray Charts: G3, G35, G36; Admiralty 236, 1054, 1055, 1099, 1644, SC 5773

İçmeler lies to the west of Keçi Adası and can be approached from either side of this island. A large unfinished hotel development is visible on the shore opposite the southern end of Keçi Adası, and there is a small islet and several rocks just in front of here that you should take care to avoid as you approach. There are also a few rocks in the waters around the western end of Keçi Adası, but they are all visible and apart from these the approach is straightforward. Strong gusts in the afternoon *meltemi* blow from İçmeler and the direction can be very confused in the entrance channel.

BERTHING AND ANCHORING

The town harbour is at the southern end of the long sandy beach backed by hotels and apartment complexes. A round light-structure is conspicuous at the end of the dock, and a new jetty extends from here. A certain amount of renovation has been done in the past few years, and although much of the harbour is occupied by local fishing and excursion boats, there is usually room for visiting yachts to tie up towards the end of the jetty.

Berthing is stern-to with an anchor rather than lazylines. The prevailing winds blow off the hills to the north so make sure your anchor is well set if you plan to spend the night here. Harbour fees will be charged.

View from İçmeler towards Marmaris

Useful information – İçmeler

FACILITIES

Water and electricity: Available on the dock.

Showers: Toilet and shower facilities have been constructed in the harbour area.

Ice: Can be bought in the village.

Laundry: A launderette, Tel: 0252 455 24 23, is situated near the PTT office.

Gas: Can be obtained from mini-markets and gas company offices in the village.

Rubbish: Rubbish bins are located in the car park next to the harbour.

Telephone: Several public phone boxes are situated throughout the village, with cards sold in mini-markets and souvenir shops. Mobile phone reception here is good.

Internet: There are a few internet cafés in the village, and some of the restaurants and cafés along the beach also offer WiFi connection to their clients.

YACHT SERVICES AND CHANDLERY

Available in Marmaris, see page 163.

PROVISIONING AND SERVICES

Grocery shops: There are a couple of mid-sized supermarkets in the village, including Dia and Tansaş. Basic provisions are also available from the many mini-markets throughout the village.

Bakery: A bakery and a butcher are situated in the village.

Local market: Is held on Wednesdays in the market area next to the main road from Marmaris.

Banks: All of the major Turkish banks have branches in İçmeler where you can withdraw money and change currency. ATM machines are plentiful, both within the town and along the beachfront.

Pharmacy: Several pharmacies can be found in the village.

Post office: There is a small PTT office towards the back of İçmeler close to the main road to Marmaris.

EATING OUT

İçmeler has plenty of restaurants which are mainly located along the beachfront and in the few streets behind. Many of these are billed as so-called 'fun pubs', meaning loud disco music, mediocre food and 'entertaining' waiters. However, if this is not your thing there are also several other options, including a number of Chinese, Indian and Italian restaurants if you fancy a change from Turkish cuisine. The Taj Mahal restaurant is a well-established subsidiary of the main restaurant in Marmaris, Tel: 0252 455 45 80. The Cavaliere restaurant, Tel: 0252 455 41 53, is located next to the Laguna Hotel at the north end of the beach and has a good Italian menu. For excellent Turkish cuisine served in traditional surroundings look for the Kerem restaurant situated next to the canal and opposite the Kanarya Hotel. Main courses and *meze* are home-cooked to traditional recipes, and be sure to leave room for the baked cheesecake dessert. Seating is limited in this ottoman-style house, so it may be necessary to reserve a table earlier in the evening. Tel: 0252 455 48 69.

ASHORE

İçmeler does not have a bazaar area, but there is no shortage of shops selling clothing, jewellery, handbags, DVDs and much more. A collection of stalls that stock local handcrafts and other items runs along the sides of the canal, which stretches inland from the middle of the beachfront.

The same kinds of trips and excursions are available from İçmeler as from Marmaris, and there are a number of dive schools that offer tuition and diving trips from boats based within the harbour.

The beach in İçmeler is more attractive than the one in Marmaris; wider, sandier and less crowded, and is a pleasant place to while away a few hours in the sun. There are a number of watersports companies where you can try your hand at waterskiing and parasailing or enjoy being towed on a variety of inflatables.

TRANSPORT

Car hire: You will discover a selection of travel and car rental agencies in İçmeler, all of which are very easy to find in the streets behind the beachfront.

Taxis: Several taxi ranks are situated along the beachfront and within the village, including one near the harbour area.

Dolmuş: İçmeler dolmuş buses are coloured orange and run every 10 minutes or so from the village centre to Marmaris Tansaş.

Coach: The otogar is located next to the main road and the various coach companies have ticket offices here. You can also buy tickets from travel agencies in the village centre.

Ferry: None, although water taxis are available to Marmaris and Turunç.

Air travel: The nearest airport is at Dalaman.

USEFUL INFORMATION

Local tel code: Muğla area, 0252, İçmeler 455.

Medical: The Ahu Poliklinik private health clinic with emergency service is located next to the main road and near the PTT office, Tel: 0252 455 38 68/31 39. For hospitals see Marmaris on page 168.

Lighthouse in İçmeler harbour

Marmaris town quay, with the castle in the background

Marmaris Limanı

South of entrance light: 36°47'.78N 28°15'.68E
Between Netsel entrance and town dock:
36°51'.06N 28°16'.60E
North-east of Yacht Marina: 36°49'.26N 28°18'.64E
South-west of Pupa jetty: 36°49'.64N 28°18'.61E
West of Albatros entrance: 36°50'.63N 28°17'.11E

Marmaris Limanı is a natural harbour that is one of Turkey's biggest yachting centres and a major tourist destination.

NAVIGATION

Charts: Turkish Hydrographic Charts: 311, 312, 3121; Turkish Hydrographic Leisure Folio 3001: 3001_1, 3001_5, 3001_11; Imray Charts: G3, G35, G36; Admiralty 236, 1054, 1055, 1099, 1644, SC 5773

Vessels approach Marmaris Limanı through Dış Limanı, which lies to the south. The 402m peak of Yıldız Adası island is conspicuous, and the smaller Keçi Adası is situated immediately west of here. Vessels must pass to the west of Yıldız Adası, but can pass to either side of Keçi Adası. Beware of strong gusts blowing from the direction of İçmeler as you head through this channel. There are lights on the southern tip of Keçi Adası (Fl R 2s) and on the north-west tip of Yıldız Adası (Fl 3s).

The harbour and resort of İçmeler lie to the west of Keçi Adası (see page 158), and the resort town of Marmaris stretches along the long beach on the north-west side of Marmaris Limanı. An aquapark is visible on the hillsides above the town roughly half way along the beach, and the town harbour and marina are at the far eastern end of the town. As you near the town quay you get a sight of the ancient castle standing over the town, at which point the marina wall and rows of gulets come into sight.

BERTHING AND ANCHORING

The town dock

The town dock runs west from the marina around the base of the castle hill and up to the start of the long beach. Most of this dock is occupied by the local gulet, day tripper and charter boat fleet, particularly during the busy weekend turnaround periods. However, visiting yachts are welcome to tie up here if there is space and the harbour master will call by to collect his fees. Berthing is stern-to with an anchor.

Anchorages within Marmaris Limanı

Vessels can free swing in 5-10m along the beach to the west of the old town and also in the vicinity of the Pupa Yacht Hotel between Albatros Marina and Marmaris Yacht Marina. Beware that the buoys near Albatros Marina are laid in very shallow water. It is also possible to anchor on the northern side of Yıldız Adası, opposite

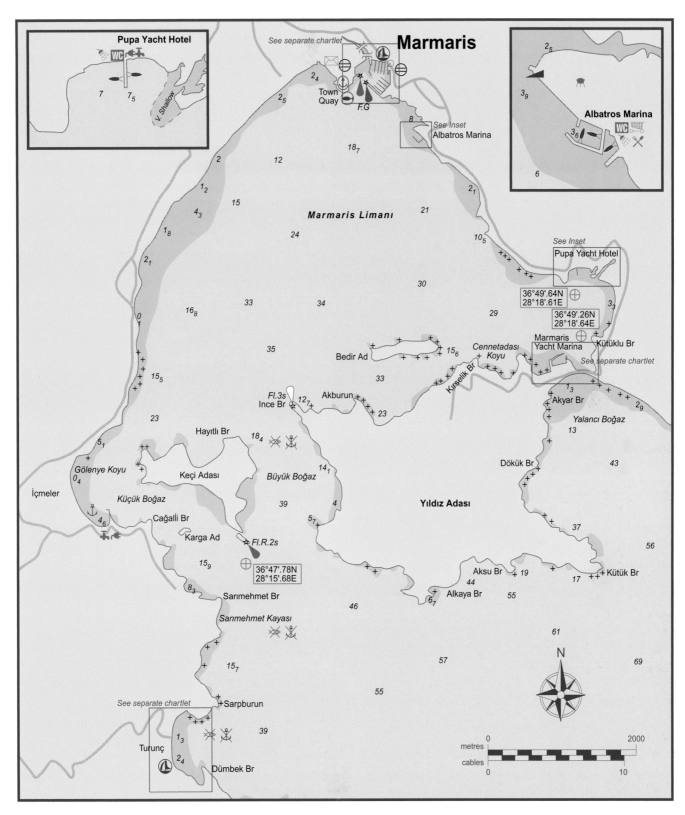

Pupa Yacht Hotel

See separate chartlet

Marmaris

Town Quay

F.G

8

See Inset
Albatros Marina

18₇

Marmaris Limanı

2₄

2₅

2

1₂

15

4₃

1₈

12

24

2₁

21

21

10₅

See Inset
Pupa Yacht Hotel

36°49'.64N
28°18'.61E

36°49'.26N
28°18'.64E

3₃

33

34

30

16₈

29

Marmaris
Yacht Marina

Kütüklu Br

See separate chartlet

35

Bedir Ad

15₆

Cennetadası
Koyu

1₃

Akyar Br

2₉

33

Kırselik Br

Akburun

23

Yalancı Boğaz

13

0₁

15₅

23

Fl.3s
Ince Br

12₇

Dökük Br

43

Hayıtlı Br

18₄

5₁

Gölenye Koyu

0₄

Keçi Adası

Büyük Boğaz

14₁

Yıldız Adası

37

İçmeler

Küçük Boğaz

39

4

56

4₆

Cağalli Br

5₇

Karga Ad

Fl.R.2s

Aksu Br

19

17

Kütük Br

15₉

44

Alkaya Br

55

36°47'.78N
28°15'.68E

8₃

6₇

Sarımehmet Br

46

61

Sarımehmet Kayası

57

57

69

N

55

15₇

See separate chartlet

Sarpburun

39

metres   0   2000

Turunç

1₃

2₄

cables   0   10

Dümbek Br

the smaller island of Bedir Adası, and in various other coves along the northern side of this island.

Marmaris Netsel Marina
Netsel Marina is Marmaris' city centre marina and is long established in its location at the eastern end of the town dock. The marina has in-water berthing for around 750 vessels up to 40m in length, as well as two travel lifts and a hard standing area. All berthing is stern-to with lazylines, and the marina attendants will assist with berthing procedures. You should call the marina on VHF Ch 06 for instructions as you approach. The marina can also be contacted on Tel: 252 412 27 08, Fax: 252 412 53 51, email: info@netselmarina.com, website: www.netselmarina.com

Facilities include water and electricity at every berth, toilets and showers for visitors and a fuel dock at the entrance to the marina. Domestic waste bins, segregated recycling and waste oil disposal services are all on hand. There is an internet terminal in the reception

Marmaris Netsel marina, with the town quay and castle area on the right of the picture

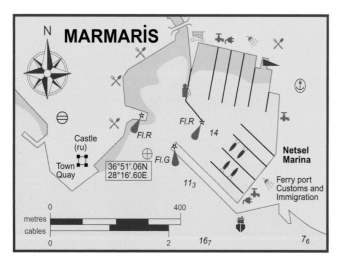

boats will be out with clients, resulting in more space for visiting yachts. The marina can be contacted on Tel: 252 412 34 30, Fax: 252 412 07 55, email: info@offshore-sailing.net, website: www.offshore-sailing.net

Water, electricity and fuel are available at every berth, and there are shower and toilet facilities ashore. The marina also has WiFi coverage, public card phones, a small provisioning and souvenir shop and an excellent restaurant that offers regular barbecues and other events.

office, WiFi is available all over the marina and public phones can be found in the marina shopping centre. A swimming pool is located within the marina, but you have to pay a small charge for using this, and the shopping mall linked to the marina incorporates some attractive shops and restaurants.

Albatros Marina

Albatros Marina is situated a mile or so along the coast to the south-east of Netsel Marina (see inset on page 161). It is operated and managed by Offshore Sailing. The marina has space for around 80 boats, mostly in stern-to berths with lazylines. It is busiest at the weekends, but during the week many of the charter

Albatros Marina

Pupa Yacht Hotel and Marina

This small development lies between the Albatros and Marmaris Yacht Marinas (see inset on page 161), and consists of just one jetty with stern-to berthing and lazylines along either side for about 30 yachts. Electricity and water are provided free of charge, as are toilet and shower facilities. Internet access is available in the office as well as phone and fax services.

You can contact the marina on VHF Ch 72 as you approach or for more information call Tel: 0242 413 18 53, Fax: 0252 413 48 99, email: marmaris@pupa.com.tr, website: www.pupa.com.tr

Marmaris Yacht Marina

Marmaris Yacht Marina is a large marina and boatyard complex situated on the narrow spit of land that connects Yıldız Adası with the mainland. This area is known as Yalancı Boğaz, which translates as false channel, and although there appears to be passage past the island here, it is closed by a narrow spit of land. Yacht Marina has berthing space available for up to 630 vessels and you should call them to request a berth on VHF Ch 72 or 73 as you approach. The marina can also be contacted on Tel: 252 422 00 22/54, Fax: 252 422 00 49, email: info@yatmarin.com, website: www.yatmarin.com

Facilities include metered water and electricity at every berth, toilets and showers ashore and WiFi coverage in the marina. Additional services comprise a library, fitness centre, pool and hairdressers.

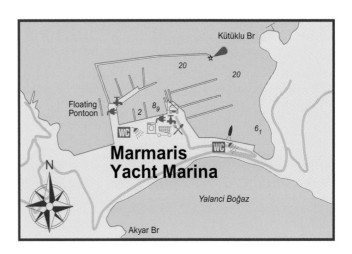

Marmaris Yacht Marina

FORMALITIES

Marmaris is a port of entry to Turkey where all vessel formalities can be completed. Transit logs are purchased from the Chamber of Shipping office, which is situated upstairs in a building next to the canal between Netsel Marina and the sports centre. The customs patrol, coastal health office and immigration offices are all located within the customs area at the ferry port next to Netsel Marina. The harbour master's office can be found on the waterfront of Kordon Cadessi, close to the Tourism Information office.

If you are staying down in Marmaris Yacht Marina then there is a customs agent based here who can complete all formalities on your behalf for a fee.

Useful information – Marmaris Limanı

Türk Telkom public phones

FACILITIES

Ice: Is available from many of the mini-markets and supermarkets mentioned below.
Laundry: Yacht Marina has its own laundry service for guests, and the Marina Laundry Service in Netsel Marina will collect from and deliver to your boat free of charge. Neither of these offer dry cleaning, but this is available from the Mavı Beyaz laundry service just on the other side of the canal from Netsel Marina.
Gas: Gas bottles can be purchased from the chandlery in Yacht Marina

and from various locations in the streets behind Netsel Marina.
Telephone: Public phones are located throughout the covered bazaar and harbour areas in Marmaris – in particular there is a large bank of them near the PTT office.
Internet: Many of the bars, cafés and restaurants within Netsel Marina and around the harbour offer WiFi connection to their clients. There are also plenty of small internet cafés in the narrow streets around the covered bazaar area.

YACHT SERVICES AND CHANDLERY

Marmaris is the major yachting centre along this section of coast and is a popular winter location for many private and charter boats that have cruised

the Turkish coast during the summer. Accordingly there are many technical operators and tradesmen who have started up businesses to cater for all these boats. As always, the best recommendation is word of mouth, and you will usually be able to tap into the local 'yachtie' network to find out who is the best person to approach for a particular job.

Marmaris Yacht Marina has the largest boatyard facility in the area, with three travel lifts of 50, 70 and 330 tons, purpose-built cradles for storage and a huge hard standing area that can accommodate several hundred boats, with water and electricity available throughout. The marina is always packed during the winter, with a crowded yard that is

Useful information – Marmaris Limanı (continued)

Albatros Marina boatyard and travel lift

organised very much on a 'first out-last in' basis. Try to confirm your winter booking as far in advance as possible, as most years both the marina and boatyard are full to capacity.

Netsel Marina also has two travel lifts of 30 tons and 100 tons, and storage ashore for around 130 boats. This marina is the base for several charter companies, which do most of their hauling out in the month before the start of the season, so it may be worth bearing this in mind if you plan to lift your boat out here.

Albatros Marina has a small boatyard with a 20 ton travel lift and space for 50 or so boats. Again the boatyard is busy prior to the start of the season with the Offshore charter boats, but they are happy to lift out and work on private boats as well. The marina has a small but good technical team, which

covers Jeanneau warranty work for the local dealer and has an excellent carpentry workshop amongst other things. Members of the team are also happy to take on private work when they can fit it into their schedule and can be contacted through the marina office.

Marmaris Yacht Marina has a number of tenant businesses that cover pretty much all trades between them and will also take on project management for larger yachts and motor cruisers. Outside contractors are allowed to enter the marina and work, but they will be charged a daily fee that is likely to be passed on to the customer. The marina office maintains a very useful 'yellow pages' directory that is full of recommendations and suggestions made by marina residents, and is a useful place to check the reputation of the tradesman

or company that you are planning to employ.

Netsel Marina has a small workshop area in the boatyard, which may be enlarged in the coming years to allow more businesses to set up shop within the marina itself. In the meantime though, outside contractors are welcome to work on boats within the marina, providing they have the correct insurance. Many of these companies have premises either in the streets behind the boat park and sports centre or in the sanayi industrial area on the way to the suburb of Beldebi.

There are several large companies that will take on almost any kind of work and organise it through either their own staff or trusted local contractors. Examples of these are below, and there are many other smaller companies with equally good credentials:

Gino Marine (based in Netsel Marina) Tel: 0252 412 06 76, Fax: 0252 412 20 66, email: info@ginogroup.com, website: www.ginogroup.com
Technical Marine Service (based in Yacht Marina) Tel: 0252 413 07 95, Mob: 0532 276 47 91, email: tms-marmaris@gmx.de, website: www.tms-marmaris.com

For **sail-making**, repairs and servicing or canvas work there are several companies that will visit your boat to make the appropriate measurements and give advice first:
Doyle Sailmakers (based close to Netsel Marina) Tel: 0252 413 67 39, Fax: 0252 412 11 23, email: nihat@doyleturkey.com, website: www.doylesails.com
Moby Sails (distributors for Elvstrom and located in the sanayi area) Tel: 0252 419 23 51, Fax: 0252 419 23 52, email: info@mobymarina.com.tr,

Useful information – Marmaris Limanı (continued)

PTT post office

website: www.mobymarine.com.tr
Hood Sail and Service (based in Netsel Marina) Tel: 0252 413 08 38, Fax: 025 412 06 89, email: sailservicehood@superonline.com, website: www.hood-sails.com

Yacht Marina has its own well-stocked **chandlery** shop where you can buy a variety of useful products such as charts and clothing, paints and resins, plumbing and electrical spares, mechanical parts, cordage and general yacht equipment. The helpful staff are happy to place orders for specific items as well.

In Marmaris town there are a number of chandlery stores in the area to either side of the small canal behind Netsel Marina. English is spoken in most (but not all!) of these shops, and if they do not have the item you are looking for they are generally quite happy to order it or to suggest another supplier that might. Anfora (stocks general spares but especially paints and antifoulings) Tel: 0252 413 00 96, email: anforayachting@superonline.com, website: www.yatmalzemeleri.com
Alev (general chandlery)

Tel: 0252 41217 12, email: alevyat@superonline.com, website: www.alevyacht.com Atlantis/Bosun's Locker (general chandlery) Tel: 0252 413 06 78, email: atlantis@atlantismarin.com, website: www.atlantismarin.com Marlin (service agents for Yanmar and also stocks a wide variety of mechanical spares) Tel: 0252 412 14 41, email: info@marlin.com.tr, website: www.marlin.com.tr

PROVISIONING AND SERVICES

Grocery shops: There is a small mini-market in Albatros Marina where you can get the majority of essential provisions. Yacht Marina has a large supermarket that stocks most things you could require, and Netsel Marina has a small Migros supermarket which sells all the basics. The most convenient large supermarket nearby is the Tansaş superstore located in the town centre. A large Migros store is situated about two-thirds of the way along the beachfront road, and a Kipa (Tesco) hypermarket can be found on the main road heading out of town towards Datça. Both of these require a taxi or dolmuş (bus) journey to reach them. For everyday shopping there are a large number of smaller supermarkets (Pehlivanoğlu, Dia, Soğutlu) as well as a host of mini-markets located all around the covered bazaar and old town area. Many of these stores will deliver large purchases to your yacht if asked.
Bakery: There are several bakers as well as butchers, green grocers and fishmongers in the streets around the covered bazaar area.
Local market: The main market day is a Thursday and it is held in a specially-built covered market that you reach by walking down the G Mustafa Muğlalı street behind Tansaş. The

ground floor is for produce and the top floor is for clothing and textiles. A produce-only market is also held here on Sundays. The Sunday market in the suburb of Beldibi can be reached by dolmuş, as can the Wednesday market in İçmeler (see page 159).
Banks: Most of the bank branches in Marmaris are located along the main Ulusal Egemenlik street that runs away from the beach past Tansaş. ATMs are situated throughout the old town and around the harbour, and often dispense euros and sterling currency as well as Turkish Lira. You can also find ATM machines within both Netsel Marina shopping mall and Marmaris Yacht Marina.
Pharmacy: Several pharmacies can be found throughout the covered bazaar and town centre area.
Post office: The PTT office is located within the covered bazaar and is signposted from the harbour street of Kordon Cadessi.

EATING OUT
Both Yacht Marina and Albatros Marina have on site restaurants that offer varied menus at reasonable prices and are popular with the residents of these out of town marinas. Guests at the Pupa Marina are also welcome to use the hotel restaurant. But it is those staying in Netsel Marina or on the town dock that have the best choice of all, mainly within easy walking distance.

Marmaris has such a bewildering number of restaurants that you wonder how any of them manage to make any money, and indeed a fair proportion reopen under new management each year. There are a handful of restaurants within Netsel Marina itself, including the popular Pineapple restaurant, Tel: 0242 412 09 76, which has a reasonably priced menu and does excellent breakfasts. For the best döner kebab in

Marmaris do as the locals do and visit Barış Usta at the La Fortune restaurant on the waterfront in Netsel Marina. The meat is cooked over charcoal rather than gas and is served in freshly baked pittas. It is so busy at lunchtimes that you may have to wait for a table.

The old harbour and castle area is lined with waterfront restaurants that may be atmospheric but do not always offer the best value. Read the menus and check the prices before sitting down, and don't be afraid to move on if you don't like what you see. Neighbours restaurant is a few doors down from the footbridge to Netsel Marina and is one of the better established restaurants, which is as popular with the locals as it is with visitors and stays busy all year round. Other places worth a visit along the waterfront are the Liman restaurant, Deniz restaurant and the Caria restaurant, but there are plenty of other alternatives that may take your fancy. If you can face several flights of narrow stone stairs then the Hillside restaurant next to the castle has fantastic views across the harbour and a quiet atmosphere compared to the bustle at street level.

Marmaris is full of restaurants promising the delights of an English-Turkish-Indian-Chinese-Italian menu, but if this seems like all the dishes will be cooked in the same pan and taste identical (they do) then there are a few more authentic options available. The Golden River Chinese is actually run by a Chinese family, so the food ought to be good and it is. They are located beneath the castle area. The Taj Mahal Indian restaurant is about 20 minutes walk along the beachfront road opposite the Point Centre shopping mall, and can also be reached by getting on a green Siteler dolmuş (bus) outside Tansaş. The head chef is from England's curry capital

Useful information – Marmaris Limanı (continued)

of Bradford and the menu features all the usual Indian dishes as well as a selection of chef's specials. There are a couple of reasonable Italian restaurants in Marmaris. Uno Momento is found along G Mustafa Muğalı street, and Il Primo is part of the Blue Bay hotel at the far end of the main beachfront road.

Some of the best restaurants in Marmaris are of course the Turkish ones and among the best of these are the type referred to as Öcak Başı, which specialises in tasty meats and kebabs cooked on a large charcoal grill known as a mangal. Çihan restaurant is located at the far end of the Marmaris beach road, one of the last buildings before you start heading towards İçmeler. You can get there on a green Siteler dolmuş, but it may be easier to jump in a taxi. La Kebab restaurant is located in the nearby

suburb of Armutalan and can be reached on a blue No 1 Armutalan bus or by taxi. It is well worth making the effort to get to these restaurants. You will be rewarded with a fantastic selection of *mezes* to start with followed by a mixed grill selection or other simple meat dishes if you have any room left. The atmosphere is authentic, the prices very reasonable and you are likely to be surrounded by more Turks than tourists.

ASHORE

Marmaris is one of Turkey's busiest resort towns, so there is no shortage of things to do ashore, which is good news for the many boat owners who choose to winter here each year.

The principal shopping area is the covered bazaar, between the castle and the main town centre. Although it seems bewildering at first,

the streets within are laid out in a basic grid pattern and the many small shops and stalls have similar stock to a large degree. Bargaining is expected in most shops unless the items are individually priced, and there are a number of cafés and small *lokantas* where you can have a pit stop to keep your energy levels up. During the summer the shopping area extends all the way along the main beach road through the hotel district and there are a few small shopping malls along here as well.

The beach in Marmaris is a fairly sparse strip of sand that is nothing to write home about. For the most part it is crowded with sun loungers and pink tourists and is backed with noisy 'fun' pubs and beachfront restaurants. There are a number of watersports concessions along the beach though, so if you fancy trying to waterski, paraglide, or being towed

behind a speed boat then these activities are available.

Marmaris has a huge fleet of gulets and day tripper boats that tour the nearby islands and bays, usually stopping at either Turunç or İçmeler for a bit of shopping before the journey home. There are also several scuba diving company boats that offer tuition courses and excursions for qualified divers. Most of these boats are based along the Kordon Cadessi harbour, which faces the long beach, and many of them can offer tuition in several different languages.

A host of small travel agencies and tour operators have sprung up to provide excursions and activities to visiting tourists. Jeep safaris and village tours usually take in the Turgut waterfall and village of Bayır on the Hisarönü peninsula, and sometimes the carpet village near Bozburun. Other local activities include

Marmaris old town and castle area

Useful information – Marmaris Limanı (continued)

Albatros Marina restaurant

Go-Karting, horse riding, cycling and hiking trails, and paintballing. It is also easy to arrange trips from Marmaris to further afield locations such as Ephesus, Pamukkale and Capadoccia, either independently or as part of a tour group.

Marmaris has a large public sports centre located just behind Netsel Marina and is open to everyone. You can purchase temporary membership that allows access to the gym facilities as well as to the regular classes in aerobics, pilates and dancing that are run throughout the year. Other facilities include a number of tennis courts outside and a small bowling alley and games arcade on the top floor.

A small cinema in the Point Centre shopping mall on the main beach road has three screens that show a selection of recent Hollywood releases and Turkish films. English language films usually

have Turkish subtitles and the current showings are displayed on posters near Netsel Marina and in the centre of town.

Nightlife is Marmaris' other big attraction and the majority of bars and clubs are located either along the long beach strip about 20 minutes walk from the town centre or within the old town's Bar Street area behind the waterfront. This area is rather close to Netsel Marina and the noise can be a problem for some visitors as the night clubs are open until 0400 every night in the summer. Clubs and bars come and go between seasons; the music on offer ranges from R'n'B to house music, rock music and even traditional Turkish music. Areena night club at the far end of the street is one of the biggest, and like several of the others is open-air and features imported dancers and regular live music as well as guest DJs.

TRANSPORT
Car hire: There are numerous car hire agencies around Marmaris, including Sesi Car Rentals, Tel: 0252 413 42 84, which has a small office within Netsel Marina, and Trio rent-a-car, Tel: 0252 412 12 12, website: www. triotourism.com

Taxis: Taxi ranks can be found within both Netsel and Yacht Marina, and others are located through Marmaris town.

Dolmuş: Local minibuses in the Marmaris area are colour coded and can be caught from the bus stations outside the Tansaş supermarket or hailed anywhere along their route. Green buses marked Siteler run up and down the main beach road, and blue buses numbered 1-4 and marked Armutalan reach the dolmuş station in this nearby suburb by a variety of routes. Orange buses to İçmeler also depart from outside Tansaş, whilst red buses marked Beldibi depart from

the side street opposite the supermarket, as do the pink buses marked Yalancıboğaz that travel in the direction of Albatros Marina and Marmaris Yacht Marina.

Other dolmuş services to villages along the Datça and Hisarönü peninsulas depart from the main dolmuş station, which is a block further down from Tansaş and back from the main road.

Coach: The town otogar is located on the Mustafa Munir Elgin street, which is the main road that runs past Netsel Marina towards Yalancıboğaz. Most of the coach companies also have offices beside the Tansaş supermarket building and run free service buses that will collect you from here and take you to the otogar to meet your coach.

Ferry: The ferry port is right next to Netsel Marina and is also where visiting cruise ships tie up several times a week during the summer and winter months. There

Useful information – Marmaris Limanı (continued)

Marmaris tourist information office

are two fast catamaran services a day to the Greek island of Rhodes during the summer, and usually two services per week during the winter, weather depending. Tickets can be obtained from various travel agencies around the town, but the ferries are actually operated by a company called Yesil Marmaris, which has offices beneath the castle area and on Kordon Cadessi, Tel: 0252 412 64 86, website: www.yesilmarmaris.com

Water taxis will take you across to İçmeler or Turunç from the harbour at the eastern end of the long beach, and Marmaris Yacht Marina runs a free ferry service twice a day between the marina and Marmaris town.
Air travel: Marmaris is served by both Bodrum airport (2 hours by car) and

Dalaman airport (1 hour 15 minutes by car). Both airports have daily charter flights from all over Europe during the summer, and at least one flight a week to the UK during the winter. Both also have daily flights to İstanbul all year round.

USEFUL INFORMATION
Local tel code: Muğla area, 0252, Marmaris 412/413, Yalancıboğaz 422.
Marmaris International Yacht Club: Has a club house on the canal next to Netsel Marina and is responsible for organising various annual events such as the charter yacht show, spring festival, Marmaris Race Week and Channel Regatta, website: www.miyc.org
Tourist information office: Is located at the bottom end of Kordon Cadessi near the

Fishing boats near Netsel Marina

castle and open seven days a week during the summer.
Medical: Ahu Hetman Private Hospital offers a full range of facilities, including dentistry and eye tests as well as emergency and in-patient care. The hospital has five ambulances and a separate dialysis centre, Tel:

0252 417 77 77, website: www.ahuhetman.com

There are also a number of private medical clinics in Marmaris as well as several dentists. Yacht Marina has a small medical clinic with a doctor in residence several times a week. Ask at the reception office for details.

Hillsides surrounding Marmaris town

Gulets anchored in Skopea Limanı

Chapter four
The Lycian coast – Ekincik to Antalya

**Charts: Turkish Hydrographic Charts: 312, 313, 321, 322,
Turkish Hydrographic Leisure Folios: 3001, 3002; Imray
Charts: G3, G36, G40; Admiralty 236, 1054, SC 5773**

The Lycian coast runs south-east from Marmaris
towards Antalya and is known for the many ruined
settlements that can be observed here, including
distinctive rock tombs carved into cliff sides.

The area has a mixture of lively resort towns and
more sophisticated village destinations, and is
fast becoming popular with visitors who like to get
away from the crowds and explore a country
more independently.

The prevailing winds bend around the coastline,
becoming more westerly towards the southerly end of
this coast. There are several ports of entry in this area,
which is a popular departure point for vessels heading
towards Cyprus and the eastern Mediterranean.

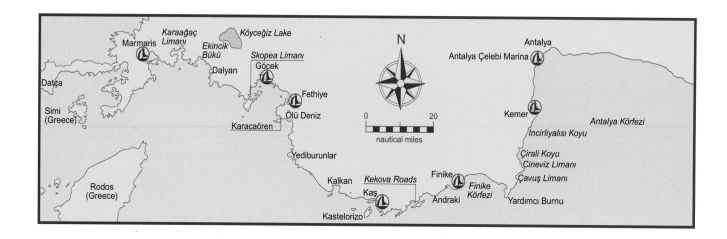

Karaağaç Limanı

Edmond's Rock: 36°46'.48N 28°23'.73E
South of Yalıncık Adası: 36°45'.91N 28°26'.24E

NAVIGATION

Charts: Turkish Hydrographic Charts: 312;
Turkish Hydrographic Leisure Folio 3001: 3001_1;
Turkish Hydrographic Leisure Folio 3002: 3002_1;
Imray Charts: G3, G36; Admiralty 236, 1054, 1055,
SC 5773

This double-headed bay between Marmaris and
Ekincik is the location of a Turkish naval base
and access is forbidden to all private boats. The
area is indicated on nautical charts, and the
waters north of an imaginary line between the
Turnalı Burun and Gökyar Burnu headlands are strictly
a prohibited area.

To the south of here a restricted area lies between
the south of Turnalı Burun and the south of the Güdük
Burun headlands, encompassing the island of Yılancık
Adası. Private vessels may pass through here to either
the north or south of the island, but they should not
dawdle or try to anchor off the island as they may well
be under observations from ashore.

The Turnalı Kayası (also known as Edmond's Rock)
is a rock and shoal area that lies approximately 1M

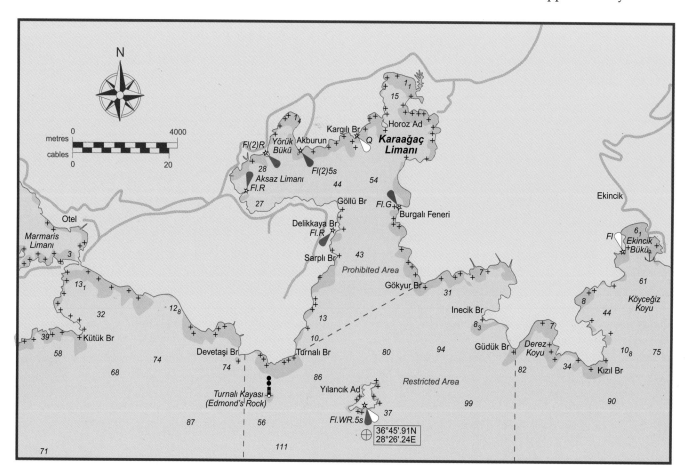

west of the island. It is dangerous to navigation and is marked with an isolated danger buoy that can be spotted as you pass by. The buoy on Edmond's Rock is lit (Fl (2) 4s), and the position of the shoal is also indicated by a sectored light on Yılancık Adası (Fl WR 5s); avoid the red sector.

Ekincik Bükü

Entrance to bay: 36°49'.21N 28°33'.36E

Ekincik Bükü is a popular place for boats to stop overnight when they are travelling between the Marmaris and Göçek areas, and has the added bonus of close proximity to the attractions in nearby Dalyan.

NAVIGATION

Charts: Turkish Hydrographic Charts: 312; Turkish Hydrographic Leisure Folio 3002: 3002_1, 3001_2; Imray Charts: G3, G36; Admiralty 236, 1054, 1055, SC 5773

Distinctive rock formation at Kızıl Burun

Ekincik Bükü lies on the northern side of the larger bay of Köyceğiz Koyu, which encompasses the long stretch of beach protecting the Dalyan river delta at its southern end.

Vessels approaching from the west must pass around the restricted area next to the naval base near Marmaris (see page 170), and will then clear the Kızıl Burun headland, which is easily identified by the distinctive pinnacles of rock lying just off it. From here you can head north up the coastline into Ekincik Bükü.

Vessels approaching from the south must pass the Dişibilmez Burnu headland, which is an area where the seas can be very confused with large steep waves that can catch a yacht unawares. It is advisable to stand off this coastline by a few miles until you are further north, level with the beach at Dalyan. As you pass the long beach you will be able to identify the small island of Delik Ada at the northern end. This is also known locally as Hole Island, and the reason for this becomes clear as you approach. This island is lit at night (Fl (2) 5s).

As you enter Ekincik Bükü itself you will be able

Hole Island (Delik Ada) off İztuzu Beach at Dalyan

to identify another light structure on the headland to the west of the entrance (Fl 5M). The village and anchorage will be seen immediately to the north of this, and the My Marina development lies tucked away on the eastern side of the bay.

BERTHING AND ANCHORING

My Marina can accommodate around 30 boats on its wooden T-jetty and quayside. Berthing is mainly stern-to with lazylines, and a member of staff is usually available to show you to a berth and help you to tie up. Overnight berthing fees are not charged if you make a reservation in the restaurant overlooking the harbour.

Over by the village on the northern side of the bay there is a very small jetty at the western end of the beach, but this is generally full up with day tripper boats. There is plenty of room to anchor off the beach though. You can free swing in around 5-10m of water and go ashore by dinghy.

There are also several other small coves along the western side of Köyceğiz Koyu where you can anchor with a line ashore to take shelter for the night.

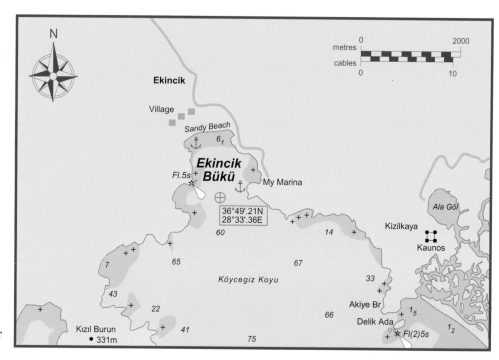

The light structure on the headland to the west of the entrance

Anchorage at Ekincik village

Useful information – Ekincik Bükü

Yachts berthed at My Marina

FACILITIES
Water and electricity:
A fresh water and electricity supply is on the dock in My Marina.
Showers: Available at My Marina.
Ice: May be stocked at mini-markets in Ekincik village and at My Marina.
Rubbish: Segregated recycling bins at My Marina. Normal rubbish bins can be found in Ekincik village.
Telephone: Public phones available in both My Marina and Ekincik village. Mobile reception here is good.

PROVISIONING AND SERVICES
Basic provisions can be bought from a few small shops in Ekincik village, where there is also a pharmacy.

EATING OUT
The My Marina restaurant, Tel: 0252 266 02 76, is built into the hillside above the harbour and provides fantastic views across the bay. The walls are full of photos of the rich and famous who have eaten here in the past, and the restaurant is known for the

quality of its service and the choice of fresh fish. You are not shown a menu, but rather a trolley selection of dishes is wheeled to the table whilst the charismatic head waiter runs through the contents and makes his recommendations.

As you can expect, all of this does not come cheaply, so if you are on a budget then do ask to check the prices before you order. The quality of the food does live up to the stunning surroundings. A word of caution though; you reach the restaurant by walking up some fairly steep and slippery stone steps, and it is not an easy climb for anyone who has trouble walking. There is a small funicular lift that can take you from the harbour to the restaurant, but it is not always operational. It may be an idea to call ahead to check if you are planning to visit with crew who may struggle with this. The bad news is that the toilet and shower block is also half way up these stone steps, so using your facilities on board is perhaps an easier option during the night.

Over in the village of

Ekincik are a couple of small beach restaurants with much more modest prices than My Marina. The Likya restaurant, Tel: 0252 266 00 45/02 57, is located right on the beach and serves Turkish and Mediterranean specialities, with an option to sample some traditionally brewed *chai* afterwards or smoke a Turkish water pipe.

ASHORE
Ekincik is the place from where you can organise a day trip to take in the attractions of the Dalyan river area (see page 174). Whether you stay on the

dock in My Marina or at anchor off the village beach, a representative from the Dalyan River co-operative will pop by in the evening to enquire whether you wish to arrange a trip for the following day. Prices are fixed by the co-operative and all boat operators are licensed, so there is no hard sell and no chance to get stung on the price.

TRANSPORT
Dolmuş: There is one dolmuş per day from Ekincik to the lake town of Köyceğiz. You can catch further buses from here to take you towards Marmaris, Fethiye and beyond.
Air travel: Dalaman airport is only about 25 minutes from Köyceğiz, but the initial trip to there from Ekincik takes at least this long as well.

USEFUL INFORMATION
Local tel code: Muğla area, 0252, Ekincik 266.

The funicular rail track at My Marina

A Dalyan river boat

Dalyan

**South-east of Delik Ada
island: 36°47'.57N
28°35'.95E**

NAVIGATION

Charts: Turkish
Hydrographic Charts: 312;
Turkish Hydrographic
Leisure Folio 3002:
3002_1, 3002_2; Imray
Charts: G3, G36; Admiralty
236, 1054, 1055, SC 5773

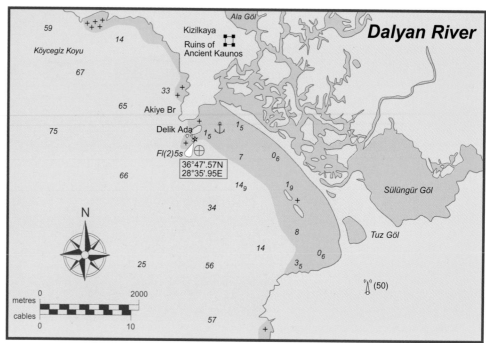

The long stretch of İztuzu
beach is exposed to the
prevailing winds and swell,
and is not a good spot to
anchor. The small island of
Delik Ada at the northern
end does offer a degree of protection
and it is possible to anchor for a
few hours in the lee of the island.
Approach and depart around the
southern side to avoid the shallow
areas to the north of the island.

The depths shelve dramatically
from over 60m to around 10m,
causing the swell to pile up and
break on the beach behind you, so
the anchorage is always rolly and
is not recommended for overnight.
There is a small rickety jetty where
the tripper boats put their passengers
ashore onto Delik Ada (known locally
as Hole Island), so you can dinghy

Day-tripper boats using the jetty at Delik Ada

The Dalyan river delta

across to here if you want
to explore the island and
walk through the hole in the
middle yourself.

Although you may be
approached by some of
the Dalyan river boats
whilst at anchor, it is not
recommended that you leave
the boat unattended here
during the several hours
that the river trips are likely
to take. It is much better
to head around to Ekincik
Bükü for the night (see page
171) and organise your trip
from there.

Skopea Limanı

Charts: Turkish Hydrographic Charts: 312, 3122, 313; Turkish Hydrographic Leisure Folio 3002: 3002_1, 3002_2, 3002_5, 3002_6; Imray Charts: G3, G36; Admiralty 236, 1054, SC 5773

The Yacht Mola restaurant jetty at Boynuz Bükü

Skopea Limanı comprises a host of smaller bays and inlets running along the coast to the south-west of Göcek village. Although generally uninhabited, these bays are home to a number of small restaurants that make a living from the boats and day trippers visiting from nearby Göcek and Fethiye. There are several small islands and rocky outcrops in this area, which constitutes a playground for the numerous craft based nearby. Most of the anchorages within Skopea Limanı have a number of alternative names in Turkish and English, as used by the various day tripper and blue cruise yachts that frequent the area. Alternative names are given alongside but you can expect to encounter even more local names for some of these bays when you are actually in the area.

It is not permitted to tie shorelines to trees along the coast of Skopea Limanı. The local council have erected concrete mooring posts along the shoreline to give vessels a secure point to tie up to and to save the trees from damage.

A small barge provided by the belediye council tours the islands and anchorages within Skopea Limanı every day to collect rubbish left by visiting yachts and charter boats. A shocking amount of rubbish is collected this way and I would urge private yachts to minimise their contribution to this by storing their waste on board until they are able to dispose of it themselves at the next town or village they visit that has proper disposal facilities, such as Göcek or Fethiye.

Göcek Adası

Within anchorage: 36°43'.79N 28°56'.75E

Göcek Adası is the closest island to Göcek village and has a couple of small bays suitable for daytime anchorage along the north-east side. In one of these you will find the Göcek Ada restaurant, Mob: 0532 549 37 79, 0535 644 00 17, website: www.gocekada.com.tr, which has a small pontoon with lazylines where a few vessels may stay the night or stop for lunch. Facilities are fairly rustic, although there are toilets and showers here. The restaurant also operates a pick-up service from Göcek village and has sun loungers on the beach for visitors.

Valley Bay

Within anchorage: 36°43'.59N 28°54'.85E

This attractive bay immediately to the west of Göcek Adası provides a sheltered spot from the prevailing winds for overnight anchoring, although there are no facilities ashore. The bay is deep so it is necessary to take a line ashore rather than free swing.

Boynuz Bükü

Centre of bay: 36°42'.64N 28°54'.14E

This deep and indented bay provides some of the best shelter within Skopea Limanı. Depths in this bay shelve more gently than in Valley Bay to the north, so it is possible to free swing here in 10-15m of water, although if it is crowded it is better to take a line ashore.

There is a small restaurant (Yacht Mola restaurant Mob: 0542 634 09 75, 0543 790 38 43) at the far end of the bay and this has a long wooden jetty where 25-30 boats can berth stern-to using lazylines. Water for boats is available here, although electricity is not.

Vessels sailing in this area should be aware of the rocky reef lying between the entrance to Boynuz Bükü and the north end of Yassıca Adaları. This is indicated with an isolated danger mark, although it is not always lit at night. There is safe passage to the west and east of this mark between the mainland and Yassıca Adaları.

Round Bay/Killeiskelesi Koyu

Within anchorage: 36°41'.95N 28°52'.73E

This is suitable as a daytime anchorage only but has a nice beach and pleasant views towards Tersane Adası and Yassıca Adaları.

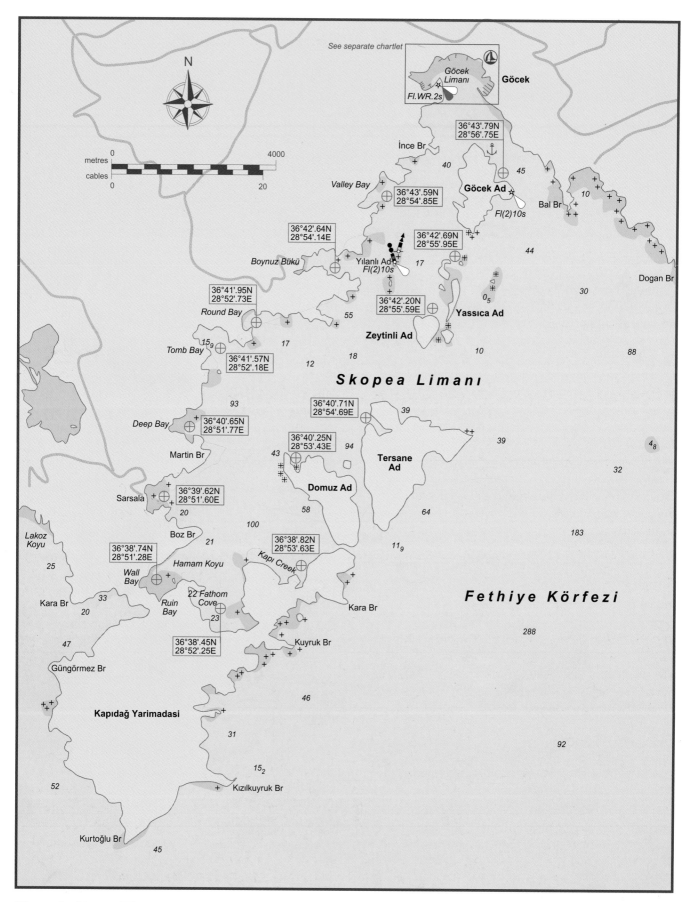

N

metres 0   4000
cables 0   20

See separate chartlet

Göcek
Limanı
Göcek

Fl.WR.2s

36°43'.79N
28°56'.75E

İnce Br

40

45

Valley Bay

36°43'.59N
28°54'.85E

Göcek Ad

Fl(2)10s

Bal Br

10

36°42'.64N
28°54'.14E

36°42'.69N
28°55'.95E

Boynuz Bükü

Yılanlı Ad
Fl(2)10s

17

44

Dogan Br

36°41'.95N
28°52'.73E

36°42'.20N
28°55'.59E

Round Bay

55

Zeytinli Ad

Yassıca Ad

30

5

0

Tomb Bay

15 9

17

12

18

10

88

36°41'.57N
28°52'.18E

Skopea Limanı

93

36°40'.71N
28°54'.69E

39

Deep Bay

36°40'.65N
28°51'.77E

36°40'.25N
28°53'.43E

39

39

Martin Br

43

94

Tersane
Ad

32

4 8

Sarsala

36°39'.62N
28°51'.60E

Domuz Ad

20

58

64

183

Lakoz
Koyu

Boz Br

21

100

36°38'.82N
28°53'.63E

11 9

36°38'.74N
28°51'.28E

25

Hamam Koyu

Kapı Creek

Fethiye Körfezi

Wall
Bay

Ruin
Bay

22 Fathom
Cove

23

Kara Br

288

Kara Br

33

20

36°38'.45N
28°52'.25E

Kuyruk Br

Güngörmez Br

47

46

Kapıdağ Yarimadasi

31

92

15 2

52

Kızılkuyruk Br

Kurtoğlu Br

45

Tomb Bay/Taşyaka Koyu

Within anchorage: 36° 41'.57N 28° 52'.18E

This bay takes its name from the ancient rock tombs
embedded in the hillsides surrounding the bay and is a

popular destination for gulets and day trip boats from
Göcek and Fethiye.

There is a short wooden jetty on the northern side of
the bay where vessels can berth using an anchor. This
area is not particularly well-sheltered so is best used

Nomad restaurant at Tomb Bay

is a popular spot for locals wanting to spend a day at the beach, and there are usually taxis waiting to take visitors back to civilisation or even the airport if necessary (check with the restaurant if you want to book in advance).

A small indent in the southern side of the bay is home to the popular Sarsala Gözde restaurant, Mob: 0532 638 63 03, 0532 347 49 61, website: www.sarsala.com, where you can get excellent *meze* and home-cooked food. A long wooden jetty provides stern-to berthing with lazylines and there is plenty of space to anchor stern to the shore around the rest of the bay.

as a lunchtime stop only. A large stylised fish can be seen on the rocks behind the jetty here, painted by the Turkish artist Bedri Rahmi during one of the first 'blue cruises' around the area. Further around the bay is the Nomad restaurant, Mob: 0536 605 58 83, 0543 595 80 40, which has its own wooden jetty and lazylines for visitors. Rubbish bins are situated on the shore near here, and there is a small, well-appointed hut on the beach where you can have a haircut, shave or massage.

Deep Bay/Sıralıbük Koyu
Within anchorage: 36°40'.65N 28°51'.77E

This is another bay with no facilities ashore, but despite the name it is shallow enough to anchor stern to the shore with a long line and offers good protection from the prevailing winds.

Sarsala/Sarsıla Koyu
Within anchorage: 36°39'.62N 28°51'.60E

This beautiful bay offers unrivalled views across Skopea Limanı all the way back towards Göcek itself. There are attractive beaches in the small coves around the edge of the bay, and a circular road leads from the northernmost of these towards Göcek village. This

Sarsala restaurant jetty

Manastır Koyu/Hamam Koyu
Within anchorage: 36°38'.74N 28°51'.28E

This double-ended bay comprises Wall Bay to the north and Ruin Bay to the south. The Wall Bay restaurant, Mob: 0544 325 10 39/0542 366 15 11/0544 401 39 57, on the northern side, has a wooden jetty where visiting boats can tie up alongside. The ancient stone walls for which the bay is known run parallel to the shore to the south-west of here and it is possible to anchor stern-to with a line ashore in this part of the bay.

Ruin Bay is named after the semi-submerged ruined buildings that line the shore and are reputed to be the remains of one of Cleopatra's bathing houses. These days they offer great snorkelling possibilities. There are no jetties or facilities here so take a long line ashore to the rocks and go ashore by dinghy to explore the ruins.

Seaside hairdresser's at Tomb Bay

A gulet anchored amongst the ruins in Ruin Bay

A 45-minute walk over the hills brings you to some impressive ruins of an ancient city.

There is a small island in the entrance to the bay that you need to look out for. Make sure you pass to the north of this, as depths are very shallow between the island and the southern side of the bay.

Kapı Creek

22 Fathom Cove
Within anchorage: 36°38'.45N 28°52'.25E

This stunning bay surrounded by pine clad hills lies between Manastir Koyu and Kapı Creek. A small cove on the western side offers reasonable protection but indifferent holding, so is useful only as a lunchtime stop rather than overnight. The eastern side of the bay was once home to a small restaurant, although that is now closed. The remains of a wooden jetty are still usable for stern-to berthing with an anchor, and rather bizarrely a large white seagull is visible carved into the shoreline just behind this.

Kapı Creek
Within anchorage: 36°38'.82N 28°53'.63E

The small restaurant in this sheltered bay has long been a favoured destination for visitors to this area and remains so today. Wooden jetties run along the shore to either side of this narrow inlet, providing plenty of space for boats to berth stern-to with the lazylines provided. A small barber's shop and massage hut is situated on the beach near the restaurant, and a walk up onto the ridge behind provides fantastic views over the bay or across the gulf towards Fethiye.

Göbün Kapı Creek restaurant can be contacted on Mob: 0555 357 09 87/0532 789 44 63.

Domuz Adası
Within anchorage: 36°40'.25N 28°53'.43E

This is a privately-owned island so do not try to go ashore here. However, it is possible to anchor in the small bay on the north-west side known as the 'aquarium' for the clear waters and vast numbers of fish that can be seen. There are some sunken ruins in the middle of the bay, so be careful to avoid these when dropping your anchor, although they do make for interesting snorkelling.

Day-trippers at Domuz Adası

Tersane Adası
Within anchorage: 36°40'.71N 28°54'.69E

This slightly larger island lying opposite Domuz Adası has a well-protected bay on the north-west corner. There is a small restaurant here, Tersane Kafeterya, Mob: 0536 677 21 40, with a private wooden jetty for visitors. Berth stern-to using one of its lazylines, pick up one of its laid moorings, or anchor around the bay and take a line ashore. The ruins of what may have been an ancient shipyard can be seen in the bay and it is possible to explore these close to.

Anchored off the beach at Yassıca Adaları

Yassıca Adaları
South anchorage: 36°42'.20N 28°55'.59E
North entrance: 36°42'.69N 28°55'.95E

This cluster of small islets and rocky outcrops is considered off limits for many charter clients, although it is quite possible to pick a passage through them during daylight hours with good visibility. Vessels can be seen at anchor as you approach, but be careful not to enter from Domuz Adası to the south as depths are very shallow in this channel. It is possible to enter from the northern or western sides, taking care to avoid the isolated danger mark mentioned earlier.

The northern end of the anchorage tends to be used by smaller boats, whilst the deeper southern end is used by bigger ones. A waterskiing school runs from the long beach to the east of the anchorage, and there is also a souvenir shop ashore here, although it seems to be fairly temporary in nature. Thirsty visitors can get a cold beer from the Kalyon floating bar, which is anchored just off the beach and open during the afternoons and evenings.

The restaurant jetty at Tersane Adası

Göcek Limanı

Entrance to bay: 36°44'.86N 28°56'.17E

Between the Skopea Marina and Belediye Marina jetties:
36°45'.14N 28°56'.29E

Port Göcek Marina entrance: 36°44'.94N 28°56'.44E

Between Club Marina and MarinTurk Göcek Village Port:
36°45.10N 28°55.71E

South of MarinTurk Exclusive: 36°44.48N 28°55.61E

Aerial view of Port Göcek Marina

The once sleepy village of Göcek has become one of the major yachting centres along the Turkish coastline and is a fashionable destination for Turkish as well as foreign tourists. The area rose to prominence during the 1980s as the then Turkish Prime Minister's holiday destination of choice. These days the area boasts six marinas and two boatyards, and is the starting location for many charter gulets following 'Blue Cruise' routes.

NAVIGATION

Charts: Turkish Hydrographic Charts: 312, 3122, 313; Turkish Hydrographic Leisure Folio 3002: 3002_1, 3002_2, 3002_6; Imray Charts: G3, G36; Admiralty 236, 1054, 1644, SC 5773

Göcek Limanı lies at the northern end of Skopea Limanı, on the western side of Fethiye Körfezi. The entrance to the bay is immediately north of Göcek Adası, and approaching vessels can pass safely to either side of this island.

Entering the bay you will see the village buildings immediately ahead of you and many boats at anchor or berthed in front of these. A headland opposite the village is marked with a sectored light (Fl WR 2s).

BERTHING AND ANCHORING

Göcek is immensely popular as a cruise destination, charter base and home for private boats, so berthing space is always at a premium and it is worth calling ahead to reserve a place, particularly during high season in July and August.

The dock area along the village waterfront is the location of Skopea Marina, which has one pontoon, and the village-operated Belediye Marina, which has two pontoons extending into the bay.

Port Göcek Marina is part of a development lying immediately east of the village. Göcek Club Marina is operated by the same company as Skopea Marina and is tucked behind a headland opposite the village. MarinTurk is currently developing two new marina facilities in Göcek, both of which opened for business in 2009 and should be finished with construction in 2010. The Göcek Village Port is located between Göcek village and the Camper & Nicholsons boatyard operated by Port Göcek Marina. It comprises a

Looking south towards Kızıl Ada and Deliktaş Adalar islands in Fethiye Körfezi

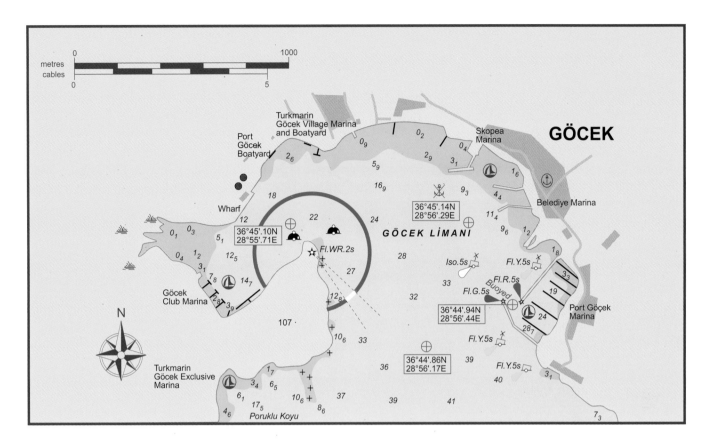

boatyard facility, residential development and L-shaped jetty with berthing for visi ting yachts. The Göcek Exclusive facility is located around the headland that is immediately south of Göcek Club Marina. It accepts vessels over 18m and is intended to become the premier facility for superyachts and large private vessels visiting the area. The floating

pontoons have distinctive 'verandah-awnings' and services will include a private beach, swimming pool and sun-lounging areas, and a floating café on one of the docks.

All of the marinas have stern-to berthing with lazylines, although some of the waterfront berths in the Belediye Marina require an anchor, but are

Aerial view of the new Göcek Village Port marina, with the lifting area for the new boatyard at the bottom of the picture

mainly used by charter gulets to collect their customers. All of the marinas have a full range of facilities. You should call the marinas on VHF Ch 72 or 73 as you approach to check berthing availability and request mooring assistance.

The marinas can be contacted on the following numbers:

Port Göcek Marina: VHF Ch 73, Tel: 0252 645 15 20, Fax: 0252 645 18 97, email: enquiries@portgocek. com (main office), Tel: 0252 645 22 88, Fax: 0252 645 21 09, email: boatyard@portgocek.com (boatyard), website: www.portgocek.com

Göcek Club Marina: VHF Ch 72, Tel: 0252 645 18 00, Fax: 0252 645 18 04, email: clubmarina@superonline.com, website: www.turkeyclubmarina.net

Skopea Marina: VHF Ch 72, Tel: 0252 645 17 94, Fax: 0252 645 17 93, email: skopeamarina@gmail.com

Göcek Belediye Marina: VHF Ch 13, Tel: 0252 645 19 38, Fax: 0252 645 14 52, website: www.gocekmarina.net

MarinTurk Göcek Village Port: VHF Ch 73, Tel: 0252 645

Marina office at Göcek Club Marina

22 29, Fax: 0252 645 15 78, email: villageport@marinturk. com.tr, www.marinturk.com.tr

MarinTurk Exclusive: VHF Ch 73, Tel: 0252 645 22 29 Fax: 0252 645 15 78, email: exclusive@marinturk.com.tr, www.marinturk.com.tr

If you want to join the boats free swinging at anchor then you can find a space in 5-10m in front of the village.

Useful information – Göcek Limanı

Göcek Club Marina

FACILITIES
Water and electricity: Available on the pontoons at each of the marinas.
Fuel: Port Göcek Marina, Göcek Club Marina and the Belediye Marina all have fuel docks where you can fill up with diesel or petrol.
Showers: Shower facilities are available at all of the marinas and are also offered by some of the restaurants in the village.

Ice: Is sold at various supermarkets in the town and also on site at Port Göcek and Göcek Club Marina.
Laundry: A laundry service can be found in the village.
Gas: Available from supermarkets in the village and also at Port Göcek and Göcek Club marinas.
Rubbish: Rubbish bins are situated throughout the town and in all marinas. Port Göcek Marina has disposal facilities for waste products such as oil and bilge water.
Telephone: Public phone boxes are located throughout the village and in both Port Göcek and Göcek Club Marina. Phone cards can be purchased at kiosks and supermarkets. Mobile reception here is good.
Internet: Many of the restaurants, cafés and bars along the waterfront offer WiFi internet connection to customers.

YACHT SERVICES AND CHANDLERY
The Camper & Nicholsons boatyard operated by Port Göcek Marina is a small yard located on the western side of the bay next to Göcek Club Marina. This has a 70 ton travel lift and a secure hard standing area. All technical services should be arranged through Port Göcek Marina.

A larger facility opened next to this in 2009, and is operated as part of the MarinTurk Göcek Village Port development. This boatyard has two travel lifts (200 ton and 75 ton), a 40 ton boat mover, and space for around 200 boats on its hard standing. A full range of technical services is offered by the marina, including mechanical and electronic repairs, woodwork and upholstery repairs, metalwork and refrigeration/ air-conditioning servicing. Speak to the marina office for details.

As a major yachting centre, Göcek offers plenty of technical services as well as a number of agencies that can take on project management for major programmes and supply contractors for almost any kind of work, including mechanical, electrics and electronics, glass fibre and carpentry, air-conditioning and refrigeration, sails and rigging. You can contact Blues Yachting, Tel: 0252 645 14 35/16 52, website: www.bluestechnic.com, or Gino Yachting, Tel: 0252 645 10 84, website: www. ginogroup.com, for further details. You can also speak directly to the office staff in Port Göcek Marina to arrange any technical work to be done at its facilities.

There are several chandlery shops in the centre of Göcek village where you can buy general spares, cordage, charts etc. Blues Chandlery is

Useful information – Göcek Limanı

Hammocks for sale in Göcek village

at the eastern end of the main street. Mavi Marin Chandlery is in the new plaza at the eastern end of the village. Sanlı Marina Chandlery is also in this plaza.

PROVISIONING AND SERVICES

Grocery shops: There is a medium-sized Tansaş and a small Migros supermarket in Göcek village, as well as several markets that cater for yachts and gulets and offer free delivery to your boat on the town dock. Both Port Göcek and Göcek Club Marinas have small supermarkets on site.

Butterfly Manav is an organic greengrocer that sells fruit, vegetables and locally made organic honey in Göcek village.

Bakery: A bakery and a butcher are situated in Göcek village.

Local market: A village market is held every Sunday just behind the main street in the village.

Banks: There are branches of several banks along the main street in Göcek village, including Akbank, Finansbank, Garantı Bank and Yapı Kredi. All have money changing facilities and ATMs. There are also ATMs in Port Göcek Marina.

Pharmacy: Several in Göcek village.

Post office: The PTT office in Göcek is located just behind the main street at the eastern end of the village.

EATING OUT

Göcek is full of restaurants and cafés that line the waterfront, main street and Port Göcek Marina complex. Menus range from traditional Turkish to modern European and even Asian specialities, and there is a choice to suit every budget.

Blues Café, Bar and Restaurant on the waterfront next to the Blues Hotel offers a bar snack menu that includes excellent homemade beef burgers as well as an *à la carte* restaurant menu with a mixture of Turkish and European dishes.

Kebab Hospital straddles the waterfront and main street at the western end of the village. Despite the unpromising sounding name, it offers a good choice of traditional *meze* and freshly prepared charcoal-grilled kebabs.

Yilmaz Restaurant is just next to Skopea Marina and specialises in fish supplied directly from the local fish market.

The Bay Restaurant is located at Göcek Club Marina and serves modern Turkish dishes in natural surroundings, Tel: 0252 645 14 56, website: www.thebayrestaurant.com

Sundowner's Restaurant and Bar at Port Göcek Marina has an *à la carte* menu as well as open buffet evenings such as seafood buffet, Turkish cuisine or barbecue evenings.

ASHORE

Göcek village has developed over the years but still has a relatively small centre with just one main street running parallel with the waterfront. You will discover plenty of small shops and boutiques along here where you can buy carpets, jewellery, handmade souvenirs and clothing.

There is a hamam (Turkish bath) building at Göcek Club Marina, where you can enjoy a full range of scrubs and massages as well. This is open every day from 0700 until midnight.

If you want to hire a car and explore the region then the beach, ruins and mud baths of Dalyan are approximately 20 minutes to the west, and the town of Fethiye is approximately 45 minutes east of Göcek.

Various agencies in the village can organise parasailing and watersports activities in the bay, diving trips and instruction, jeep safaris of the surrounding area and white water rafting trips to Saklıkent.

TRANSPORT

Car hire: Orion Car Rental, Tel: 0252 645 19 16, is in Port Gocek Marina. Oscar Rent-a-Car, Tel: 0252 645 26 54, is part of the VIP Airport Transfers group with an office in the Göcek plaza at the eastern end of the village.

Taxis: Taxi ranks are located at both ends of Göcek main street, as well as in Port Göcek and Göcek Club Marinas.

Dolmuş: Buses run from the village to surrounding villages.

Coach: Coaches operating between Fethiye and Marmaris stop at the petrol station at the western end of the village. There are booking offices in town for some of the bus companies where you can check timetables and buy tickets, or pay when you board the coach.

Ferry: A free ferry operates between Skopea and Göcek Club Marinas every couple of hours during the day. A timetable is posted in both locations.

Air travel: Dalaman International Airport is about 20km to the west of Göcek, with daily flights to major European destinations throughout the summer.

USEFUL INFORMATION

Local tel code: Muğla area 0252, Göcek 645.

Customs office: Between Göcek Club Marina and the village.

Göcek Yacht Club: www.gocekyachtclub.org

Doctor: There is a first aid and medical centre at Port Göcek Marina.

Dentist: In Göcek village.

Hospital: The nearest hospital in is Fethiye.

The Bay Restaurant at Göcek Club Marina

Aerial view of Ece Saray Marina. The private jetty belonging to the Yacht Plaza Hotel can be seen at the top of the picture

Fethiye Limanı

South-east of Katrancık Adası: 36°41'.43N 29°00'.74E
Light on Kızıl Ada: 36°39'.19N 29°02'.65E
Between cardinal mark and Fethiye Adası:
36°38'.95N 29°05'.57E
Ece Saray Marina entrance: 36°37'.55N 29°06'.10E
Western bay: 36°37'.69N 29°06'.00E

The modern harbour town of Fethiye is located on the site of the ancient city of Telmessos, and various ruins can be seen in or around the town today. It is a port of entry to Turkey and is the location of a large hotel and marina complex as well as several smaller yacht facilities and boatyards.

NAVIGATION

Charts: Turkish Hydrographic Charts: 312, 3122, 313; Turkish Hydrographic Leisure Folio 3002: 3002_1, 3002_2, 3002_7; Imray Charts: G3, G36; Admiralty 236, 1054, 1644, SC 5773

Fethiye Limanı lies on the eastern side of Fethiye Körfezi and is sheltered by a headland to the west and the island of Fethiye Adası to the north. Vessels must approach the town from the north, passing through the waters of Fethiye Körfezi.

There is a chain of small islands and rocks strung along the north of the gulf between Fethiye and Göcek. The most westerly of these is Katrancık Adası, which is about half way between the two towns. Approximately 1M to the south-east of here is a small group comprising Tavşan Adası, Deliktaş Adalar and the larger Kızıl Ada. A patch of shoal water to the west of Tavşan Adası is indicated with an unlit west cardinal mark, and there is a light structure on the southern tip of Kızıl Ada (Fl 5s).

The tip of the Çamlı Burnu headland is another 1M south-east of Kızıl Ada, and a north cardinal mark indicates the Batıkkaya reef just to the east of here (VQ). Fethiye Adası lies across the entrance to Fethiye Limanı and vessels must pass to the west of this island as the passage to the east is shallow, rocky and dangerous to navigation. The entrance to Fethiye Limanı is indicated at night by red and green lights on the western tip of Fethiye Adası (Fl R 3s) and the northern tip of Paçarız Burnu headland (Fl G 3s).

Once within Fethiye Limanı you will be able to see the town immediately to the south. Stay on the western side of the bay as you approach the town, avoiding the shallows that extend from the eastern side. Two west cardinal marks show the approach to Fethiye harbour and are lit at night (Kuzey Sığlığı VQ (9) 10s and Guney Sığlık Q (9) 15s). An isolated danger mark on the western side of the bay indicates the location of a shallow wreck. It is supposed to be lit at night (Fl 5s) but this is not always the case.

As you near Fethiye town you will see the commercial dock at the eastern end, with the town dock running between here and the large Ece Saray Marina to the west. A number of other jetties and yachting facilities line the bay west of here.

BERTHING AND ANCHORING

The Fethiye town dock is used mainly by local fishing, charter and excursion boats, although there is often some room for other vessels to berth for a few hours during the day or overnight. In this case you will need to drop an anchor and approach the dock stern-to.

Most visiting boats, however, head for the large Ece Saray Marina, which can accommodate around 460 boats up to 60m in length. You should call the marina on VHF Ch 73 as you approach to request

Ece Saray Marina office

berthing instructions. Wait for the marina staff to show you where to go and give you assistance with berthing if necessary. Berthing is generally stern-to with lazylines. The marina can also be contacted

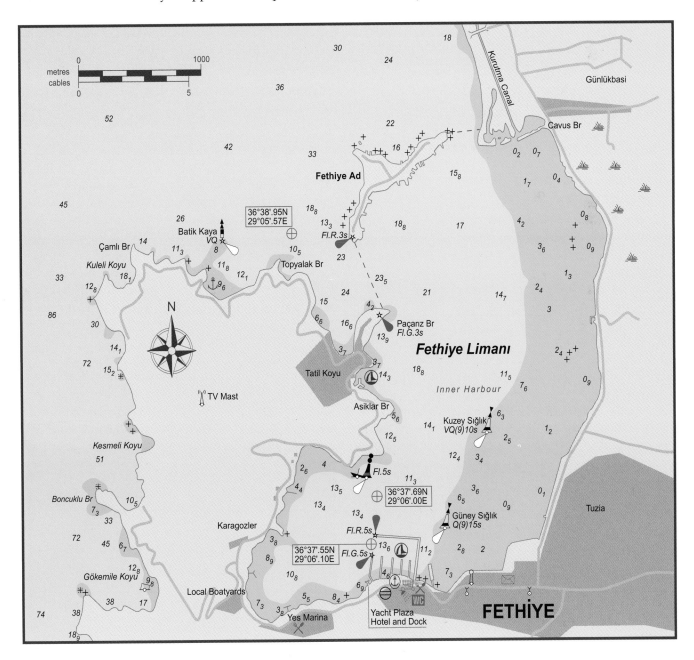

The Yacht Plaza Hotel jetty

Right next to here is another jetty backed by a small sports arena. It doesn't seem to be operated by anyone, but there are usually several local boats berthed stern-to along here.

FORMALITIES

Customs clearance in Fethiye is fairly easy as all of the offices are located close to each other and to the marina. The health office is across the street from the Ece Saray Marina. The customs patrol and harbour master offices

on Tel: 0252 612 50 05, Fax: 0252 612 50 08, email: marina@ecemarina.com, website: www.ecesaray.net

Immediately west of Ece Saray Marina is a newly redeveloped dock that belongs to the Yacht Plaza Hotel. There is space for around 25 boats here and visitors are quite welcome to use the facilities for a small fee. The dock is used as a turnaround base by a local charter company so can be rather busy at weekends, but during the week whilst the boats are on charter there is usually plenty of room for others. Berthing is stern-to on the wooden quay and there are lazylines available. You can contact the Yacht Plaza Hotel on Tel: 0252 612 50 67, Fax: 0252 612 50 68, email: info@yachtplazahotel.com, website: www.yachtplazahotel.com

A little further around the bay is a small dock at Yes Marina, which has space for about 15 boats to anchor stern-to the wooden jetty, Tel: 0252 614 22 58, Mob: 0532 372 46 02.

The Yes Marina jetty

are housed in a small building immediately behind the marina, and transit logs can be obtained from the marina office. Beware of the fact that some or all of these offices may be closed at weekends out of high season, so make sure you do your clearance formalities during the week.

Useful information – Fethiye Limanı

FACILITIES
Water and electricity: Available on the town quay, at the Yacht Plaza and Yes Marina jetties and at all berths within Ece Saray Marina.
Fuel: Can be obtained at the fuel quay in Ece Saray Marina.
Showers: At Ece Saray Marina as well as at the Yacht Plaza and Yes Marina locations.
Ice: Can be bought from supermarkets in the town.
Laundry: Laundry can be done at Ece Saray Marina, the Yacht Plaza Hotel and also at Murat laundry, Tel: 0252 612 26 67, behind the marina.
Gas: Is stocked at Ece Saray Marina and also in the town.
Rubbish: Rubbish and waste products can be disposed

of and recycled in Ece Saray Marina, and there are also bins within the town and at Yacht Plaza and Yes Marina.
Telephone: Public phone boxes are located throughout the town and cards can be purchased easily. Mobile phone reception is good.
Internet: WiFi internet connection is available within Ece Saray Marina and also at the Yacht Plaza Hotel. There are several internet cafés within the town of Fethiye.

YACHT SERVICES AND CHANDLERY
Ece Saray Marina has a number of technical services workshops and offices at the far end of the marina docks. You should speak to the marina office

in order to arrange work on your boat. There are also several service agents with offices in the streets behind the marina.

Captain Eddy's is a well-stocked chandlery that also offers technical service and Customs agent services to boats in Fethiye, Tel: 0252 614 25 26, 24-hour mob: 0532 224 80 62, website:

www.eddysyachting.com.
Ece Saray Marina has no hard standing facilities, but there are a couple of boatyards towards the western end of the bay. These are all pretty local affairs and you could struggle to find someone in the office who speaks English, so it may be best to travel down there by bus

Technical assistance is available in Fethiye

Useful information – Fethiye Limanı (continued)

Souvenir shopping in Fethiye

first to make arrangements in person rather than trying to do so over the telephone. Facilities ashore are minimal and these are not places where you would want to spend any time actually living on your boat whilst it was out of the water, but they are cheap and functional working boatyards, so ideal for annual out of water maintenance or winterising.
Karagözler boatyard
Tel: 0252 614 43 58.
Çankayalar boatyard
Tel: 0533 726 08 63.

PROVISIONING AND SERVICES

Grocery shops: You will find a decent supermarket within the Ece Saray Marina complex and several mini-markets and small supermarkets in the nearby streets and town centre. Larger supermarkets on the road out of town can be reached by taxi.
Bakery: There is a bakery/patisserie within Ece Saray and other bakeries in the town.
Butcher: Several butchers are in the town centre.
Local market: Fethiye's weekly market is held on Tuesdays and you can buy all kinds of fresh produce, clothing, souvenirs and other items here.
Banks: There are several bank branches and change offices in the centre of the town, including Vakıf Bank,

TEB Bank, Fortis Bank and Akbank. All of these have ATM machines for cash withdrawal, and others are located around the marina and along the harbour.
Pharmacy: Several in the town centre.
Post office: The PTT office is situated in the town centre.

EATING OUT

There are a number of restaurants in Fethiye, mainly within the bazaar area or stretched along the waterfront. Generally the standard is high and prices are more reasonable than in nearby Göcek.

If you enjoy seafood then don't miss the chance to visit the Fethiye fish market, which is to the east of the bazaar area. Here you can buy fish directly from the man who caught it, then take it across to one of the nearby restaurants who will clean it and grill it for you on the spot.

Guests staying at either the Yacht Plaza or Yes Marina jetties can eat at the excellent restaurants ashore here. Yacht Plaza guests who eat at the hotel restaurant will get a reduction in the mooring costs. There is a 5 star restaurant at the Ece Saray Marina, which is also open to marina customers.

ASHORE

Although most of Fethiye is of fairly modern

construction, having been badly hit by an earthquake in 1958, many people find that this is a town that grows on them and the longer you spend here the harder it is to leave. Scattered around the town you will see various remains of the ancient settlement of Telmessos, including an amphitheatre which was excavated during the 1990s along with a collection of rock tombs and medieval fortress above the town that can be seen from the water as you approach. There is a small museum on the main street running east of the town centre where you can see archaeological remains from around the local area and also the 'Trilingual Stele', which acted as a sort of Rosetta Stone in helping scholars to decipher the Lycian language.

The bazaar area is one of the better sorts of its kind and compared with the shopping areas of Marmaris or Bodrum is relatively low key and lacking the hard sell tactics that can mar the experience for many.

The usual kinds of excursions and trips are available from travel agencies in the town (jeep safaris, boat trips, village tours and the like), but one place that may be worth a visit is the beautiful Saklıkent Gorge where you can go hiking, climbing, canyoning and rafting. It is about half an hour

drive from Fethiye.

Crews staying in either the Ece Saray Marina or the Yacht Plaza hotel can make use of the swimming pool facilities in these places.

TRANSPORT

Car hire: There are a number of car rental offices in the street immediately behind Ece Saray Marina, so it is easy to compare deals.
Taxis: Several taxi ranks in town, including one near the Ece Saray Marina.
Dolmuş: Dolmuş minibuses run regularly along the road between Yes Marina and the town centre. The main dolmuş station is east of the town centre and you can catch buses to Göcek, Ölü Deniz, Saklıkent and Kemer from here.
Coach: The main otogar is located slightly out of town and has regular departures for Marmaris, İstanbul, Antalya and other cities. Most of the bus companies have sales offices within the town and operate a free bus service to get you from there to the otogar.
Ferry: Daily ferries and a hydrofoil service operate to the Greek island of Rhodes during the summer months only. The services are operated by the Yeşil Dalyan company, which has a sales office directly behind the Ece Saray Marina, Tel: 0252 612 40 15, website: www. yesildalyantravel.com
Air travel: Dalaman airport is roughly one hour away from Fethiye by taxi.

USEFUL INFORMATION

Local tel code: Muğla area, 0252, Fethiye 612/614
Fax: 0252 612 50 68,
email: info@yachtplazahotel. com, website: www. yachtplazahotel.com
Medical: There are a number of private clinics and hospitals in the Fethiye area. Lokman Hekim Esnaf Hospital, Tel: 0252 612 64 00, website: www. esnafhastanesi.com
Tourist information office: Is situated next to the marina office.

Karacaören

North entrance to anchorage: 36°32'.59N 29°03'.61E

NAVIGATION

Charts: Turkish Hydrographic Charts: 312, 313; Turkish Hydrographic Leisure Folio 3002: 3002_1, 3002_2, 3002_8; Imray Charts: G3, G36; Admiralty 236, 1054, SC 5773

A restaurant with a number of mooring buoys is situated in this small inlet that lies on the western side of the İblis Yarımadası peninsula, opposite the Karacaören Adası island. Vessels approaching from the west will pass around the Dökükbaşı Burnu headland on the west of this peninsula, which is lit a night (Fl (2) 5s).

There is a cluster of reefs and rocky islets between Karacaören Adası and the anchorage, which can be difficult to spot through the afternoon swell and choppy waters. Although there is a passage through here immediately to the west of the island, unless the weather is calm and you have good visibility through the water, it is safer to pass around the eastern side of Karacaören Adası and to approach the bay from the north.

You should anchor around the sides of the bay and take a line ashore to prevent swinging. You may be approached by some 'friendly' locals in a boat who will offer to help take your lines for you. They will expect to be paid for this service, so don't agree unless you really do want their help and confirm what they want to be paid in advance. Alternatively, you can use one of the mooring buoys that are maintained by the family-run restaurant ashore. They will not charge you for using these if you eat in their restaurant, which also has toilet and shower facilities and sells fresh bread in the morning.

There are a number of ruins on the shore around the bay and also on the island. You can explore them yourself but make sure you have decent shoes as the ground is rough. Snorkelling around here is excellent as the waters are clear and there is plenty of fish.

Gemiler Adası

Western entrance: 36°33'.32N 29°03'.69E
Eastern entrance: 36°33'.33N 29°04'.75E

NAVIGATION

Charts: Turkish Hydrographic Charts: 312, 313; Turkish Hydrographic Leisure Folio 3002: 3002_1, 3002_2, 3002_8; Imray Charts: G3, G36; Admiralty 236, 1054, SC 5773

There are ruins on the shores of this elongated island, and several restaurants can be seen in the bay on the mainland opposite. It can be hard to make out the island against the shoreline as you approach, but you can estimate its position about 0.5M north of Karacaören Adası off the eastern tip of the İblis Yarımadası peninsula (see above).

You can pass around either end of the island, but watch out as there are rocks just off both ends, and anchor with a line ashore on the western end of the northern side. The depths shelve sharply as you approach the shore, and there are quite a number of sea urchins so wear some shoes when you take your line to the beach. As in Karacaören – see above – you may be offered assistance with anchoring but it is unlikely to be free, so check before accepting to avoid disagreements later.

It is also possible to anchor either with a line ashore or free-swinging in the bay opposite the island. To get the best protection, tuck right into the western side of this bay. Staff from the restaurants here are happy to run clients to and from the island to explore the ruins ashore, and because of all the water traffic you should be careful where you choose to swim and pay attention around you as you do so. You will have to pay a small fee to explore the ruins on the island, and be sure to wear good shoes and take drinking water with you when you go.

Kalevezi Koyu

(Beştaş Limanı, Cold Water Bay)
Middle of bay: 36°33'.70N 29°05'.16E

NAVIGATION

Charts: Turkish Hydrographic Charts: 312, 313;
Turkish Hydrographic Leisure Folio 3002: 3002_1,
3002_2, 3002_8; Imray Charts: G3, G36; Admiralty 236,
1054, SC 5773

This bay on the mainland lies to the east of Gemiler
Adası and has two coves within which you may be able
to anchor safely overnight.

The better and larger of these is on the western side
and can be identified by a white-domed building on the
headland immediately east of it. The family-run Cold
Water Bay restaurant, Mob: 0532 811 05 59, is set just
above and behind the beach and serves Turkish village
food with great views across the bay. It also has a small
mini-market where you can buy basic provisions. The
bay is quite deep and you can get close to the shore
before dropping anchor and tying onto the rocks to
prevent swinging. The bay gets its name from the fresh
water spring that bubbles up in one corner, causing the
water temperature to drop dramatically in this area.

You can take a walk from the restaurant on the
western side towards the old Greek village of
Kayaköy, which was abandoned during the population
exchanges of 1923.

On the eastern side of the bay is another small cove
where there is room for three or four vessels to anchor
with lines ashore. There are no facilities here.

Neither of these locations offers any protection from
southerly winds and swell, and they should not be used
in such conditions. The prevailing westerlies can push a
bit of sea into the bays, but this is more uncomfortable
than dangerous as long as your anchor is well set.

Ölü Deniz

Anchorage: 36°32'.75N 29°06'.70E

Ölü Deniz means 'Dead Sea' in Turkish, and is a busy
resort town that is famed for its beautiful landlocked
lagoon and long sandy beach.

NAVIGATION

Charts: Turkish Hydrographic Charts: 312, 313, 3131;
Turkish Hydrographic Leisure Folio 3002: 3002_1,
3002_2, 3002_8; Imray Charts: G3, G36; Admiralty 236,
1054, SC 5773

Ölü Deniz lies to the east of the İblis Yarımadası
peninsula and is easy to identify by the long sandy
beach running to the south of the lagoon. There are no
dangers in the approach from either direction.

MOORING AND ANCHORING

There is no harbour area at Ölü Deniz, and since 1984
the lagoon has been off limits to yachts and any other
motorised craft in order to protect the environment and
prevent pollution. It is possible to anchor just to the
south-west of the lagoon entrance, in a small bay that
is protected by the Yoğan Burnu headland to the west.
Tuck in close to the coast to get the best shelter here,
taking a line ashore to prevent swinging. You can motor
in your dinghy up to the entrance to the lagoon, but
once you are inside you must not use the engine and
will have to row.

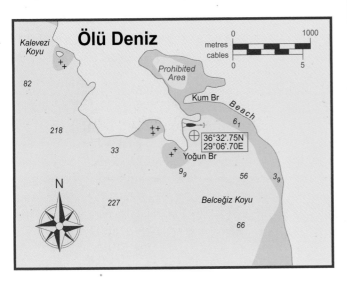

Ölü Deniz beach

Useful information – Ölü Deniz

FACILITIES

Ice: Is sold at supermarkets in the town.

Laundry: Laundry service in the town.

Gas: It may be possible to buy this in the town.

Rubbish: Rubbish bins are located ashore.

Telephone: There are public phone boxes throughout the town and mobile phone reception is good.

Internet: Several internet cafés are situated in the town and some bars and cafés have WiFi connection available to customers.

PROVISIONING AND SERVICES

Grocery shops: There are plenty of mini-markets and a few mid-sized supermarkets in the town, where you will also find several bakeries and butchers.

Local market: None, but nearby Hisarönü holds a market on Mondays.

Banks: Several bank branches are located throughout the town and cash is available from ATM machines situated along the beach and in the main shopping areas.

Pharmacy: Several in the town.

Post office: The PTT office is located on the road leading towards the lagoon from the beachfront.

EATING OUT

Ölü Deniz is actually a fairly standard package tourism resort, which has the usual array of mid-priced, mid-quality restaurants aimed at foreign tourists and their families. As well as the usual Turkish and international dishes, there are plenty of Indian and Chinese restaurants as well, including a Thai one.

There are also a number of restaurants set attractively around the lagoon area, although these may be better to visit during the day as a long row back across the lagoon in the dark may not be the best plan after a bottle of wine with dinner.

ASHORE

Ölü Deniz has all the usual facilities and attractions available in a tourist resort, with excursions to nearby locations such as Saklıkent Gorge and Fethiye town. More interestingly, Ölü Deniz is a popular centre for the sport of paragliding, where willing punters will hurl themselves off the 1,900m heights of nearby Baba Dağ mountain to ride the

Paragliding at Ölü Deniz

thermals over the lagoon and surrounding areas before landing on the beach at Ölü Deniz. There are several companies that offer the chance to experience this in tandem with a qualified instructor, and all have offices in the town and information available at the beach landing sites. The town is also the location of the annual International Air Games competition in October, so there is sure to be plenty to see if you are in the area at that time. Visit the website www.babadag. com for more information.

The nearby attraction of Butterfly Valley can be visited either by car or by boat trip from Ölü Deniz, although it is not a safe place to anchor your own boat if you wish to explore. The valley is home to the Jersey Tiger butterfly, amongst many others, and during the summer months you can see thousands of butterflies of every shape, size and colour. It is also possible to hike up to a 60m waterfall where you will come across an artistic community with performances, activities and workshops scheduled throughout the year. For more information go to www.thebutterflyvalley/ blogspot.com.

For other information about the area you can visit www.oludeniz.com

TRANSPORT

Car hire: Available from a number of agencies within the town.

Taxis: Taxi ranks are situated throughout the town.

Dolmuş: Services operate to surrounding villages.

Coach: There are regular coaches to Fethiye, where you can make onward connections to Antalya, Marmaris, İstanbul and many other places.

Air travel: The nearest airport is at Dalaman (approximately 90 minutes by road).

Ölü Deniz beach is a popular tourist destination

Yediburunlar
(The Seven Capes)
West of Kötü: 36°22'.92N 29°05'.58E

NAVIGATION

Charts: Turkish Hydrographic Charts: 312, 313;
Turkish Hydrographic Leisure Folio 3002: 3002_1,
3002_3; Imray Charts: G3, G36; Admiralty 236, 1054,
SC 5773

This section of coastline lies to the south of Ölü Deniz
and to the north of the long sandy beach at Patara. The
seven headlands in question running from north to
south are Kötü Burun, Sancak Burun, İnkaklık Burun,
Kalkamak Burun, Yassıca Burun, Kılıç Burun and İnce
Burun (also shown as Zeytin Burun on some charts).
The northernmost of these, Kötü Burun, has a light
structure so that it can be identified at night (Fl (2) 10s).

It is advisable to stand well off the shoreline as you
pass along this section of coast, and also along Patara
beach to the south. The seas in this area can be confused
and steep as the onshore swell is reflected from the
uneven coastline and steepens in the approach to the
long beach.

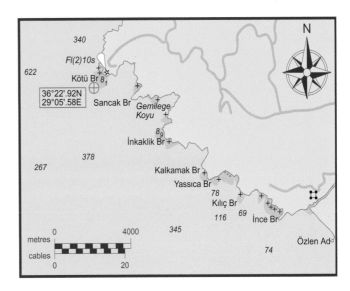

In fact the entire section of coastline between
Ölü Deniz and Kalkan is generally a lee shore that
offers nothing in the way of sheltered anchorages
for almost 30M. If you are heading south with the
prevailing winds then this is generally not a problem,
but if you are trying to head up to the north then it is
advisable to start as early as possible in the morning to
try to get past the Yediburunlar section before the wind
and swell starts to build.

Kalkan
West of Çatal Adaları: 36°12'.80N 29°20'.29E
Entrance to bay: 36°14'.08N 29°23'.41E
Harbour entrance: 36°15'.65N 29°24'.92E

The pleasant town of Kalkan (meaning 'shield' in
Turkish and known in Greek as 'Kalamaki') has a
sheltered harbour and is one of the main stopover
points for vessels travelling along the Seven Capes
stretch of coastline. Like nearby Kaş, the town has
Ottoman Greek origins but lost much of its population
in the Population Exchange that took place in 1923.
Also like Kaş, it retains a laid back but sophisticated
atmosphere with strong historical connections that
sees it frequently named as one of Turkey's best kept
secret destinations.

NAVIGATION

Charts: Turkish Hydrographic Charts: 313, 3131;
Turkish Hydrographic Leisure Folio 3002: 3002_1,
3002_3, 3002_8; Imray Charts: G3, G36; Admiralty 236,
1054, SC 5773

Vessels approaching from the north past the Seven
Capes should be able to pick out the islands of Çatal
Adaları as they leave the long expanse of Patara beach

to port. The western tip of the larger island can be
identified at night with a light (Fl 5s). You can pass
either to the north or the south of this pair of islands,
but do not try to pass in between.

Vessels approaching from the direction of Kaş will
need to avoid the few islands that lie along this route,
and in particular watch out for the isolated danger mark
above the 2m shoal at WPT 36°11'.60N 29°29'.00E. Once
you have rounded the southern end of Heybeli Adası
you should be able to pick out the İnce Burun headland
to the east of Kalkan bay. The winds tend to blow quite

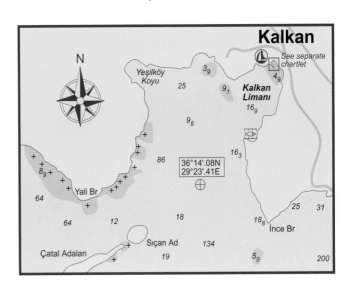

strongly from the west from early in the day, so unless you fancy a long beat upwind it is best to make an early start if heading towards Kalkan from Kaş direction.

Once you have entered the bay, continue to head north into it and the whitewashed houses of Kalkan will be clearly visible extending up the hillsides around the harbour.

BERTHING AND ANCHORING

Kalkan has a fairly roomy harbour and there is usually more space here than in nearby Kaş. A rocky mole stretches along the southern side of the harbour, and the entrance is lit at night with both red and green lights. A buoyed swimming area extends from the beach lying immediately next to the harbour entrance.

Once you are inside the harbour there is room to anchor stern-to along the quays to either side of the entrance. The far end of the harbour is shallower and tends to be occupied by dive boats and day tripper boats. There can be strong gusts blowing off the hills in the evenings and afternoons here, so ensure that your anchor is well dug in before leaving the boat.

The coastguard and harbour master's offices are located at the western end of the harbour. There is a fee for overnight berthing in Kalkan.

If you prefer to anchor then head west of the harbour towards the bay named Yeşilköy Koyu. You will find space here to free swing in 5-10m close to the beach,

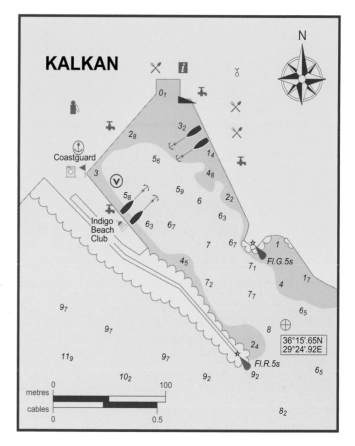

or further out with a line ashore in 10-15m. Again, you need to ensure that your anchor is well set as there can be strong gusts from the hillsides.

Kalkan harbour

Useful information – Kalkan

Kalkan beach and harbour entrance

FACILITIES

Water and electricity: Available along the dock.

Fuel: Not available unless by a visiting fuel tanker.

Showers: For a fee yachtsmen can use the shower and toilet facilities at The Indigo Beach Club.

Ice: Ice and gas can be purchased at the town markets.

Laundry: The Indigo Beach Club offers a laundry service.

Rubbish: Rubbish bins are along the quay.

Telephone: The mobile phone reception in the area is good. Public phone boxes are located throughout the town and phone cards can be bought in mini-markets and kiosks.

Internet: WiFi connection is available at the Indigo Beach Club as well as at several other bars and cafés around the harbour area.

PROVISIONING AND SERVICES

Grocery shops: There are several small supermarkets on the road that runs along the northern side of the harbour. They will deliver to your boat for free. There is also a local market held on Thursdays along the road leading away from the harbour.

Bakery: A bakery and a butcher can be found in the town.

Banks: There are branches of Yapı Kredi, Garantı Bank, Akbank and Deniz Bank in Kalkan. All have ATMs and money changing facilities.

Pharmacy: There are a few in the town.

Post office: The PTT office is located at the top end of the town near the bus and dolmuş station.

EATING OUT

Kalkan has a good choice of restaurants that cater for all budgets, although the ones surrounding the harbour area tend to be more pricey. Some of these restaurants, such as the very smart Aubergine restaurant, Mob: 0532 612 02 77, offer extras such as live music and jazz nights on certain days of the week, and many of them have terraces with excellent views across the harbour and the bay. Look out also for the Korsan Marina and Korsan Fish Terraces restaurants, Tel: 0242 844 32 60, website: www.korsankalkan.com, which are both run by the same couple and have enviable positions overlooking the harbour.

ASHORE

Kalkan town stretches up the hillsides surrounding the harbour area and is full of narrow streets and twisting alleys to explore. The usual range of Turkish products and souvenirs is on offer here, but the commercial atmosphere is more relaxed than in many places, making it pleasant to browse the shops at your own pace.

Diving and watersports are popular activities in Kalkan, as are the boat day trips to nearby Kekova. Blue Marlin Water Sports, Tel: 0242 844 27 83, website: www.bmwatersports-kalkan.com, has an office right next to the harbour from where you can organise fishing trips, speed boat rental, dinghy sailing and waterskiing activities.

Diving trips and instruction are available from a few outfits in town, including the Dolphin Scuba Team, Tel: 0242 844 22 42, website: www.dolphinscubateam.com, and C & C Scuba, Mob: 0532 311 76 10, website: www.ccscuba.com.

If you feel like exploring inland by car then there is plenty to see. Patara beach is 15km to the west of the town and is not accessible by boat due to the lack of shelter from the prevailing winds. The ruins of an ancient port and a modern sleepy Turkish village form the backdrop to the beach, and the town was the birthplace of St Nicholas. The 18km long beach is a protected nesting site for the area's sea turtles.

Other nearby sites of interest include the ruins of ancient Xanthos at modern day Kınık on the Xanthos river, and the shrine to the God Leto at nearby Letoön, both of which are recognised as UNESCO World Heritage sites. The impressive Saklıkent Gorge is only 40km from Kalkan, with opportunities for trekking and white water rafting.

TRANSPORT

Car hire: Available from several travel agencies and hire companies in the town. Enes Rent-a-Car has an office right next to the harbour, Tel: 0242 844 39 61/ 36 74, website: www.enesrentacar.net

Taxis: There is a taxi rank close to the harbour.

Coach: The otogar is at the top end of the town next to the Fethiye-Antalya main road. Coach services operate frequently to Antalya and other large cities.

Dolmuş: Dolmuş minibus services operate to Fethiye and Kaş.

Air travel: The nearest airports are at Dalaman (145km) and Antalya (210km).

USEFUL INFORMATION

Local tel code: Antalya area 0242, Kalkan 844.

Harbour master: Office next to the harbour.

Medical services: The Tuana Medical Centre is a small clinic with 24-hour emergency cover and some outpatient services, Tel: 0242 844 22 44.

Hospital: The nearest large international hospital can be found in Fethiye.

Local information websites: www.kalkan.org.tr – an online guide to the town. www.kalkanturkey.com – a general guide produced by a local property sales company. www.enjoykalkan.com – an independent residents' website with information about the town and its surrounding area.

Kalkan harbour master's office

Kaş Limanı

Entrance to Bucak Denizi: 36°11'.65N 29°34'.54E
Between Kastelorizo and Kaş: 36°10'.69N 29°35'.70E
Harbour entrance: 36°11'.73N 29°38'.50E
Anchorage entrance: 36°11'.11N 29°38'.40E

Kaş is a gem of a town tucked into a bay and located conveniently between Kalkan and Kekova Roads. It is founded on the Lycian town of Antiphellos and both rock tombs and sarcophagi from this era are visible around the town today. Many of the town's original inhabitants were Greeks who were expelled during the population exchange after WWI, but the area seems to have recovered since then and still has close ties with the nearby Greek island of Kastelorizo (Meis Adası in Turkish). The town has a laid back atmosphere and is gathering a reputation as one of Turkey's premier outdoor activities destinations. There is plenty to explore in the winding streets that surround the harbour and extend up the hill, as well as in the nearby countryside, or you can just relax and do a bit of shopping in the town.

NAVIGATION

Charts: Turkish Hydrographic Charts: 313, 3131, 321, 3211; Turkish Hydrographic Leisure Folio 3002: 3002_1, 3002_4, 3002_9; Imray Charts: G3, G36, G40; Admiralty 236, 1054, SC 5773

Light structure at the entrance to Kaş harbour

Kaş lies approximately 12M to the east of Kalkan and the same distance west of Kekova Roads. The Greek island of Nisos Meyisti (also known as Kastelorizo) lies opposite the entrance to the bay, with smaller uninhabited Greek islands to either side. If you are approaching from the Kalkan direction there are a number of submerged rocks, shallow areas and small islands to look out for. The islands are fairly easy to identify in daylight, and a passage of due east from the south end of Öksüz Adası should bring you safely into Kaş Limanı.

Vessels approaching from the east also have a few islands to look out for, particularly between Kastelorizo and the Turkish mainland. If you can hug the coast

Approaching Kaş. The harbour is on the left

Bucak Denizi, the location of the new marina that is planned to open in 2010

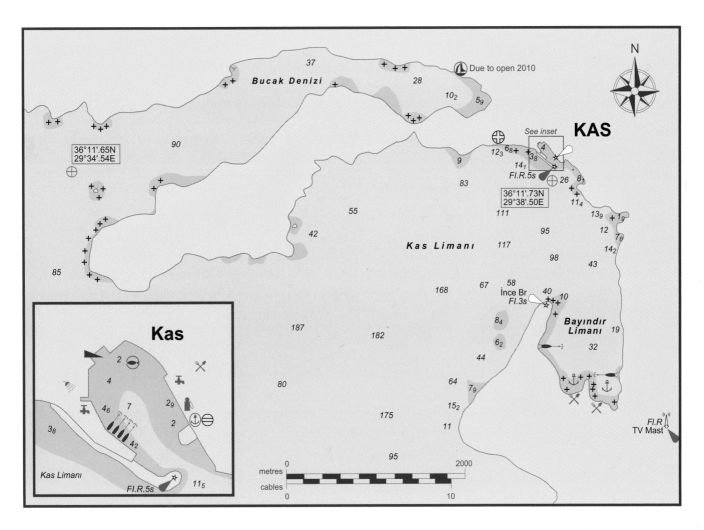

Light structure and rocks at the entrance to Bayındır Limanı

around Gata Burnu you will easily avoid these areas.

There are a few lights to guide you if you are approaching the area in the dark. Kastelorizo has one on its northern tip (Fl WR 4.5s) and Nisos Strongili has one on its southern end (Fl 5s). A sectored light (Fl WRG 10s) guides you towards the docking area in Bucak Denizi, and a white light (Fl 3s) marks the headland at the entrance to Bayındır Limanı. The entrance to Kaş harbour is marked with a red light (Fl R 5s).

Once you are within Kaş Limanı the town buildings can be easily spotted on the hillside surrounding the harbour, which is in the north-east part of the bay. Entrance to the harbour is straightforward and free of any dangers, although you will see buoyed swimming areas just next to the entrance.

BERTHING AND ANCHORING

The majority of berths in Kaş harbour are permanently occupied by day trippers, fishing boats and dive boats, which leaves fairly few spaces for visiting yachts. It is worth making the effort to arrive a little earlier than usual if you want to be sure of a place on the dock. Otherwise you can overnight quite securely in one of the nearby anchorages. If you do make it into the harbour then berthing is stern-to with an anchor wherever you can find space. The northern end is shallow and used only by small fishing boats, and there is a customs area immediately to your right as you enter the harbour. A fee is charged for overnight mooring in Kaş. Work has been done in 2009 to extend the quay within the harbour walls, so there should be more space available for berthing in 2010, although this is likely to be taken up by local diving and day-tripper boats.

If you prefer to anchor or there are no spaces left in the harbour then you can head approximately 1M to the south into Bayındır Limanı. This large double bay provides plenty of space to anchor in 10-15m, either free swinging at the southern end or with a line ashore around the edge of the bay. Although the bay is well sheltered from the prevailing winds, the holding is not always the best as the bottom is weedy in places, so try to dig your anchor through the weed as you lay it. Another anchorage lies off the Çukurbağ Yarımadası peninsula, just to the north of Condur Burnu.

To the north of this peninsula is Bucak Denizi inlet, which is the site of a proposed marina development. After being postponed for several years, work was restarted on this project by Makyol Construction in 2009, and it is planned to open the marina for business in 2010. A breakwater has been constructed from material excavated from the Kaş-Kalkan road construction project, and pontoons should be installed over the 2009/2010 winter. You can view plans for construction on the website www.kasmarina.com.tr. Hopefully the new breakwater will provide protection to the berths behind, as the prevailing winds can push an uncomfortable swell in here. Eventually the marina will have berths for up to 438 yachts on several floating pontoons, and the surrounding area will be landscaped to accommodate bars, restaurants, shops, chandleries and technical services, and an attractive promenade to walk along into Kaş town.

Useful information – Kaş Limanı

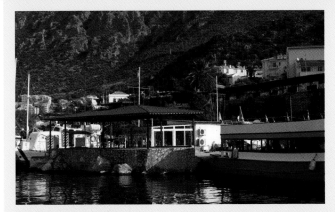

Coastguard office in Kaş

FACILITIES

Water and electricity: On the dock in Kaş harbour.

Fuel: Available by truck only.

Showers: For 6TL you can use the showers near the harbour.

Toilets: Public toilets next to the mosque cost 0.50TL. Others are located in the shower/laundry block and cost the same amount.

Ice: Is sold in mini-markets and from an ice seller near the showers and laundry area.

Laundry: Available near the harbour.

Gas: Ask at the mini-markets in the town.

Rubbish: Bins along the quay are emptied daily.

Telephone: Public phone boxes are located near the mosque and next to the PTT.

Internet: WiFi connection is available from several bars and restaurants in the town. There is an internet café opposite the PTT.

PROVISIONING AND SERVICES

Grocery shops: Several mini-markets in town stock most supplies, including a couple very close to the harbour. Most will deliver to your yacht for free. A larger Gempa supermarket is on the road leading out of the town towards Kalkan.

Bakery: There is a choice of bakeries and butchers in the town.

Banks: There are a few ATMs in the town, and also a branch of TC Ziraat bank next to the PTT.

Pharmacy: Several in the town.

Post: The PTT office is on Bahçe Sokak, just to the north of the harbour next to the belediye park.

EATING OUT

There is a wide choice of restaurants in Kaş, most of which are concentrated in the area surrounding the harbour and main shopping streets. Prices are generally higher than in other places as Kaş is a rather upmarket destination; so take care, particularly when ordering fish and wine.

ASHORE

Kaş is a very pleasant town to explore, with plenty of narrow winding streets to give it ambience, an attractive bazaar area and several Lycian sarcophagi dotted around the streets and hillsides. There is a definite arts and crafts theme to many of the shops in the town, and you can buy some very attractive pieces, including original artwork like paintings and sculpture, often depicting the characteristic Lycian architecture of the region. Carpets are also a popular product here, and keep an eye-out for locally produced oregano, said to be the best in Turkey.

Kaş is a good base from which to explore the surrounding area. Boat trips depart daily for Kekova Roads and the Greek island of Kastelorizo. There are also a number of dive companies that offer tuition as well as a range of diving trips for the already qualified. Many of the tour operators in town have an emphasis on ecological activities, which seem more interesting than the usual bus trips and jeep safaris (although these are available as well). The Dragoman Outdoor Activities Centre, Tel: 0242 836 36 14, website: www.dragoman-turkey.com, offers a variety of guided hiking trails, sea kayaking trips around Kekova Roads and the novel sport of 'coasteering' – ie, exploring the coast at sea level by swimming, climbing, wading and jumping.

There are several areas of well preserved archaeological remains in the vicinity of Kaş, all of which can be visited either as part of a tour or independently with a hire car.

If you are visiting towards the end of June then you may be in time for the annual Kaş Lycian festival, which usually features traditional

Kaş harbour

Useful information – Kaş Limanı (continued)

Stone sarcophagus in Kaş

music and dancing and means that the town will be especially busy.

TRANSPORT

Car hire: Available from several tour operators in the town.

Taxis: There is a taxi rank right next to the harbour.

Coach: The otogar is located on the road out of town and is the start point for intercity coach services that run daily to Fethiye and Antalya, where you can change for other destinations.

Dolmuş: Local services run to Kalkan and various other nearby villages.

Ferry: The Meis Express operates between Kaş and the Greek island of Kastelorizo. There are departures every weekday morning during the summer and twice a week during the winter – always weather dependent. You can book directly in the harbour or through a tour operator in town, Tel: 0242 836 17 25, Mob: 0532 331 97 59, website: www. meisexpress.com

Air travel: The nearest airports: Antalya (190km) and Dalaman (166km).

USEFUL INFORMATION

Local tel code: Antalya area 0242, Kaş 836.

Kaş Marina: Tel: 0212 351 4151; Fax: 0212 351 4165; email: info@kasmarina.com. tr; website: www.kasmarina. com.tr

Coastguard and harbour master office: Situated immediately to the right of the harbour entrance.

Tourist information office: In the main square next to the harbour, Tel: 0242 836 12 38.

Doctor: There are several doctors' surgeries that are used to dealing with tourists. Dr Munis Ozun speaks English and has a 24-hour call service, Tel: 0532 582 20 54. The surgery is close to the harbour.

Dentist: A few in town, including one near the PTT.

Hospital: A small state hospital can be found in the town, and several large private and teaching hospitals in Antalya.

Carpet displays and typical Kaş architecture

Waterfront ruins on Kekova Adası

Kekova Roads
(Ölü Deniz)

Western entrance 1 (W): 36°10'.08N 29°49'.85E
Western entrance 2 (E): 36°10'.26N 29°50'.36E
Eastern entrance off Kekova Burnu: 36°12'.13N
29°54'.50E

Kekova Roads is the name given to the area between Kekova Adası and the mainland, approximately 15M to the east of Kaş. It is also known locally as Ölü Deniz (Dead Sea), similar to the lagoon area just to the south of Fethiye.

The area is the site of the preserved ruins of several ancient settlements, dating from Byzantine times, which can be observed both above and below the water. The whole area is under a preservation order, meaning that tourism has remained low key and fairly unobtrusive. Most visitors come by private boat or by daily trip boats from nearby towns, although several small pansiyons have now sprung up to cater for the determined overland visitor.

One of the main attractions here is the partially submerged ruins lying off the northern side of Kekova Adası. This once flourishing settlement was destroyed by a series of earthquakes in the second century AD, and partially slid off the island into the sea. Anchoring, snorkelling and diving are all forbidden in this area

to prevent damage to the remains and discourage the taking of 'souvenirs'. The best way to view the area is on one of the glass bottomed tripper boats that depart regularly from Kaleköy and Üçağız. Otherwise you could take your dinghy across from the anchorage at Tersane and hang your head over the side with a face mask on.

Semi-submerged ruins

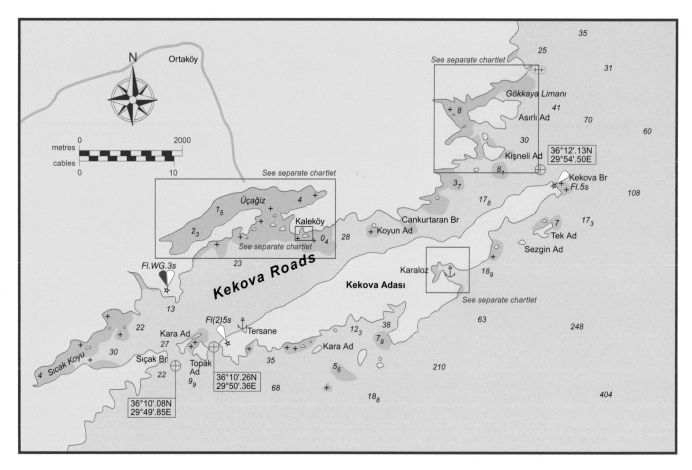

NAVIGATION

Charts: Turkish Hydrographic Charts: 321, 3212; Turkish Hydrographic Leisure Folio 3002: 3002_1, 3002_4, 3002_10; Imray Charts: G3, G36, G40; Admiralty 236, 1054, SC 5773

Vessels approaching from the Kaş direction should have a good downwind blast for most of the way. It is easy to just follow the coastline as you head east away from Kaş, which will enable you to keep well clear of the various islands that lie to the south of here. Watch out for a group of rocks that break the surface closer inland just before you reach the Ulu Burnu headland. Once around here you can head for the southern end of İç Adası and then follow the coastline north-east directly towards Kekova. It is also possible to pass between İç Adası and the Sıcak Yarımadası peninsula, and this may be a better route to take on the return journey to avoid the strong afternoon winds and swell that are generated by the *meltemi*. There are a couple of small bays on the southern sides of İç Adası and Sıcak Yarımadası where it is possible to anchor and take some shelter from the prevailing winds, but these are often occupied by gulets, leaving no space for other boats.

The western entrance to Kekova Roads lies between the mainland headland of Sıcak Burun and the western end of Kekova Adası, which is lit at night (Fl (2) 5s). There are two channels that lie to either side of a cluster of islands and rocks in the centre of the entrance. The western channel is easier to follow; just hug the coastline around Sıcak Burun and it will take you in. It is also indicated with a sectored light on the mainland opposite (Fl WG 3s); just stay in the central white sector to ensure safe entry.

The other channel lies between Topak Adası and the western end of Kekova Adası. Take care not to pass between Topak Adası and Kara Adası by mistake as there is no passage through here. In fact there is an anchorage between these two islands that is much used by charter gulets. Entrance is from the south only and you have to exit in the same direction. It is open to the prevailing winds so not recommended in strong weather or overnight. A shoal extends north of the

Anchorage amongst the islands in the western entrance to Kekova Roads

western end of Kekova Adası, so give this a wide berth if you are planning to head east from here.

Vessels approaching Kekova Roads from the east will have a clear run along the coast from Finike, although it will be upwind all the way and is best started early before the wind and swell have a chance to build. The eastern end of Kekova Adası is lit (Fl 5s) and the entrance here is free of dangers.

Once you are within Kekova Roads the hilltop castle at Kaleköy is an obvious landmark and you can use this to orient yourself.

Sıcak Koyu
Sıcak Koyu: 36°10'.32N 29°49'.20E

This long narrow bay provides plenty of space to anchor in about 5m of water for lunch or overnight, or take a line to the southern shore. The bay is sheltered from the prevailing winds although there are sometimes gusts from the hillsides. At night the entrance can be partially obstructed with fishing nets, so make sure you are here before dusk so that you can spot these.

There are a couple of restaurants ashore with basic facilities. A 20-minute walk across the isthmus connecting Sıcak Yarımadası to the mainland will bring you to Asar Bay and the ruins of a settlement named Aperlai, which are partially underwater. Snorkelling is permitted here but do not be tempted to collect souvenirs as this is illegal.

Tersane anchorage

Tersane
Tersane anchorage: 36°10'.34N 29°50'.75E

This small bay lies on the western end of Kekova Adası and faces north towards Üçağız and Kaleköy. It is perfect for either lunch or overnight, although the small size means there is only room for three to four boats at most. Take a long line to the western shore but beware of sunken walls that extend underwater from here. These are the remains of the old naval dockyard belonging to the sunken town further along the island (*tersane* means dockyard in Turkish) and more ruins can be seen ashore, including a large archway right on the beach. The water is clear and good for snorkelling.

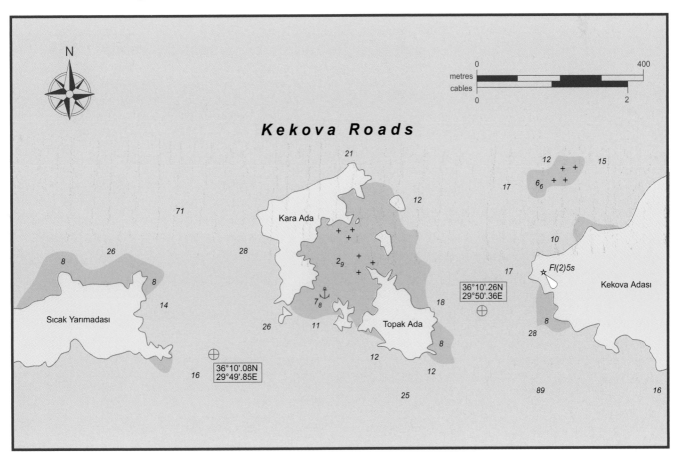

View from the castle at Kaleköy towards Üçağız

Üçağız

Entrance to Üçağız: 36°11'.38N 29°51'.13E

This long thin bay lies almost due north of Tersane anchorage and the entrance is situated to the west of the castle at Kaleköy. Many small islets and rocks extend from the shore to either side of the entrance, several of which have ruined buildings on them. There is a slightly larger island in the middle of the entrance

proper, and you can pass to either side of this and continue towards the village or one of the anchorages within the bay.

Üçağız can be reached by road so there is more in the way of restaurants and facilities here. Three restaurants near the village mosque (Onur's, Hassan's and Ibrahim's) have jetties right next to each other where you can tie up alongside. All of them listen on VHF Ch 16 if you want to call them up

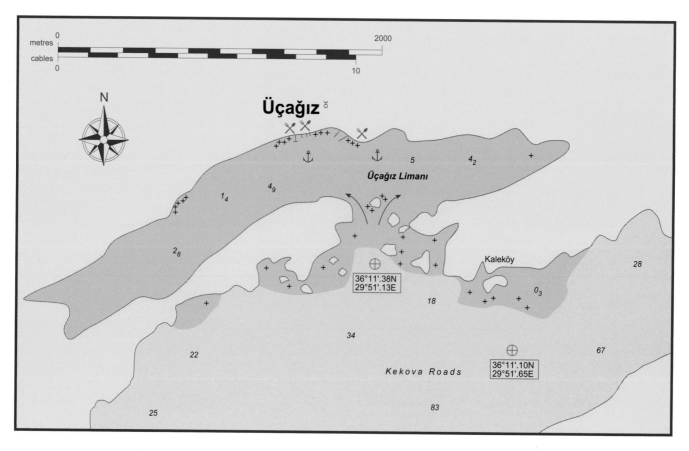

Rocky entrance to Üçağız

and book a spot, a boat trip or to arrange to be collected from your boat at anchor. Water and showers are available here but no fuel or electricity. The Marina restaurant is at the western end of the village, and has a dock with lazylines for stern-to berthing. The Theimussa restaurant and pansiyon at the eastern end of the village has a small dock suitable for dinghies only. Other docks in the village are used by day tripper and glass-bottomed boats, and also the coastguard who is on hand to check for any illegal diving activities.

Vessels can anchor in 5-10m to either side of the village, leaving a clear passage for the tripper boats that come and go from the village jetties. There is plenty of room to free swing but the far end of each side of the bay is very shallow so stay in the middle.

The village has several other restaurants and cafés,

Ruined buildings and sarcophagi along the shoreline

and a couple of small markets where you can buy basic provisions and ice. The ruins of ancient Teimiussa can be explored along the shore to the east of the village. There is little water movement because of the narrow entrance channel, so swimming is not advised in this bay. Dolmuş services operate between here and Kaş to the west and Demre (Kale) to the east.

Restaurant jetties in Üçağız

Restaurant jetties at Kaleköy

Kaleköy

Approach to Kaleköy: 36°11'.10N 29°51'.65E

This small village occupies the site of ancient Simena and is dominated by a castle that is situated immediately above the entrance and makes a conspicuous landmark to aim for. Clusters of small rocks lie to either side of the entrance but these are easy to spot and pass between. There is space to free swing at anchor just off the village in about 10m of water, or you can tie alongside one of the private jetties belonging to one of three restaurants (Hasan's Roma, Hassan's

Rocks line the approach to Kaleköy

Deniz and Smile's Likya). All of these offer water, electricity, toilets and showers, and some even claim WiFi access.

Buildings straggle up the hillside towards the castle and it is well worth the short hike to get up here. Entrance costs 8TL and once inside you will be rewarded with spectacular views towards Üçağız to the north, Kekova Adası to the south and the Kekova Roads area stretching away east to west. The castle also boasts a small amphitheatre, reputed to be one of the smallest discovered.

There are a couple of small mini-markets where you can buy basic provisions, including bread and ice.

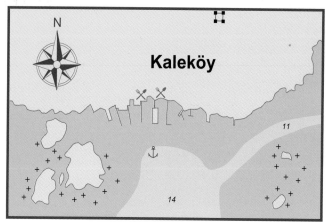

Kaleköy castle

Karaloz

Karaloz anchorage: 36°11'.05N 29°53'.48E

This small and stunning bay is located on the southern side of Kekova Adası, roughly in the middle. It is surrounded by steep hillsides and hooks around to give good shelter from the *meltemi*. A cave on the northern side of the entrance helps to identify it from the surrounding hills. The bay is quite deep so always take a line ashore and do not attempt to stay here if southerly winds are predicted. There are no restaurants or facilities ashore.

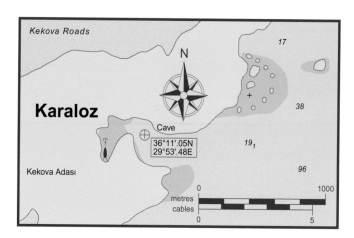

Gökkaya Limanı

Gökkaya Limanı (between islands): 36°12'.40N 29°54'.20E

This beautiful bay is on the mainland just to the north of the eastern end of Kekova Adası. Several small islands lie in the entrance to the bay, and you should

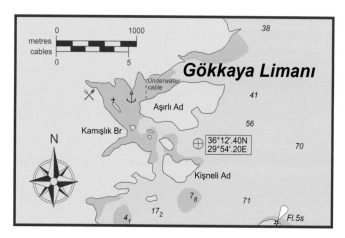

pass to either side of the larger Asırlı Adası. Do not try to pass between Kişneli Adası and the mainland as there are shallow areas and submerged rocks here. An underwater cable running north from the western end of Asırlı Adası supplies power to the island, so do not attempt to anchor near here.

Vessels can free swing at anchor in around 5m off the restaurant in the northern arm of the bay. There are natural springs ashore here and a water taxi service operates to the nearby town of Kale (Demre), home of St Nicholas. A variety of provisions and services can be found here, and it is also a good place from which to explore the impressive ruins at ancient Myra.

Alternative anchorages exist around the bay in various inlets and small coves. Space is restricted in these areas so you will need to take lines ashore to prevent swinging. There is a waterline cave on the southern end of Asırlı Adası. Although it is not possible to anchor here, you can reach it by dinghy from the mainland anchorage.

Useful information – Kekova Roads

FACILITIES
Water and electricity: Are both available at restaurant jetties in Üçağız and Kaleköy.
Showers: Restaurants in Üçağız and Kaleköy offer shower facilities to visiting yachtsmen.
Ice: Can be bought in Üçağız and Kaleköy.
Rubbish: Rubbish disposal services are in Üçağız and Kaleköy.

Telephone: The mobile reception in the area is good. Public phones are available in Üçağız.
Internet: WiFi is advertised in some restaurants in both Üçağız and Kaleköy.

PROVISIONING AND SERVICES
Limited provisions available in the villages of Üçağız and Kaleköy. There are no banks or pharmacies, but there is a small PTT office in Üçağız.

Beautiful flowers at Kaleköy restaurant

Restaurant in Üçağız

Andraki

Entrance to the bay: 36°13'.41N 29°56'.31E

NAVIGATION

Charts: Turkish Hydrographic Charts: 321, 3212;
Turkish Hydrographic Leisure Folio 3002: 3002_1,
3002_4, 3002_10; Imray Charts: G3, G36, G40;
Admiralty 236, 1054, SC 5773

The bay of Andraki lies approximately 2M north-east
of Gökkaya Limanı and offers a sandy beach, some
facilities ashore and reasonable shelter. The bay was
once the main port for the ancient town of Myra,
although these days it has become silted up by the river,
which empties into the sea nearby and is no longer
usable as a deep water harbour.

A rocky mole has been constructed to protect the bay
from southerly conditions, and the quay is home to
numerous day tripper boats that cater for visitors from
the town of Demre (also known as Kale). These boats

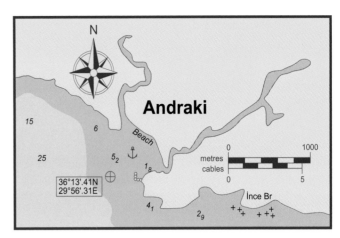

return to the harbour each evening, so there is rarely
space on the quay for visiting yachts. You will find
room, however, to free swing in 5-10m off the beach.

Water is available on the quay, and a few cafés
and restaurants are ashore, along with a mini-market
where you can get basic provisions. You can travel
into Demre by dolmuş minibus or taxi during the
summer season.

Finike

South of headland: 36°15'.97N 30°09'.27E
Marina entrance: 36°17'.70N 30°09'.15E

Finike is the location of a modern marina and is also
a port of entry for vessels arriving in and departing
from Turkish waters. The marina is a popular place for
cruising boats to overwinter, and is also a good location

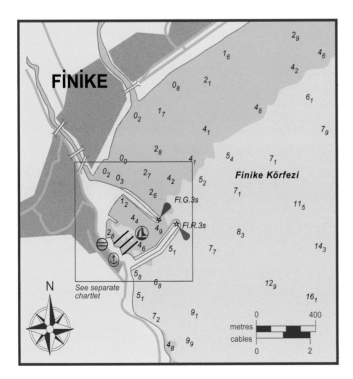

Aerial view of Setur Finike Marina

to spend a couple of days if you want to organise some
overland trips to the ruins of Myra, near Demre, or to
the natural flames of the Chimera and ruins of Olympos
further to the east.

NAVIGATION

Charts: Turkish Hydrographic Charts: 321, 3131;
Turkish Hydrographic Leisure Folio 3002: 3002_1,
3002_8; Imray Charts: G40; Admiralty 236, 237, SC 5773

Finike town lies at the western end of the long bay
of Finike Körfezi, which is easily identified as you

approach. If you are coming from the west you will not be able to see the harbour until you have rounded the headland to the west and are close-to. There is a light on this headland (FR) and also the marina entrance is lit on either side (Fl G 5s & Fl R 5s).

BERTHING

Setur Finike Marina has berthing spaces for around 270 boats up to 70m long. Call the marina on VHF Ch 73 as you approach to request a berth and they will send someone in a dinghy to guide you in and assist with berthing. All berthing is stern-to with lazylines. The marina can also be contacted on Tel: 0242 855 50 30, Fax: 0242 855 50 32, email: finike@seturmarinas.com, website: www.seturmarinas.com

FORMALITIES

All formalities can be completed here as the customs patrol, harbour master and health offices are all located within the marina.

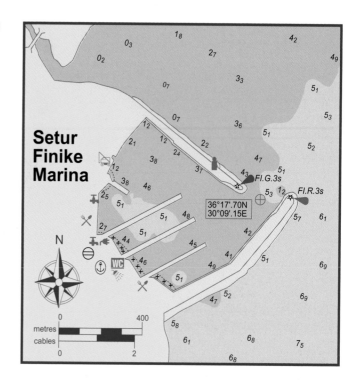

Useful information – Finike

FACILITIES

Water and electricity: Each berth is equipped with water and electricity.
Fuel: The fuel dock is immediately to your right as you enter the marina.
Showers: Toilet and shower blocks are at the marina.
Ice: Is sold in the marina supermarket.
Laundry: There is a self-service laundry facility in the marina.
Gas: Available at the marina.
Rubbish: Rubbish disposal and recycling bins ashore, and also waste oil and bilge disposal facilities in the boatyard.
Telephone: Public phones are situated in the marina and the mobile phone reception here is good.
Internet: WiFi connection is offered throughout the marina and visitors can use a PC terminal in the marina office.

YACHT SERVICES AND CHANDLERY

The marina has an 80 ton travel lift and a hard standing area that can accommodate up to 150 boats. Water and electricity are available throughout the boatyard, and there are a number of workshops and companies offering technical

support and professional standards of workmanship. Contact the marina office for more information.

The Öztürk Marin Chandlery in the marina stocks a good range of spares and is happy to order anything else that may be required. It can also arrange for sail repairs and technical service on boats, Tel: 0242 855 48 30/31, Mob: 0532 437 58 30.

PROVISIONING AND SERVICES

Grocery shops: The well-stocked Toprak supermarket is located in the marina and can deliver to your yacht. There are a few others within walking distance.
Bakery: Fresh bread is available from the Toprak market in the marina.
Butcher: In the town.
Local market: Held on Wednesdays and Saturdays in central Finike.
Banks: There are several bank branches in the town, all with ATM machines, including Yapı Kredi bank opposite the marina entrance.
Pharmacy: A few pharmacies can be found in the town.
Post office: The PTT office is in central Finike.

EATING OUT

There are several restaurants located within the marina, including Altın Sofra, Tel: 0242 855 12 81, Finike restaurant, Tel: 0242 855 50 02, and the Pergole restaurant. There are other options within walking distance of Finike town.

ASHORE

Finike is a good place to base yourself for a few days to explore the surrounding area, which is rich in ruins, remains and attractions.

The town of Demre (also known as Kale) is about 30km to the west of Finike, and is renowned for being the home of St Nicholas, better known to us as Father Christmas. Turkish legend has it that St Nicholas overheard the three sisters of a poor family plotting to sell themselves one at a time to afford the dowries that would enable each of them to get married and relieve the burden on their family. To save the sisters from this fate he collected a bag of gold and threw it through the open window for two years in a row on 25 December. On the third occasion he found the

window closed due to the cold weather so threw the coins down the chimney instead, where they fell into the stockings that the youngest daughter had hung up to dry. The Church of St Nicholas can be visited in Demre town centre and used to hold the bones of the saint until they were looted by Italians in the 11th Century.

Close to Demre are the fantastic ruins of ancient Myra where St Nicholas was once a bishop, and you can still see examples of ancient tombs and amphitheatres today.

Travelling in the other direction brings you to the ruins at Olympos, where you can stay overnight in one of the treetop camps if you fancy something really different. You may also witness the spontaneous fires caused by gases seeping out of the ground and bursting into flames on contact with the area. This phenomenon is known as the Chimera, and was originally attributed to the mythical beast of that name, which is also associated with the Sicilian volcano Mount Etna.

TRANSPORT
Car hire: Toprak Rent-a-Car has an office in the marina, Tel: 0242 855 24 16, and there are other agencies in the town.
Taxis: There is a taxi rank at the entrance to the marina and others in the nearby town.
Coach: The bus station is located about 500m from the marina and has regular connections to Antalya and the surrounding areas.

Air travel: The nearest airport is in Antalya, which is 125km from Finike, approximately a 90-minute drive. Dalaman airport is 225km in the other direction, approximately 3 hours.

USEFUL INFORMATION
Local tel code: Antalya area, 0242, Finike 855.
Medical: There are medical facilities at the marina and a hospital is situated close to the town.

Entrance to Finike Marina

Yardımcı Burnu
(Gelidonya, Beşadalar)
**Safe water between the headland and first island:
36°12'.29N 30°24'.30E**

NAVIGATION
Charts: Turkish Hydrographic Charts: 321, 322, 3223; Imray Charts: G40; Admiralty 236, 237, SC 5773

The Yardımcı Burnu headland has proved to be treacherous to vessels in the past and is the location of the wreck of a 13th century Phoenician trading ship, one of the first ever to be scientifically excavated in 1960 after discovery by a sponge diver. Artefacts recovered from the wreckage are on display in Bodrum's Museum of Underwater Archaeology (see page 100).

The cape is easily identified by the islands lying to the south of it, which make up the Beşadalar (Five islands) group that was the cause of the Phoenician shipwreck. There is depth and searoom enough to pass between the islands and the mainland.

Çavuş Limanı

Entrance to bay: 36°18'.53N
30°29'.22E

NAVIGATION

Charts: Turkish
Hydrographic Charts: 321,
322, 3223; Imray Charts: G40;
Admiralty 236, 237, SC 5773

Çavuş Limanı is a large
sheltered bay situated
between the headlands of
Fener Burnu and Çavuş
Burnu, approximately 6M
north of the Yardımcı Burnu
headland (see page 209).

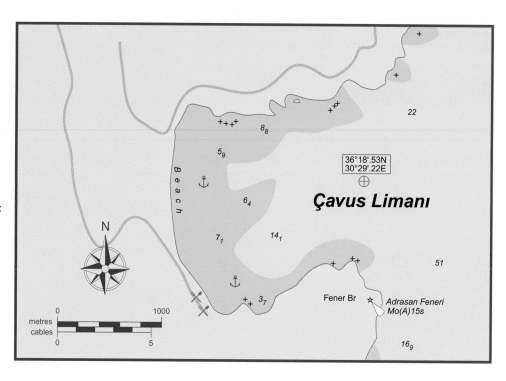

Vessels approaching from
the south will be able to identify the rocky island of
Sulu Ada, and can pass safely to either side of this.
Do not venture too close to the island, especially in
rough weather, as there are numerous rocks in the
surrounding waters and they are not always easy to
spot amongst the breaking swell. There is a light on the
Fener Burnu headland (Mo (A) 15s).

Vessels approaching from the north will identify the
smaller island of Pırasalı Adası off the Çavuş Burnu

headland, and can also pass safely to either side of this.

The long beach at the head of the bay is easy to
identify as you approach, and you can free swing at
anchor in 5-10m off the beach or take a line ashore if
you plan to stay the night. Shelter is generally good
from the prevailing southerly winds, but the bay is
open to any weather coming from the north or east.

There are some facilities ashore, including a couple of
small hotels, a mini-market and some beach restaurants.

Cineviz Limanı

Entrance to bay, just north of the group of rocks:
36°22'.31N 30°29'.97E

NAVIGATION

Charts: Turkish Hydrographic Charts: 321, 322, 3223;
Imray Charts: G40; Admiralty 236, 237, SC 5773

Cineviz Limanı is a remote anchorage that offers
good shelter from the prevailing southerly conditions.
It is tucked away on the northern side of an
isthmus connecting Cineviz Adası to the mainland,
approximately 2.5M north of Çavuş Burnu. Sazak Koyu,
on the southern side of this isthmus, is occupied by
several fish farms and is not a good place to anchor.

It is sometimes difficult to pick out the entrance to the
bay as you approach. Vessels coming from the south
can follow the coastline north from Çavuş Burnu until
they reach Cineviz Adası and can head into the bay.
Vessels approaching from the north should be able to

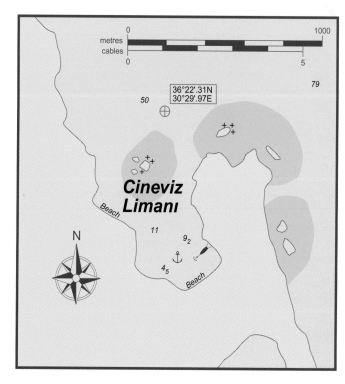

identify the long beach in Çıralı Limanı as they sail past, and then make out the entrance to the bay as they get closer. Look for the 883m peak of Eren Tepe mountain behind the bay.

A cluster of small rocks in the middle of the entrance help to identify the location. You can pass safely to either side of these rocks and anchor in 5-10m off the beach or rocky shore, taking a line ashore to prevent swinging. There are no facilities here and the anchorage is remote and dramatic.

Çıralı Koyu

Entrance to the bay: 36°24'.03N 30°29'.33E

NAVIGATION

Charts: Turkish Hydrographic Charts: 321, 322, 3223; Imray Charts: G40; Admiralty 236, 237, SC 5773

This is a wide open bay that does not offer particularly good shelter and is suitable as a daytime stop only. The anchorage is identified by a long beach approximately 2.5M to the north of Çıralı Koyu, and you can free swing at anchor in 5-10m of water off the beach.

This is the place to stop if you want to go ashore and explore the overgrown ruins of ancient Olympos. A couple of small restaurants on the beach cater for day trippers visiting the ruins from nearby resorts. The natural gas flames of the Chimera can be observed by following the track from the village, but this is a phenomenon best observed at dusk and therefore on a trip from a more sheltered anchorage such as Kemer.

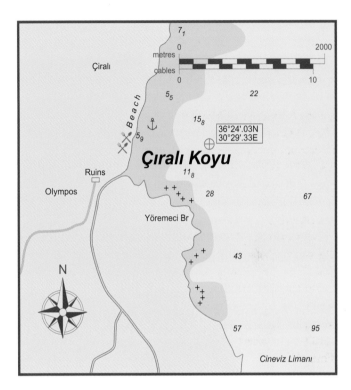

Ruins at Çıralı Koyu

İncirliyalısı Koyu
(Tekirova, Ancient Phaselis)

Southern anchorage: 36°31'.11N 30°32'.79E
Northern anchorage: 36°31'.45N 30°33'.45E

NAVIGATION

Charts: Turkish Hydrographic Charts: 322, 3222;
Imray Charts: G40; Admiralty 236, 237, SC 5773

This fantastic spot offers visitors the chance to anchor within the ancient harbour and explore the ruins ashore at their leisure. The anchorage is located approximately 5.5M south of the Koca Burun headland near Kemer and is split into two areas by a small headland in the middle of the ancient settlement.

Vessels can anchor in either the northern or southern bays, but great care is needed as you approach in order to avoid the numerous rocks and the remains of several ancient breakwaters.

The ruins are scattered all around the shoreline and up into the surrounding hills, and the site is a protected area. The village of Tekirova is just to the south of the anchorage and has facilities to cater for the many visitors to this ancient site. It is useful if you need to top up on basic provisions but has none of the charm and tranquillity of Phaselis.

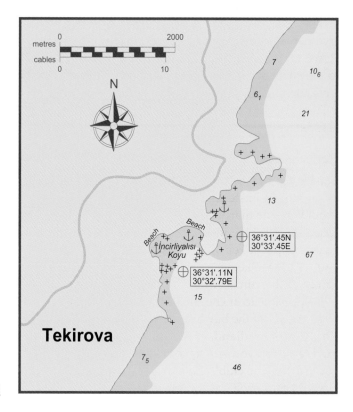

Kemer

North-east of Koca Burnu headland:
36°36'.20N 30°35'.58E
Entrance to the bay to the east of
the marina:
36°36'.07N 30°34'.94E
Marina entrance: 36°36'.12N
30°34'.34E

Kemer is a coastal resort town that lies approximately half way between the harbours at Finike and Antalya, and makes a convenient stopping place for vessels travelling between these places. The backdrop of the high Taurus mountains makes for a spectacular setting, and the town has all the facilities a visiting yacht could require.

Aerial view of the Kemer Turkiz Marina

NAVIGATION

Charts: Turkish Hydrographic Charts: 322 3222;
Imray Charts: G40; Admiralty 236, 237, SC 5773

Kemer is located immediately to the north of the 320m high Koca Burun headland, which also has a light structure on it (Fl 10s). Vessels approaching from the south will not be able to see the town until they have passed this point and should keep a distance offshore as they round the headland to avoid the rocks at the base of the cliffs here.

Yachts approaching from the north and east should

be able to identify the headland from some distance away and will see the buildings of the town as they get closer in. The Kirli Saha shoal lies approximately 0.5M to the north of the marina entrance and is marked with a beacon and a light structure (Fl (2) 10s).

The entrance to the marina is lit at night (Fl R 5s and Fl G 5s).

BERTHING AND ANCHORING
The Kemer Turkiz Marina has in-water berths for 230 boats, mainly in stern-to berths with lazylines. You should call the marina on VHF Ch 73 as you approach to request berthing instructions. The marina can also be contacted on Tel: 0242 814 14 90, Fax: 0242 814 15 52, email: marina@kemerturkizmarina.com, website: www.kemerturkizmaina.com

It is possible to anchor in 5-10m of water on the western side of the bay between the marina and the Koca Burun headland. This is the location of a Club Med resort, so you will have to share the bay with guests using the club's watersports facilities, and some areas off the beach are buoyed for swimming. The small jetty in the bay is private and not suitable for yachts.

FORMALITIES
Kemer is a port of entry to Turkey and all vessel clearance formalities can be completed here. The customs, harbour master and immigration offices are all next to the marina office, and the marina staff are happy to complete formalities on behalf of vessels staying in the marina if necessary.

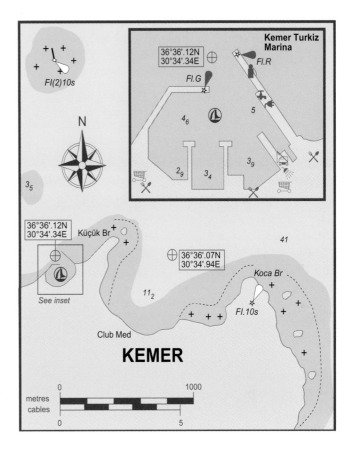

Useful information – Kemer

FACILITIES
Water and electricity: Available at every berth.
Fuel: The fuel dock is located at the entrance to the marina.
Showers: In the marina.
Ice: Is stocked at the Tobacco Shop general store in the marina.
Laundry: The marina offers laundry facilities.
Gas: Bottles can be exchanged at the Tobacco Shop.
Rubbish: Segregated recycling bins ashore in the marina, as well as disposal of household waste, sewage removal and waste oil disposal facilities.
Telephone: Public phone boxes are located within the marina and throughout the town, with phone cards available from the Tobacco Shop and other mini-markets in the town. Mobile reception here is good.
Internet: WiFi internet is offered throughout the marina and there is an internet terminal in the front office. There are also several internet cafés within walking distance of the marina.

YACHT SERVICES AND CHANDLERY
The marina has a 60 ton travel lift, 10 ton crane and 20 ton boat mover and can accommodate up to 140 boats in its hard standing area. Water and electricity can be obtained throughout the boatyard. Technical services are available through the marina and include a painting workshop, engine workshop, upholstery and sail workshop, carpentry workshop, mechanical workshop, electrical and electronics services. Contact the marina office for more information.

The Marina Yacht Chandlery is located next to the marina office and stocks a range of chandlery items for yachtsmen.

PROVISIONING AND SERVICES
Grocery shops: The Tobacco Shop is a general store located within the marina and stocks essential items for provisioning. There are several other mini-markets situated in the town, as well as a couple of larger supermarkets such as the Carrefour Express.
Bakery: Fresh bread is available at the Tobacco Shop.
Butcher: Several in the town.
Local market: Is held on Fridays.
Banks: There are several banks in the area where you can withdraw or change currency over the counter. Vakıf Bank and Akbank both have ATM machines next to the marina.
Pharmacy: Several in the town and one in the marina.

Post office: The main PTT office is located in the town near the New Kemer Mosque.

EATING OUT
There are plenty of restaurants in the resort, although several of these will be closed if you visit out of high season. There are also a number of options for eating out within the marina area and these are open all year round.

The Café du Port has a good location right on the waterfront and the Surf bar and restaurant is also nearby. The Navigator restaurant is the marina's main restaurant, with separate terrace and bar areas.

ASHORE
Kemer is a lively resort in the summer and has not yet been overdeveloped.

Useful information – Kemer (continued)

The marina has an active liveaboard community that organises activities throughout the year, making this a popular place for cruisers to overwinter their boats.

Excursions to the surrounding areas can be organised through any of the tour operators in the town, or independently by hiring a car or travelling on the local dolmuş minibuses.

The ruins of Olympos and the burning flames at Çıralı are easily visited from Kemer, as is the city of Antalya. If you are fond of mountainous scenery then don't miss the chance to go up the cable car to the top of the 2,365m Tahtalı Dağı mountain (www.tahtali.com). The nine-minute cable car ride operates throughout the year.

Keen divers will be interested to explore some of the nearby dive sites such as the wreck of *Paris II* and the Üç Adalar (Three islands), which are actually four islands with underwater canyons and reefs surrounding them.

If you like horse-riding then you can visit the Berke Ranch for lessons and woodland trekking expeditions. For more information go to www.hotel-berkeranch.com

In the bay immediately to the east of the marina are the ruins of the ancient settlement of Idyros, which include a Byzantine church with mosaic floor.

TRANSPORT

Car hire: There are a number of rental agencies in the resort, including the Maxwell Travel Agency, located within the marina complex, Tel: 0242 814 15 41.

Taxis: A taxi rank is situated immediately outside the marina entrance gate and others are located throughout the town.

Coach: The town's otogar station is on the main road between Antalya and Finike, and service buses will take you here from the bus companies' office in the town. Services operate to Antalya, Finike, Fethiye, Ankara and other large towns.

Dolmuş: Local minibuses will take you to visit the sites of Olympos, Phaselis and other nearby villages.

Air travel: The nearest airport is 55km away in Antalya. The marina has heliport facilities.

USEFUL INFORMATION

Local tel code: Antalya area, 0242, Kemer 814.

Port Authority: Next to the marina office, Tel: 0242 814 52 62.

Tourist information office: In the square close to the marina, Tel: 0242 814 11 12.

Medical: There are three hospitals in the vicinity of Kemer: the state hospital, Tel: 0242 814 15 50, and two private hospitals, the Anadolu, Tel: 042 814 59 70, and the Yaşam, Tel: 0242 814 55 00. There are also two general Polikliniks – the Ata, Tel: 0242 814 38 38, and the Medica, Tel: 0242 814 31 11.

Antalya

Entrance to the commercial harbour:
36°50'.17N 30°37'.06E
Entrance to Çelebi Marina: 36°49'.90N 30°36'.48E
Entrance to Kaleiçi harbour: 36°53'.02N 30°42'.06E
South of wreck near entrance to Kaleiçi harbour:
36°52'.79N 30°41'.83E

The city of Antalya is the administrative centre of the Antalya province and the centre of the tourist region known as the 'Turkish Riviera'. It has long been an important seaport and centre of international trade and is one of the largest and wealthiest cities in Turkey. The modern seaport and yacht marina are located 12km from the centre of Antalya's old town (Kaleiçi) and medieval harbour, which is used only by local fishing craft, gulets and day tripper boats.

NAVIGATION

Charts: Turkish Hydrographic Charts: 322, 3221, 3222; Imray Charts: G40; Admiralty 236, 237, 242, SC 5773

The city of Antalya stretches around the north-west part of the Antalya Körfezi gulf, and the commercial harbour lies approximately 5M south-west of the centre of the town. The approach is in deep water with no dangers to avoid other than any commercial traffic that may also be using the harbour.

There are a number of ship mooring buoys located along the coast to the south of the commercial harbour, and although they are not lit, they are easy to avoid by standing off the coast by a mile or so. The exact locations of all the buoys are given on the Çelebi Marina website (see page 215).

The harbour can be identified as you approach by the various storage tanks, cranes and other shipyard construction ashore. Entrance to the main harbour is lit

Antalya's old harbour at Kaleiçi

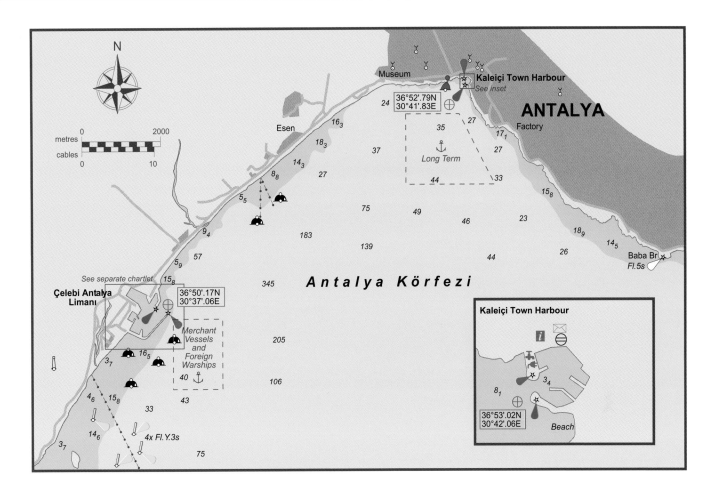

(Fl R 3s & Fl G 3s), and so is the entrance to the yacht marina, which is situated in the south-east corner of the harbour to the south of the cruise ship dock.

The Kaleiçi town harbour lies under the medieval town walls and is difficult to identify until you are quite close-to. The entrance is protected by a mole extending from the southern side, which is lit (Fl R 3s & Fl G 3s). A wreck lying in approximately 4m of water is situated to the south-west of the harbour entrance. It is usually marked by a buoy, but this is not an official marker and is not lit. The Yivli Minare (fluted minaret) is conspicuous on the hillside behind the harbour as you approach the entrance.

If the wind is blowing strongly it can push quite a swell towards the harbour entrance, making passage difficult or impossible, and shelter within uncomfortable at the least. Generally it is better for yachts to make for the marina in the commercial harbour, where there is more likely to be space and better shelter.

BERTHING AND ANCHORING

The Çelebi Marina has berths for 230 vessels up to 30m in length. All berthing is stern-to with lazylines. You should call the marina on VHF Ch 09 as you approach and request mooring instructions. They will usually send out a dinghy to guide you to your berth and assist with mooring. The marina can also

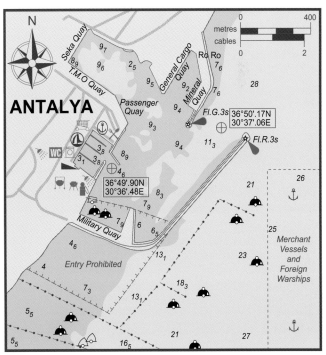

be contacted on Tel: 0242 259 32 59, Fax: 0242 259 10 10, email: info@celebimarina.com.tr, website: www. celebimarina.com.tr

As mentioned above, space in the Kaleiçi town harbour is extremely limited and it is generally advised that vessels head for the Çelebi Marina. However, if conditions are fair for entry and there seems to be space,

Aerial view of Antalya's commercial port and Çelebi Marina

then it is both an atmospheric and central location. You can call the harbour master on VHF Ch 73 to request berthing instructions, which will generally be stern-to using a laid mooring.

There are no sheltered anchorages in the vicinity of Antalya.

FORMALITIES

Antalya is a port of entry to Turkey, so all entry and exit formalities can be completed here. There are customs and harbour master offices at both the Kaleiçi harbour and at the cruise port next to the Çelebi Marina. The marina office is able to assist with all formalities and you can also purchase transit logs from here.

A rough entrance to the old harbour in Antalya's Kaleiçi district

Useful information – Antalya

FACILITIES
Water and electricity: Supplies are installed at all berths in Çelebi Marina and on the dock in Kaleiçi harbour.
Fuel: Fuel is available in Çelebi Marina and from a fuel dock located at the entrance to the Kaleiçi harbour.
Showers: Toilets and showers are part of the facilities offered by Çelebi Marina, and there are also public toilets and showers located within the Kaleiçi harbour area.
Ice: Can be bought from

mini-markets close to both harbours.
Laundry: Available in Çelebi Marina.
Gas: Bottles can be refilled at Çelebi Marina.
Rubbish: There are segregated recycling bins and waste oil disposal facilities in Çelebi Marina as well as general rubbish bins around the Kaleiçi harbour.
Telephone: Public phones are located around both the marina and the harbour, with phone cards on sale at local shops. Mobile phone reception here is good.
Internet: WiFi coverage

is provided at berths in Çelebi Marina and there is an internet terminal in the office. Several cafés in the vicinity of Kaleiçi harbour offer WiFi connection to customers.

YACHT SERVICES AND CHANDLERY
Çelebi Marina has three travel lifts (60, 75 and 200 tons), a 12 ton boat mover and a hard standing area that can accommodate up to 300 boats. Water and electricity are available throughout the boatyard and there are a number of

workshops and companies that can cater for any kind of work required on sailing and motor vessels, including painting, carpentry, mechanical, electrical and electronics, sail and canvas repair, glass fibre repair and surveying.

The Pelikan Yat Market stocks a range of chandlery products and will order anything else that is required, Tel: 0242 259 20 40.

PROVISIONING AND SERVICES
Grocery shops: A supermarket is on site at

Useful information – Antalya (continued)

the Çelebi Marina and offers a provisioning service for yachts. There are also a couple of small markets around the Kaleiçi harbour area and plenty of others located throughout the town.

Banks: A Garantı Bank ATM machine can be found in the car park just above the Kaleiçi harbour. There are also several ATM machines within the Çelebi Marina. All of the Turkish banks have branches in the town centre where you can withdraw or change money.

Pharmacy: A number of pharmacies are situated throughout the town.

Post office: There are several post offices amongst the streets of Antalya, but the most convenient one is a small branch next to the Kaleiçi harbour.

EATING OUT

A couple of restaurants housed in the marina complex include the Yoma bar and restaurant (next to the Yoma Beach), and the Seamen's restaurant and cafeteria.

There is a far greater choice of restaurants within Antalya itself, and many of these are situated within the Kaleiçi old town and harbour area, so a taxi ride back to the marina will be required. The options range from basic and cheap *pide* and kebab restaurants and *locanta* to the more expensive tourist-orientated and specialist restaurants offering fine ottoman and

international cuisine, fresh fish and other delicacies. Many of these restaurants have atmospheric locations either around the harbour area or within restored ottoman buildings.

The Ekici Restaurant has a prime spot next to the old harbour and specialises in seafood that is freshly caught by the local fishing fleet, Tel: 0242 247 81 90, Mob: 0533 336 76 48, website: www. ekicigroup.com

The Ayar restaurant in the centre of the old town is an example of the traditional meyhane, where you can enjoy live Turkish music as you eat. This is a fashionable and popular spot, so bookings may be required at weekends and on special occasions, Tel: 0242 244 52 03/0242 248 67 60, website: www. ayarmeyhane.com

The Villa Perla is a charming restaurant and guesthouse combination in an old ottoman house and courtyard. The hostess is effusive and welcoming, and as full of character as the surroundings, and you can always stay the night in one of the individually furnished rooms if you can't tear yourself away from the place after your meal, Tel: 0242 248 97 93, website: www. villaperla.com

ASHORE

There is plenty to see and do within the city of Antalya and in the surrounding

The old and the new in close proximity in Antalya's Kaleiçi district

Hadrian's Gate

area, and it is a popular choice for cruising vessels overwintering in Turkey.

The Kaleiçi, or old town area, is full of the kind of antique yet lived-in buildings that unfortunately seem to be rather rare along much of Turkey's modern coastline. Traffic access to the area is restricted, so you can wander the cobbled streets on foot and explore the various shops and boutiques, quaint cafeterias

and attractive architecture that you will come across. The Kaleiçi area is bordered by medieval stone walls that remain largely intact and access to the streets within is through a number of gates and portals, including Hadrian's Gate (Hadriyanüs Kapısı) on the eastern side and the fortified Castle Gate (Kale Kapısı) on the northern side. There are also a number of notable mosques, monasteries, minarets and

Attractive ottoman courtyards in the old town

Useful information – Antalya (continued)

Narrow streets and ottoman architecture in Antalya's old town

other religious structures, such as the Fluted Minaret (Yivli Minare).

The Kaleiçi Museum, www.kaleicimuzesi.com, is located in the centre of the old town and is open from 0900-1200 and 1300-1800 every day except Wednesdays. The museum is housed in a restored ottoman mansion, with different rooms decorated to illustrate the lives of the area's past inhabitants, and also includes an exhibition hall in the restored Christian church of St George (Aya Yorgi) where you can see collections of fine ceramics and other ottoman treasures.

The Antalya Archaeological Museum contains one of the county's most important collections of ancient artefacts and monuments, mainly from the surrounding Antalya region. It is located between the town and the marina at the starting point for the city tramline, and is open from 0830-1730 every day except Mondays. Exhibits include a collection of fossilised remains found in the area, classical sculpture depicting Roman gods and emperors, mosaics and sarcophagi discovered in the surrounding regions, collections of ancient coins and writings and much more.

If you are staying in the area for an extended period and want to explore further afield then it is easy to do so, either by joining a tour organised by one of the many travel agencies in the city, or by hiring a car and exploring by yourself. Popular day excursions include trips to the Düden waterfalls and Karain Cave, explorations of the ancient sites at Termessos, Perge and Aspendos, rafting trips along the Bridge River (Köprü Irmağı) and visits to various beaches along the coast. The fantastic landscapes of Cappadoccia are also within striking distance of Antalya and are well worth a few days' visit if you will be in the area for a while.

TRANSPORT

Car hire: Car hire is available through the marina reception office and also from various agencies within the town centre.

Taxis: There are taxi ranks close to the marina and cruise port as well as near the Kaleiçi harbour and all over the town.

Coach: The main otogar coach station is some way out of the town centre and has regular services to destinations all over Turkey. Shuttle buses will take you from the bus companies' booking offices in the town out to the otogar, and if you are travelling in by coach then you can usually ask the driver to drop you off as he passes through the town on the way to the main station.

Dolmuş: Dolmuş minibuses operate regular services along the coast road between Çelebi Marina and the town centre.

Tram: Antalya has a useful tram system that runs along the seafront from the museum through the centre of town, past the stadium and beyond.

Air travel: Antalya's airport is located approximately 10km from the city centre and is one of the country's busiest, with regular flights from abroad throughout the year.

USEFUL INFORMATION

Local tel code: Antalya area, 0242, Antalya 259, 247, 241.

Çelebi Marina Technical Services: Tel: 0242 259 32 59, extension 103, Fax: 0242 259 10 10, email: service@celebimarina.com.tr

Antalya Port Authority: Tel: 0242 259 12 12.

Passport Police: Tel: 0242 259 13 80.

Customs: Tel: 0242 259 13 24.

Customs Patrol Authorities: Tel: 0242 259 14 31.

Coastal Health Authorities: Tel: 0242 259 09 55.

Tourist information office: Located on Cumhuriyet Caddesi, close to the Kale Kapısı fortress gate just to the west of the Kaleiçi area. Opening hours are 0800-1900, Tel: 0242 241 17 47.

Antalya weather service: Tel: 0242 247 34 87.

Medical: Medikal Park Hospital, Tel: 0242 444 44 84; Lara Hospital, Tel: 0242 349 40 40; Yasam Hospital, Tel: 0242 310 80 90; Antalya Devlet (State) Hospital, Tel: 0242 238 53 53; Medical Faculty University Hospital, Tel: 0242 249 60 00.

Local information websites: www.antalyafestivals.org is a useful website listing all of Antalya's cultural festivals and activities, including the annual Aspendos festival (see pages 31-33). www.antalyaguide.org is an online guide to the city and its surroundings, with listings of restaurants, accommodation and visitor facilities.

The Kaleiçi walled city

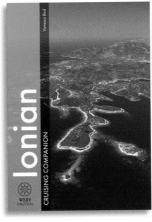

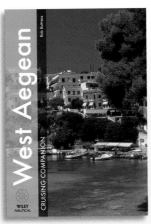
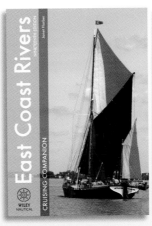

TURKISH ALPHABET

The modern Turkish alphabet is Latin-based and was introduced by Atatürk in 1928, replacing the Arabic-based Ottoman-Turkish alphabet in use before then. Words are always pronounced phonetically, so once you have learnt the alphabet you can read most written Turkish words out loud. The majority of the sounds are very similar to English apart from the following:

C is always pronounced as a *j*.
Ç and Ş are pronounced as *ch* and *sh*.
İ (with a dot) is pronounced *Ee*, much like the English 'I'. Don't confuse this with I (without a dot), which should be pronounced as *uh*.
Ğ is pronounced as a silent 'g'.
Ö and Ü are pronounced towards the front of the mouth, whilst O and U (also used in Turkish) are pronounced at the back. This distinction is difficult for native English speakers to pick up but you can get by without it.

There is no X or V in the Turkish alphabet; the letters *ks* and *w* are usually substituted. The letters J and Q are also omitted, apart from in a few words adopted from other languages such as *jandarma*.

USEFUL WORDS AND PHRASES
General pleasantries

Hello	*merhaba*	mer-ha-bah
Goodbye	*görüşürüz*	gor-uh-shuh-rus
Pleased to meet you	*memnun oldum*	mem-num ol-dum
How are you?	*nasılsınız?*	nah-sul-sun-us
I am fine	*iyim*	ee-yim
Good morning	*günaydın*	gun-aye-dun
Good day	*iyi günler*	ee-yi gun-ler
Good evening	*iyi akşamlar*	ee-yak-sham-lar
Good night	*iyi geceler*	ee-gej-eh-ler
Please	*lütfen*	loot-fen
Thank you	*teşekkür ederim*	tesh-eh-kur ed-er-im
Thank you	*sağol*	sah-ol
You're welcome	*birşey değil*	beer-shay deh-ill
Cheers!	*şerefe!*	Sher-eh-fey

Numbers

1	*bir*	beer
2	*iki*	icki
3	*üç*	ooch
4	*dört*	dirt
5	*beş*	besh
6	*altı*	al-uh
7	*yedi*	yed-ih
8	*sekis*	sek-is
9	*dokuz*	dock-uz
10	*on*	on
20	*yirmi*	yir-mih
30	*otuz*	ot-uz
40	*kırk*	krk
50	*elli*	el-ih
60	*altmış*	at-mush
70	*yetmiş*	yet-mish
80	*seksen*	seck-sen
90	*doksan*	dock-san
100	*yüz*	yooz
1000	*bin*	bin
0	*sıfır*	suh-fur

Questions

How much (cost)	*ne kadar*	neh kah-dar
How many (number)	*kaç*	katch
How	*nasıl*	nah-sul
Who	*kim*	kim
When	*ne zaman*	neh zah-man
Where	*nerede*	neh-reh-deh
Why	*neden*	neh-den
Which one	*hangi*	hang-ee

Food, drink and shopping

Bread	*ekmek*	ek-mek
Cheese	*peynir*	pay-neer
Meat	*et*	et
Beef	*dana*	dah-nah

(technically this means 'veal', but not the kind of milk-fed veal we know in the UK)

Lamb	*kuzu*	kuh-zuh
Chicken	*piliç or tavuk*	pill-ich/tav-ook
Beer	*bira*	beer-ah
Wine (red)	*şarap (kırmızı)*	shar-ap (kur-muh-zuh)
Wine (white)	*şarap (beyaz)*	shar-ap (bay-az)
Milk	*süt*	soot
Water	*su*	soo
Bakery	*fırın*	fir-in

Butcher	*kasap*	kah-sap
Greengrocer	*manav*	man-av
Pharmacy	*eczanesi*	eck-san-eh-see

General vocabulary

Yes	*evet*	ev-et
No	*hayır*	hah-yur
OK	*tamam*	tam-am
Maybe	*belki*	bell-kee
Possible	*mümkün*	moom-kun
Very good	*çok iyi*	chock ee-yee
OR		
Very good	*çok güzel*	chock goo-zel
Now	*şimdi*	shim-dee
Later	*sonar*	son-rah
Left	*sol*	sol
Right	*sağ*	saah
Hot	*sıcak*	suh-jack
Cold	*soğuk*	soh-uk

Nautical terms

Harbour Master	*Liman Başkanı*	lih-man bash-kan-uh
Customs Patrol	*Gümrük Muhafaza*	gum-ruk muh-ah-fah-zah
Passport Police	*Pasaport Polisi*	pass-ah-port poll-eeh-see
Coastal Health Control	*Sahil Sağlık Denetleme*	sah-hil saah-luk den-et-leh-meh
North	*kuzey*	kuh-zay
South	*güney*	goon-ay
East	*doğu*	doh-oo
West	*batı*	bat-uh
Sea	*deniz*	den-iz
Wind	*rüzgar*	rooz-gar
Port	*liman/limanı*	lih-man/lih-man-uh
Harbour	*iskele*	iss-keh-leh
Bay	*koyu*	koy-oo
Village	*köy*	koy
Island	*ada/adası* (plural: *adalar*)	ad-ah/ad-ah-suh
Headland	*burun/burnu*	bur-un/bur-noo

(**NB** The word for headland changes according to whether the preceding name is a proper noun or an adjective. Names such as *Kara* (black) and *İnce* (narrow) are followed by Burun; proper nouns are followed by *Burnu*)

Gulf	*körfezi*	kor-feh-zee
Peninsula	*yarımadası*	yah-rum-ad-ah-suh
Strait	*boğaz*	bo-aaz
Channel	*yol* (also means road)	yol
Lighthouse	*fener*	fen-er
Rock/reef	*kayası*	kay-ah-suh
Hill	*tepe*	teh-peh
Mountain	*dağ*	daah
Lake	*göl*	gol

Hayıt Bükü jetty